Let this be our secret

Let this be our secret

Deric Henderson

Gill Books

Gill Books
Hume Avenue
Park West
Dublin 12
www.gillbooks.ie

Gill Books is an imprint of M.H. Gill & Co

978 07171 4770 0

Typography design by Make Communication
Print origination by O'K Graphic Design, Dublin
Printed by ScandBook AB, Sweden

This book is typeset in 10.5/13 pt Minion.

The paper used in this book comes from the wood pulp
of managed forests. For every tree felled, at least one tree
is planted, thereby renewing natural resources.

A CIP catalogue record for this book is available
from the British Library.

5 4

This book is dedicated to my wife Clare and our two sons, Deric Jnr and Edward.
Where would I be without them?

'Then, after desire has conceived, it gives birth to sin; and sin, when it is full-grown, gives birth to death.' (JAMES 1:15)

Contents

Acknowledgements

The late Liz Johnston, a former mayor of Coleraine, was the first person I interviewed. It was April 2009. Her health was failing, but she yearned to know the truth, because Trevor Buchanan, a friend and neighbour, had called at her home just hours before his body was found. Liz died in October 2009 without knowing all the circumstances.

John Hansford, who was the pastor at Coleraine Baptist Church at the time of the deaths, talked to me at length, as a howling wind and driving rain rattled the conservatory doors and windows of his hillside home overlooking the Mediterranean on Spain's Costa Blanca.

Trevor McAuley sat with me at the kitchen table of a house in Portstewart and shared his memories of the woman with whom he spent eight years of his life. He referred to her as 'Buchanan' throughout—never Hazel.

Pat Chambers, an old friend of Lesley Howell's, spoke at length over coffee in a smart Dublin store, while Chris Clarke, Lesley's only brother, recalled his memories in a hotel room, as we watched the tide go out on the Lancashire coast. Valerie Allen, one of her bridesmaids, gave me access to letters written by Lesley before and after she married the man who was to kill her a decade later.

The brothers and sisters of the late Trevor Buchanan generously shared their thoughts and recollections—all of them wonderful people, but still hurting.

Lesley's aunt, the indefatigable Alice Berry, agreed to see me at her home in Lurgan, County Armagh.

Others who opened their doors or took my calls include Robin Hastings, a former Coroner who was in charge of the 1992 inquest; John Wray, Trevor Buchanan's lifelong friend, and his wife Sheila; Trevor's friends Derek Ewing (Coleraine) and John Doherty (Castlederg); Robin Butler, a friend of the late Harry Clarke, Lesley's father; Hamilton Houston, a retired Chief Superintendent who was involved in the 1991 police investigation into the deaths; and Dorothy

Moody, the owner of a health studio outside Coleraine and one of the last people to see Lesley alive.

I conducted almost 50 separate interviews, but the identities of many of those who reflected on the lives and times of the four central characters cannot be disclosed. They wanted to remain anonymous. That was the deal before the notebook was produced, and I am grateful for their patience, understanding and assistance.

Mark Jamieson, five times Northern Ireland Regional Press Photographer of the Year, was heavily involved in the project from day one. We had our moments, but he became a great friend and confidant. Is there anybody in Coleraine he does not know? Fellow journalists were also on hand to advise and encourage when the head dropped—among them Eamonn Mallie, Des Magee, Chris Ryder, Fionnuala O'Connor, Ivan McMichael, Ivan Little, Brian Rowan, Hugh Jordan, the PR consultant Austin Hunter, Sam Smyth (Dublin), Ray Managh (Dublin) and David Armstrong (Portadown)—but especially the outstanding David McKittrick, who has been down this road many times before.

My Press Association colleagues in Belfast and Dublin, notably David Young, who worked with me covering Hazel Stewart's trial, as well as my editor Jonathan Grun and his number 2 in London, Teilo Colley, allowed me all the space I needed. Two personal friends, Ernie Telford and Kieran Campbell, were hugely supportive as well.

It was manic towards the end, but the excellent and ever-helpful Susan Feldstein made sure the manuscript was edited and delivered on time to my publisher, Fergal Tobin in Dublin, where the staff of Gill & Macmillan could not have been more accommodating. Thanks too go to my agent, Paul Feldstein of The Feldstein Agency.

There was unwavering support from all sides of the family. My sister Gloria White and mother-in-law Mary Carlin proved once again that the power of prayer does work and Auntie Jean Gregory never lost faith either.

My wife Clare and our two boys, Deric Jnr and Edward in London were always there for me. They knew when to engage and when to stand back, especially on days when there were few words on the screen and I thought this project would never end. I would not have crossed the finishing line without them. They were fantastic.

Foreword

I broke a promise to write this book.

Having spent the best part of my adult life intruding on grief while reporting on the violence which once dominated so much of day-to-day life in Northern Ireland, I vowed I would never again arrive unannounced on the doorstep of victims' relatives. The pledge was made as I sheltered under an umbrella on a wet and miserable Sunday morning in June 1994 in the village of Loughinisland, where six men were shot dead as they watched a World Cup soccer match on a pub television.

A bereaved woman had answered my knock on her front door. She was wearing a black dress covered in specks of white fluff. The garment had obviously been hurriedly retrieved from the bottom drawer for a period of mourning. Her eyes were red and glazed and she twisted a white handkerchief in her hands. Excusing herself for looking so tired and weary, she politely refused my request for an interview.

I never walked up a driveway or garden footpath again to seek out personal testimonials from those in mourning—not even when my home town of Omagh was bombed in the summer of 1998, leaving 29 people dead, including a mother pregnant with twins. I left it to others to apologise for calling at such a bad time, before being invited inside to pose the difficult and painful questions.

The arrests of Colin Howell and Hazel Stewart in January 2009 changed all that.

Even though an entry in my diary for 20 May 1991 records the incident—'Couple die in suicide at Castlerock'—I did not recall the deaths of Trevor Buchanan and Lesley Howell. The tragedy barely registered outside Coleraine in County Londonderry, where they both lived. But I remember the time well. The affable Peter Brooke was Secretary of State for Northern Ireland, the British Government was in secret talks with the leadership of the IRA—and I was just out of hospital after a major health scare. The first faltering steps were being taken towards a peace settlement, and the attention of those of us who waited to challenge the politicians emerging from the depressing

Castle Buildings in Belfast was far removed from that beautiful stretch of the North Coast where the two bodies were discovered. Fast forward 20 years, and who would have believed so many column inches and air time would be devoted to a tragedy that had more or less passed us by?

It was a crime of passion which went undetected for so long because of the cunning and guile of the two people who carried it out: Colin Howell, a narcissistic but seemingly harmless small town dentist, and his obedient lover, Hazel Stewart. The ingenious and ruthless way in which they murdered his wife Lesley and her husband Trevor Buchanan—before fooling investigating officers into believing their partners had killed themselves—means their evil deeds will live long in the memory. They left behind a trail of emotional carnage. Not just for those closest to them, especially their children and their wider family circles, but, in Howell's case, for the women patients the dentist abused while they were heavily sedated and under his care.

I found this a tough and demanding assignment. Many of the people interviewed made a deep and lasting impression on me, especially the brothers and two sisters of Trevor Buchanan. Listening to them was almost like witnessing their dead brother being brought back to life. The most poignant moment of all was when Victor Buchanan told how his grief-stricken father reached into his son's coffin, gathered him into his arms and cried out: 'Why did you do it, son? Why didn't you come to me? Why didn't you come to me?' Journalists can become detached and unfeeling, but this was the first time in over 40 years in the business that I had to set down my pen and walk away to compose myself.

Colin Howell and Hazel Stewart had practically everything they ever wanted, except peace of mind. Howell emerged from a working class background to make a good career for himself—and a lot of money. He regarded himself as a born-again Christian, as did Hazel Stewart, who led a fairly ordinary life until she started cheating on the man who worshipped the ground she walked on.

Howell's guilty conscience finally got the better of him, and, although Stewart continues to protest her innocence following her trial earlier this year, no one in the courtroom in Coleraine last March will forget the moment a jury found her guilty at the end of 15 unprecedented and dramatic days of evidence and legal submissions. It has been a horrendous ordeal for so many people—particularly the

Buchanans, Chris Clarke, Lesley's only brother, and the many young adults and children who have been left behind to struggle to come to terms with the circumstances surrounding two murders so callous they almost defy belief.

The Howell and Buchanan couples were devout Baptists and this book also examines how their church dealt with the whole affair. Perhaps those in their church could have done things differently; perhaps they, like other people and institutions, stood little chance of penetrating Howell's web of deception and Hazel Stewart's lies.

But the most pointed question of all must concern the incompetent police investigation which allowed the two perpetrators to get away with murder for so long. Even though she was troubled and in a loveless marriage, why would a young mother devoted to her children climb into the boot of a car and kill herself, just hours after she booked a session on a sunbed for a couple of days later? Why would a police officer who had never before harboured thoughts of suicide—even in the depths of despair—suddenly change his mind and take his own life?

Researching and writing this book has been an extraordinary experience. Above all, it has been humbling and sometimes painful to witness the quiet dignity and integrity of the many decent and blameless people who were so deeply affected and whose lives may never be the same again. In their struggle to come to terms with their pain, and their refusal to become embittered by hatred, all of them have surely shown what the meaning of true Christianity is.

Deric Henderson
Belfast, June 2011

Chapter 1

'Behind the Concrete Walls in his Mind . . .'

28 JANUARY 2009

The night before he surrendered himself to the police, Colin Howell took three of his young children to the outside patio and urged them to look up at the stars. He had a pair of binoculars, and he held the youngest in his arms as he knelt down to let the others take turns looking at the magnified night sky. It was Howell's last lingering look at freedom. As a doting father, he knew this was the final time he and his children would enjoy this kind of physical closeness.

The highly successful dentist and one-time pillar of the local community and Baptist church had been living on his own at a rented caravan in Castlerock for the past month or so, after his second wife, Kyle, had ordered him out of the family home. He had recently confessed to an adulterous relationship, and a subsequent revelation, that he had squandered all the family's savings—£353,000—in a crazy investment scheme to recover missing gold bullion in the Philippines, had pushed the young mother of seven to breaking point. But the couple agreed that Howell could return each evening to read their children a bedtime story and tuck them up before they went to sleep.

As he now stood under the glare of an outside light in the back garden of the lavish family home, gazing up at the sky and holding his sons close, there were tears in his eyes. It was an emotional moment, but Colin Howell's time was up. He knew it and so did Kyle. Casual adultery and financial recklessness were the very least of his wrongdoings. At last the moment had come for all of his past iniquities to be brought—to be forcibly dragged—to the light. His dark world had finally imploded.

29 JANUARY 2009

Kyle Howell looked up at the clock on the kitchen wall: it was approaching 8.00 a.m. She was sitting at the kitchen table, with baby Susanna on her knee. The other four of her younger children were watching a Nick Jr. video. Kyle was crying. It had been another long and difficult night. Her husband was no longer the man she thought she knew, the one she had loved and had looked up to for 12 years— whose encyclopaedic knowledge of the Bible never ceased to amaze her, the one who had once delivered a compelling sermon about sexual immorality to like-minded acquaintances from their local church, and had talked so convincingly about how he had worked through his own crisis of being unfaithful. Both Kyle and Howell were 'born-again' Christians, deeply committed Evangelicals, and these principles and beliefs were fundamental to their faith.

But if Howell had managed to negotiate his way through personal and marital difficulties in the past, then his latest revelations to his wife—and the resulting situation he now faced—were in a different league altogether. This was cataclysmic. There would be no way back this time. His head was in a place where it had never been before, even with all the many crises he had faced up to this point in his life. He felt he was eternally damned, and just the night before—not for the first time—he had been contemplating taking his own life. Utterly distraught and desperate herself, it had taken every ounce of Kyle's emotional strength and presence of mind to persuade him not to take this final step. Quoting the Scriptures, she had urged him: 'There's grace. There's grace. The Lord is giving you another chance. This is your chance. If you love your life, you won't lose it.' Howell's confidence was shot, however, and, when she reminded him again of what he needed to do—unburden himself once and for all of all the darkness of his past—he had kept repeating: 'I can't, I can't, I can't.'

Refusing to accept this, she had simply replied each time: 'But you *can*, you can . . .'

And now, in the cold light of day, as three of the children gathered up their things for school, Kyle told her husband it was time for the next step in the process which they both knew was now unstoppable. She was calling in the church elders, so that they could hear the full truth about Colin Howell's past sins. Resigned, he accepted this, but said that he just wanted to take the children to school in nearby Castlerock so that he could say his goodbyes. She warned him there was to be no emotion and that he was to act normally.

Then the young mother called Graham Stirling, left a message on Andrew Brown's phone and spoke with Willie Patterson: all were elders in The Barn Christian Fellowship church to which the Howells belonged. All had been close confidants of Colin's over the years. Kyle also contacted Davy Hoy, another elder, but he was unable to come. The other three men, however, promised that they would be there at the agreed time. Earlier that morning, Howell had called his dental surgery and left a message for his PA, asking her to cancel all his appointments and telling her: 'I won't be in for the next couple of days. Something unusual has happened.'

Now all Kyle could do was sit in the kitchen, holding Susanna while she read a story to young Finn and waited for the return of her husband and the arrival of the elders.

After leaving the children off to school, and hugging them especially close before they ran into the gates of the playground, Howell went back to the caravan, collected a few belongings and then returned to the family home at Glebe Road, on the outskirts of the picturesque village of Castlerock. By the time he got home, the elders were already there. Graham Stirling had been the first to turn up, followed quickly by Willie Patterson, and then Andrew Brown.

Another friend from the church had come to help out with baby Susanna. And then, finally, Colin Howell began a protracted confession which continued almost without interruption for well over an hour. A series of revelations from the dentist—each more sensational than the last, it seemed—would culminate in a final admission which would leave those around him stunned, devastated and struggling to comprehend.

Kyle was weeping again, as her husband began to speak. Although he remained calm, he was trembling and shaking, and it was obvious to the three church elders that the powerful emotions he was struggling to keep at bay were very close to the surface. Willie Patterson would later tell police: 'Colin looked awful. I don't know how to describe it. His eyes were standing out of his head and he was in great distress.' But with a sense that now he had started, he had no choice but to finish, Howell continued, speaking quietly but distinctly, his eyes fixed on the table before him.

He began by telling them that he had been having contact with another woman. The relationship, he told them, had first begun in 2002 and at the time he had admitted to it to Kyle and a church friend. There had been no further contact for some time. But the relationship had started up again in 2005. Howell would tell Kyle he was going to the surgery to do some paperwork and then slip off to see the woman at her home. But, he was now insisting, they had never had intercourse.

The elders listened intently, but with no great sense of surprise. They had known all about this since the middle of the previous month, when their friend had told them he was increasingly tormented with guilt over his latest dalliance, and said he planned to tell Kyle all about it. Kyle had just left with some of the children for a family break over Christmas in Florida, where her parents lived on Sanibel Island. The original plan had been that Kyle would fly out first and then Howell would follow her with his father Sam, and Dan and Jonny, his two sons from his first marriage, and that they could all spend Christmas there together. In the weeks previously, when he had first shared with the elders his intention to tell Kyle about the affair, Howell had already been in a highly emotional state, claiming to his confidants that he had 'lost it' and 'was going to be damned' for what he had done.

Kyle's reaction to her husband's revelations of infidelity, when he confessed in a fraught phone call to Florida, had not been good. She told her husband not to join her in the States after all, and two days before New Year's Eve, Howell moved out of the house and into a caravan. He had paid £600 to cover the deposit, the first month's rent and a cylinder of gas. The elders knew all this too, and Stirling and Brown had been to the caravan park off Sea Road, Castlerock, to visit their friend in a pastoral capacity, as part of a bridge-building process which they hoped might end with him eventually being reunited with his family. As Stirling would later recall of Howell: 'He felt he was being fraudulent in his witness and in his life's journey. He explained that he was under powerful conviction by the Holy Spirit and was feeling exceptionally guilty about his lifestyle and the way he was doing business.'

So the admission about the relationship was nothing earth-shattering to those who had gathered that Thursday morning to hear what Howell had to say. In the preceding weeks, they had been witness to a series of other revelations on his part, in a drip-feed process of confession, noting with alarm that he seemed to be gradually losing all contact with reality and sinking into a deep depression. He was unable to function properly in the surgery and even the simple demands of everyday living seemed to be too much for him. He had told them, and then Kyle, how he had just lost all the family money in an outlandish investment scheme which involved funding a search for Japanese gold in the Philippines, but had turned out to be a scam. And although they had all already known for a number of years about his damaging addiction to online pornography, nonetheless he felt compelled to them all about this once more too.

As Graham Stirling would later confirm, it was clear to all in whom he confided, that in December 2008 and in the first weeks of 2009, Colin Howell was deep in some kind of spiritual crisis, as he contemplated suicide and then eternal damnation: 'He did say that he was very concerned with regards to his eternal security, his soul's position with regards to salvation as far as his Christian status was, or the lack of it. And then being able to come to a place where he could be accepted by God and forgiven through his repentance and his confession . . .' But all of the elders had the strong intimation too that there was something more, something beyond all of this—another affair, perhaps—which their friend needed to tell them about, if only he could bring himself to do it. And that was the reason, they surmised, that they had been summoned to the Howell home that morning.

They were right of course—in terms of his self-imposed confessional process, Howell was far from finished. Now, as they sat around him, he was telling them that, at his urging, his first wife Lesley had had three abortions in the months coming up to their wedding. This had been many years previously of course, in 1983. And, he continued, there had been another abortion in his past about which he had never spoken—this time involving his former lover,

Hazel Buchanan. It had been right at the beginning of their affair, in 1990. With each new revelation, Kyle was reeling: 'I felt like I was getting a punch in the stomach.'

Next, Colin Howell told the elders that the respectable façade of his professional life—as a gifted, highly successful and sought-after dental specialist—had also been a sham all along. While he had been building an unblemished and exemplary career as a cosmetic dentist—one who insisted on the highest of standards of surgical excellence, customer service and staff conduct—he had indecently assaulted women patients when they were under sedation and unable to fend him off. This, the elders had certainly not expected. They knew that he had struggled over the years with an unusually high sex drive, which explained perhaps his problems with pornography and his compulsion to seek sexual relationships outside the confines of his marriages. But they had never once suspected that he might have forced himself upon those in his clinical care who were too vulnerable to keep him at bay.

Yet, even while Howell's audience struggled to take on board each fresh admission, they had the unavoidable sense that there was more to come. And they were now feeling more and more apprehensive as to what it could possibly be.

Up until this point, the dentist had remained relatively composed. All at once, however, he began to falter and lose his momentum. Seeing this, Kyle shook herself out of her shocked state and became the resolute one again. She pleaded with him, imploring her husband to finally come clean with everything. She quoted passages from the Bible to strengthen her plea, saying: 'One shall have to undergo suffering to reach truth. That is why it is said that truth is eternally victorious.' Howell composed himself once more. Then, staring again at the table in front of him, and unable to make eye contact with any of those in the room, he told them that something else had been preying on his mind of late—something far worse than anything he had already admitted to.

And then he began to recount in meticulous detail exactly what had happened on the night of 18 May 1991, almost eighteen years previously.

Now, finally, he was saying it out loud, in public, in the presence of other people. He had told Kyle these things after they first married but, an innocent abroad at the time struggling with her own difficulties, she had been unable, or unwilling, to comprehend. The fact was that Colin's first wife—Lesley—and Trevor Buchanan had not died in 1991 as a result of a suicide pact as everyone had thought—but that he had been responsible for their deaths.

This, now, was the whole truth: that he, Colin Howell, had murdered not only his wife Lesley but also the man who was married to his then mistress, Hazel Buchanan. He had broken God's most cardinal law—not once, but twice. He, Colin Howell, was a double murderer.

He then explained to those assembled exactly how he had done it. How he had poisoned Lesley with car exhaust fumes, and how, as she realised that her life was ebbing away, she had called out for Matthew, their eldest son and a six-year-old child at the time. How he had then murdered Trevor in the same way, gassing him with deadly carbon monoxide as he lay in his bed unable to properly defend himself. How he had left the bodies in a car at the back of The Apostles, the landmark row of cottages which overlooked the village of Castlerock. How he had set up the scene to look like suicide, and had then run along the beach and cycled home.

Everyone in the room remembered the shocking events of 1991, when the bodies of Lesley Clarke, Howell's first wife, and Trevor Buchanan, the young policeman married to the woman with whom Howell had been having an affair at the time, were found together in a car in the garage of a house in Castlerock, the victims of an apparent double suicide pact. Everyone at the time, including the police and authorities, had believed that Lesley and Trevor had been so distressed by the ongoing affair between their spouses that they had been driven to the ultimate act of desperation. Everyone remembered how the tragedy had rocked the small seaside community to its core. Everyone except for Kyle of course, who had been barely out of her teens at the time, still living in the States and with no notion of how her life would unfold and ultimately unravel once she moved to Northern Ireland and met her future husband.

But now, apparently immune to the stunned silence of those around him, Howell was in full flow, unstoppable. The confession continued, relentlessly, unabated. His account of how he had managed to convince investigating officers that the deaths had been suicide left his listeners gasping for breath. As Graham Stirling later recalled: 'I shivered about him bragging it was so clever to fool the police . . . We were absolutely gobsmacked and shocked beyond belief, because I never in my wildest dreams, ever thought I was going to hear that sort of confession. I was coming across expecting to hear about another adulterous affair that had gone too far, or something, but did not anticipate hearing anything like that.'

Finally, it was over. All of the truth was out in the open, under the scrutiny of the harsh daylight of that cold morning in late January. The horror of what Colin Howell had done and the full extent of the lie which he had been living for so many years was plain for all to see. The façade he had spent so many years creating and maintaining—deeply committed Christian, upstanding family man, dependable pillar of the community, generous benefactor of deserving charities, dashing dentist, all-round nice guy—had collapsed. And the craven, tortured, and perhaps delusional hypocrite that was Colin Howell had been laid bare for the very first time.

The elders and Kyle sat in stunned silence for some minutes. Then all they could think of doing was to ask him if it was really true, if he was sure that the details were correct. Struggling to believe what he had just been told, it occurred to Graham Stirling that perhaps this was the ultimate evasion on Howell's part—that maybe he was just making it all up to escape the mess that his life was in, in so many ways: 'It was almost as if I felt that he was doing this as a cop-out of all the really huge financial implications and difficulties that he was in, that his business was failing, that there was a downturn in everything, and he was just floundering . . . So I asked him, was he really sure that this was exactly as it was? Colin assured us the facts were correct. Why would he confess to such a thing if it wasn't true? The evidence would match that of the police evidence at the time.'

Andrew Brown, however—a fellow dentist who had been so worried about his friend's state of mind that he had recently contacted the Dental Protection Agency because he feared that he was no longer capable of treating patients—would immediately see what had happened with Howell in another way, as the workings of Divine Providence. He later told police: 'From our perspective on it, we would say God had his hand on that, to take him there, because nothing else was going to. It had to be something of such a cataclysmic effect on him in order to shake him out of . . . [the] barriers that he put up to get this locked [away]. I mean, he must have had it behind 15–20 foot concrete walls in his mind, to stop it coming forward again and again . . .'

For all those assembled in the room that day, it was a defining moment in their lives, one which none of them was ever likely to forget.

By now, Howell had regained his composure. While his full confession had taken every ounce of resolve to deliver, and he was emotionally spent, he had known for weeks, and perhaps months, that his time as a free man was now very limited. He had already prepared himself for a long spell in jail. The night before, he had even booted up his computer to type the words 'Double Murders' into Google. On the basis of this research, he reckoned he might get a 20 to 30 year sentence. If he got 20 years, then he could be a free man by the time he was 70—leaving him another 20 years. The Howell family had a history of longevity. He was already hoping to have some kind of life after his release.

At 10.15 a.m., Willie Patterson phoned for the police to come to the house. Kyle was weeping and distraught in her sorrow and anger, and in between her sobs, she wailed to her husband: 'You sucked the life out of Lesley, and that's what you do, Colin—you suck the life out of people . . .'

While Patterson made the call, the others stayed with Howell and tried to help him come to terms with the fact that he would be leaving his family for a very long time. They assured him that they would do their best to see that his children were safe and secure, and that someone would endeavour to look into his financial affairs. Then, as they waited for the police, they all held hands and prayed.

An hour and a half later, Sergeant Soren Stewart and two women detectives, Constable Melody Kidd and Constable Kathryn Parish, arrived at the Howell home. The dentist himself opened the door to them. His first words to the Sergeant were: 'Mr Stewart—I'm sorry to bring you out here under these circumstances.' Then the officers went into the room where the elders were assembled, and, as Constable Parish took notes and Howell waited outside, Patterson explained to them what Howell was claiming he had done.

The decision was quickly taken to arrest the dentist, but when Willie Patterson went to fetch him, he was nowhere to be seen. The elder returned in a panic, saying: 'He's gone, he's gone!' Kidd and Parish glanced at each other and then both looked out of the window at the lake below. They speculated that Howell might have jumped into the water, while Stewart's first thought was that he had hung himself. But just at that moment the dentist appeared nonchalantly from one of the many bedrooms, carrying a small sports bag and wondering what all the fuss was about. He was immediately arrested by the three officers and taken to their car. He did not say a word during the 15 minutes it took them to reach Coleraine police station.

———

Even as Howell waited in his cell to be brought into a nearby interview room, he must have had time to reflect on how it had come to this. He had lost everything: his wife, his family, his glittering career, his family home, his money, his place in the church, his standing in the community—and now, finally, his liberty. It was a question which would occupy many hours of his time in the captivity to come.

Chapter 2
Howell–Clarke: To Have and To Hold

MAY 1983

Colin Howell was looking forward to a new life together with his young fiancée, Lesley Clarke. It was May, just a few months before the wedding, and he was preparing to sit his final exams in dentistry at Belfast's Queen's University. After the wedding, their plans were to move to the town of Coleraine and set up home together. Clearly full of hope for the future and passionate about his bride-to-be, a 24-year-old Howell penned a letter to her:

> 'My dearest Lesley—I was just about to go to bed when I was filled with thoughts of you. It occurred to me that I'm always too busy thinking of work to relax with you, or that there is always a reason for us to be apart early in the evening. I'm just saying that I'm looking forward to long evenings together alone when these blasted exams are over. I miss you sometimes, like now, and want to tell you I love you and I'm looking forward to our future together. I hope Coleraine brings you new friends and new commitments to God. I'm just so tired now that I can't say all that's on my mind. It's 1.10 a.m. and I need sleep. With all my love, Colin xx.'

They were married on 16 July 1983 at Windsor Baptist Church, just off Belfast's Lisburn Road. The bridesmaids wore pale blue strapless dresses. The night before the wedding, they had stayed with Lesley at the Conway Hotel near Dunmurry, on the southern outskirts of Belfast, where the reception was to be held the following day. Lesley got a bikini wax and the girls had thought it hilarious. They were all in high spirits, yelping and laughing as they made their way around the hotel. Like her fiancé, the bride-to-be was excited and full of anticipation.

There had been a heat wave that summer, and it was a fabulous day for the wedding, and for the well-attended reception afterwards. The Howells and the Butlers—Colin's mother Sarah's family—were all God-fearing Baptists, well known in north Belfast for their earnest observance of their strict religious principles. Colin's family, especially his mother, would have preferred there to have been no alcohol on the tables at the reception, but the bride's father was having none of it. Harry Clarke was himself from a devout Brethren background in mid-Ulster but he was his own man, and did not see the harm in their guests being able to enjoy a few drinks. Chris Clarke, Lesley's brother, recalls that the difference of opinion made for a slightly strained atmosphere on the day: 'It was bizarre and slightly uncomfortable. There was rigid segregation. The tables were set in such a way that there was a corridor down the middle. Drink was served at one half, but not served at the other: there were wet tables and dry tables . . . My dad made a stand that he was serving alcohol to his guests . . . I can't remember if a toast was actually proposed. My dad was a fair, but not provocative man.'

The belief that it was important to observe a particular kind of religious lifestyle was not something confined to the older generation of the Clarkes and the Howells. It was a crucial factor in the lives of Colin and Lesley too—although neither of them felt quite as strongly about the issue of alcohol as Sarah Howell. Very much in line with his upbringing, however, Colin Howell firmly believed that there should be no sex before marriage, that his bride should be a virgin and that he would remain faithful to her until death.

Lesley was his first serious girlfriend and the first woman with whom he had sex. They had slept together before they were married, however, and he felt a great deal of guilt about this. And they had transgressed what Howell would have seen as God's immutable laws in other very serious ways too. In the year before they married, Lesley had no less than three abortions—two of these only weeks apart. They had both agreed that the pregnancies should be terminated. Lesley later confided to a friend that she feared at the time that her fiancé would end the relationship if she did not concede. It was she who paid for the abortions. On each occasion, Howell had accompanied her to the same clinic in west London—the very one to which he would also take his mistress Hazel a number of years later. The guilt felt by the young couple about the abortions was overwhelming—it was a burden which Lesley in particular would carry with her for many years.

In the days before the wedding, despite his impassioned letter to his fiancée, Howell had his doubts about the marriage—or so he would tell an examining psychiatrist in the years to come. Lesley had been unsure about it too. But the young man felt very much that they were compelled to go ahead—he was convinced that no one else would want either of them after what they had been through. All the arrangements were in place: everything had been organised, and the hotel and honeymoon had been booked. And so Howell decided, because of the momentum, to go ahead with the wedding. He was determined to make a go of it, and resolute that the relationship would last forever.

Lesley's Christianity meant everything to her too. She prayed often and spoke to those close to her of her desire to get to know God better. One of her favourite passages in the Bible was James 1:2-4, which refers to trials and temptations as opportunities for spiritual growth: 'Consider it pure joy, my brothers, whenever you face trials of many kinds, because you know that the testing of your faith develops perseverance. Perseverance must finish its work so that you may be mature and complete, not lacking anything.'

Valerie Allen, one of Lesley's closest friends, who knew her from their days growing up together in Dublin, would in later years identify the rigid religious ethos to which both Colin and Lesley were so deeply committed as being at the very heart of the tragedy which later played out in their lives: 'I felt that all this had happened in a cultural structure where guilt about pre-marital sex and so on drove people together; where they were under huge pressure to make the marriage work and not to divorce at any cost . . . I felt angry that they had not had enough life and sexual experience to have been able to . . . handle this better. I'm guessing Lesley [was] the first one Colin had been with. I don't know if he was [for her] or not. [But] if they had both had a bit more sexual experience, they might not have got married. Or they might have got married and made it work, rather than be gobsmacked at an affair. I felt a lot of it was guilt and inexperience. It made them feel that they had to stay together, when they had other options open to them, like divorce, or having sex with each other and not marrying.'

———

Colin Howell was brought up in the Protestant Woodvale district of Belfast, before the family moved to the neighbouring Ballysillan area. He was the fourth of five children, and had two brothers, Gordon and Jim, and two sisters, Pauline and Maud. In later years, he had minimal contact with any of his siblings, but he was always close to his father, Sam, a former manager at a Government Training Centre. Howell would later say of his relationship with Sam: 'I was dad's little buddy.' They played golf and went fishing together and even after Lesley's death, his father did not blame his son, or regard him as being responsible for it. He felt Colin was a son he could be proud of.

Howell's mother, Sarah, loved him as well. She always busied herself with general housework, and attended diligently to the needs of her children. He had great memories of her on family camping holidays in Donegal, when they could get away from the tensions of Belfast, then a troubled and dangerous city. She always looked out for her second youngest, and he recalled one occasion in particular when she was there to reassure him—the night when, as a teenager, he had cried after giving himself an electric shock: he had forgotten to switch off his electric blanket, and accidentally touched the pins of the plug when he woke up. And he had memories too, again as a teenager, of turning away in embarrassment one afternoon in Belfast, when Sarah challenged a barber over the price of a haircut. She was a good mother, but Howell didn't have the same relationship with her as he had with his father. She died in 2007, aged 75.

The Howells and Sarah's family, the Butlers, were both staunchly religious Baptist families. From a very early age, Colin attended Shankill Baptist Church with the rest of the family, and it was more or less inevitable perhaps that by the time he was six years old, he had committed himself fully to the Baptist faith. For the remainder of his childhood and indeed into adulthood, he attended church three times on a Sunday, as well as lining up faithfully once a week with his local battalion of the Boys' Brigade. By the time he was 13, the young Colin had decided that he wanted to become an overseas missionary, just like some of the people who came to speak at his Shankill church every now and again, and those he would meet many years later when he did free dental work in both India, and in Romania where a Baptist pastor would name his adopted son after the dentist from Castlerock.

Howell was educated at Cavehill Primary School. When he sat an entrance test for a grammar school place at Belfast Royal Academy, he spent too long on the questions and narrowly failed the exam. So he went instead to The Boys' Model, a big all-boys secondary school in north Belfast which also had an excellent record in academic achievement. He conducted himself well, never got into trouble and was complimented by the teachers on his neat handwriting. He didn't, however, feel comfortable with the fairly macho, aggressive ethos among the boys in the classrooms and on the sports pitches at 'the Model', where many of the pupils came from tough, working-class districts heavily influenced by loyalist paramilitaries. He remembers suffering from a lack of confidence and low self-esteem. By the time he sat his O-levels in the mid-70s, however, his family had moved out of Belfast and he much preferred Portadown College, a mixed-sex school, where he would go on to obtain A-levels in Maths, Chemistry and Physics. He was a school prefect and a member of the Scripture Union. Former headmaster Harry Armstrong recalls of him: 'He was a perfectly reasonable, well-balanced young man, a hard worker, keen on his studies—a model pupil, really. It was obvious he had his eyes on a professional career . . .'

Howell's ambition was to study medicine once he left school, but his 'B' and two 'C' grades were not good enough for him to be able to qualify. He decided to do dentistry at Queen's University, where he spent six years, including a year out to do a Bachelor of Science degree in Anatomy. Former associates from his university days were not hugely impressed by him. With around 35 students in his year, Howell tended to keep himself to himself and rarely socialised with any of them. He shared a house with five other students at 37 Stranmillis Road, just opposite the Ulster Museum. His evangelical Protestant beliefs and fire-and-brimstone type of Christianity didn't sit well in the clubs and bars around the university which the dentistry crowd tended to frequent, and his classmates considered him something of an outsider. One ex-student, who knew him during his fourth and fifth year, remembers: 'He wasn't the brightest, but then he wasn't the dumbest either. He kept a low profile and didn't stand out. He was a bit of a loner and didn't seem to mix with the more gregarious amongst us, who might have been a touch loud, told jokes and held court. He wouldn't have been part of that crowd. He was very peripheral: quiet, shy and a bit of a country boy, really.'

Howell had just one potentially serious girlfriend before he met Lesley. It was someone he met shortly after he started university, but she had two-timed him at a summer camp. She pleaded for a reconciliation, but the young dental student was hurt and wanted nothing more to do with her. It wasn't the first time he had been let down in his romantic dealings with the opposite sex. As a teenager he had once written a letter to a girl he fancied, but she ended up going out with the boy he had charged with delivering the envelope.

As a young man, Howell's religious beliefs left him frustrated and sexually repressed. Perhaps it was no surprise then that he developed a fascination for pornography, buying his first top-shelf magazine when he was 19 and a student in Belfast. He would go on to struggle with pornography all his adult life, as the fascination soon developed into an obsession, about which, as a strict Christian, he was tormented with guilt. In later life, he made numerous attempts to break a compulsion to spend hours sitting alone at night looking at images on his computer: he even went so far as to enlist the help of church elders and some fairly sophisticated computer software, but all to no avail.

When it came to women, the young Howell was intense and possessive. He first met Lesley at a church gathering. In March 1980, when friends presented him with a bicycle for his 21st birthday at a party at the Queen's Halls of Residence, she and some of the girls she shared a house with were among the guests.

Lesley, a very attractive and gregarious girl, was a student nurse at Belfast's Royal Victoria Hospital and shared a house with others in her year. She was popular with the male sex and had been on dates with various suitors before she met Howell. The first of these worked for the BBC. His main hobby was hang gliding and he gave her a present of a Paddington bear—but the relationship lasted no more than a month. Another date collected her on one occasion in an impressive-looking car, which caused the other girls to stare with envy. At one point, she was struck with a young man called Robert, and felt hurt when the brief liaison ended abruptly. She once got talking to a nice fellow she met on the bus going home to Hillsborough one day, but he ended up asking out one of Lesley's friends. And finally, just around the time she met Howell, but before things got serious between them, she went out with a junior doctor one night. He was a Catholic from west Belfast, and she liked him and thought him a bit special. But Howell, who clearly was more serious about Lesley than she was about him, was not best pleased. He turned up at her house and waited for her to return with the new friend. When the two arrived back, Howell ended up physically ejecting the other young man from the building, in a jealous fit of rage. It was perhaps an early indication of his intense and controlling instincts when it came to women.

––––

She was born Lesley Anne Elizabeth Clarke, on 24 February 1960 in Plymouth, England, where her father Harry, who came originally from Waringstown in County Armagh, was based with the Royal Marines. Mrs May Clarke (née Marshall) had given birth to her only other child, Christopher, in Lurgan, County Armagh, some 18 months earlier. After Mr Clarke left the Marines and went into business, working for a pet food company, the family moved to Eaglesham in Scotland, and then to west Kilbride, before settling for a number of years in Dalkey, south Dublin. This is where Lesley spent the happiest years of her childhood.

She attended Wesley College for a year and then switched to Newpark Comprehensive, at the time a new and innovative coeducational school in Blackrock. Its sister school was Mount Temple Comprehensive, north Dublin, where Bono of U2 is an ex-pupil. Lesley was bright and intelligent, and a very good student. She became part of a small circle of friends who attended an evangelical youth club, the Highway Club, at Merrion Hall in the centre of Dublin. This was around 1971. She was already friendly with a girl called Hilary Scargill, who lived nearby, when she met Valerie Allen from Silchester Park, Glenageary. Valerie had been a pupil at Glengara

Girls and then moved to Newpark. Lesley and Valerie attended the same history and French classes. (Being comprehensive schools under the patronage of the Church of Ireland, both Newpark and Mount Temple were open to all denominations.)

Lesley and Valerie would go to the youth club every Saturday night, and later they sang together in a choir called 'Daybreak'. Sometimes during the Easter holidays, they would stay at Lesley's family caravan—either on their own or with the Clarke family—at Roundwood, near Glendalough in the Wicklow Mountains. They played Monopoly and ate bacon sandwiches during the day, and at night, after dressing up to disguise their teenage years, they would slip off to a nearby pub. Valerie had developed a taste for Guinness, but drank moderately. Lesley had the occasional Babycham. One weekend, as Valerie recalls, the girls went for a walk and found a pregnant sheep in danger of drowning in a bog. They eventually managed to pull it free, and the rescue operation, which seemed to last for ages, was indicative of Lesley's love of animals. At the time she had a cocker spaniel called Patsi, and she had doted on the family's previous dog, Pip, also a cocker spaniel. When she was married and living in Coleraine, she had another spaniel, Kerrie.

After the Leaving Cert school exams, Valerie went to Dublin's Trinity College and Lesley to Belfast to take up a career in nursing, which was very much a family tradition. She had an aunt who nursed in London and two cousins, who were a little older than her and great fun, who worked at hospitals in Northern Ireland. It seemed that Lesley was always destined for the wards, according to Valerie, now a professor in the English Department at John Jay College, City University of New York: 'She was demonstrative and very caring to her parents. She was also very affectionate. She had a lovely way. She would compliment us about how we looked. She was very sweet, intelligent, not quick-tempered or jealous.'

After a short spell working in a shop in Dublin immediately after leaving school, Lesley moved to Belfast to take up a place as a student nurse at the Royal Victoria Hospital in Belfast. It was 1978, the year when the DeLorean car company, backed by £56 million of British government aid, announced plans to build a luxury sports car plant at Dunmurry. Belfast was a dark and dangerous city—88 people died violently during that year, which was otherwise dominated by an escalating protest inside the Maze Prison by 250 Republicans who were demanding political status. The prisoners' campaign took the form of refusing to slop out, and smearing excrement around their cells. The then all-Ireland Catholic Primate Cardinal Tomás Ó Fiaich, who visited the jail at the time, said the cells reminded him of a Calcutta slum.

The new arrival from the Irish Republic was apolitical, but she quickly realised that life in west Belfast, where she worked, was much different from the cosseted environment of Dublin 4. Her type of evangelicalism kept her away from the sectarian politics of Northern Ireland, but friends remember that she once voted for a Unionist candidate because she was upset at having to treat young British soldiers with perforated stomachs: the result, it was said, of accepting sandwiches laced with ground glass, which had been offered to them by seemingly friendly locals on the nationalist Falls Road.

Initially Lesley missed Dublin and even though there were about 15 other trainees, including two from Co. Monaghan, she admitted that she felt lonely for the first few months, living in nursing accommodation on the city's Whitewell Road. The training on the wards was demanding and at night the student nurses would have to study in preparation for a test every Friday. More often than not, Lesley would finish top of the class.

With Lesley dressed as a cheeky schoolgirl, the student nurses held a party to mark their move from the accommodation at Whitewell Road to the nursing home at the Royal. By this time, Lesley had developed a close circle of good friends. There were half a dozen in the group, all of them Christians who enjoyed each other's company. Some of them would go home at weekends, while Lesley took time out to visit relatives from her father's side of the family, in mid-Ulster. Among these was her cousin, Eric Clarke, a gospel singer whom she liked and respected. She worried about her grandmother, Elizabeth Marshall, who lived on the Banbridge Road, Lurgan: Elizabeth suffered from high blood pressure. Lesley feared her mother would suffer from the same medical condition. Mrs Marshall died in 1981, just five years before Lesley's mum passed away from poor health brought on by heart-related problems.

Lesley was an outstanding nurse. Her early days at the Royal were spent in the geriatric unit. The work was hard and demanding, both physically and emotionally. Some of the nurses found it depressing, but Lesley got on remarkably well with the elderly women, sometimes cleaning and polishing their finger nails and putting on perfume for them in readiness for visiting time. A former colleague, a junior doctor at the time, remembers Lesley on the haematology ward, nursing an elderly lady who had undergone a bone marrow transplant. This patient later died, but Lesley had gone out of her way to make her final days as comfortable as possible. The ex-colleague recalls: 'She was extremely good to that lady, but then all the patients liked her. She was exceptionally considerate, a very caring nurse and you would be hard pressed to say anything negative about her. She was a very nice girl, bubbly with beautiful eyes. I didn't know her for very long. She was a born-again Christian. I remember having our photograph taken with that lady, Lesley sitting on one side of the bed, me on the other. The Royal, and working in medicine, was a lot different in those days. We used to play tennis on the courts outside the wards, and if you walked in still wearing your tennis gear, then nobody took a blind bit of notice. It was all so much more relaxed and civilised, and that was the type of regime Lesley worked in.'

Keen to move out of nursing accommodation, Lesley and her friends decided to check out the ads for rented accommodation in the *Belfast Telegraph*, quickly finding a house which looked suitable for them. It was a warm summer's evening when they went to investigate No. 108 University Avenue. Other girls had also gathered outside the front door. Lesley and her friends liked the location because the road was tree-lined and away from the other students, who generally preferred accommodation closer to the Royal, on the Donegall Road and off the lower end of Lisburn Road. The landlord was not hugely impressed, however, when six student nurses said they wanted to rent his property. As well as Lesley, there was Ruth Allison from Belfast, Ann Kempton from Dungannon, Co. Tyrone, Linda Patterson from Lifford, Co. Donegal, Janet Torbitt from Whitehead, Co. Antrim, and Carolyn Walker from Londonderry. Carolyn would later become one of Lesley's three bridesmaids. While at first the landlord was very reluctant, Lesley assured him that they were girls of high standing who didn't drink alcohol, and promised him there would be no wild parties. It was her negotiating skills which secured the lease. She moved into the first floor front room, which was bright, with a dining table by the window.

It was around this time that Lesley's parents moved to Hillsborough. They thought she would be pleased to be closer to the new family home, but it effectively signalled the end of her days in Dublin. Just as her mother had been sorry to leave Scotland, Lesley was heartbroken that she would no longer have a permanent base in the city she loved, and would now be living 100 miles away from her two close friends from school, Valerie Allen and Hilary Scargill. She talked a lot about her time in Dublin. Her recall was impressive if somewhat romantic, and when she went back from time to time, she felt it wasn't the same somehow. After the family move to Hillsborough, her mother May's health began to deteriorate. She had a coronary artery bypass, but problems developed with the healing process after a vein was removed from her leg. One night, while at singing practice in Windsor Baptist Church, Lesley heard that her mum had suffered a small stroke and immediately feared a much bigger one was up ahead.

The young nurse would make the short journey to the wards on an old bicycle which she had brought up from Dublin. It was a bit of a bone-shaker. Maroon in colour with a basket in front, it rattled as she pedalled along the Donegall Road before the morning rush-hour traffic started. When it rained, she pulled on waterproofs over her uniform, and wore red Wellington boots. One morning, she came across a wounded pigeon struggling to get to its feet after being struck by a passing car. She stopped and lifted the bird onto the footpath. There was nothing she could do to save it, but she didn't want it to be run over again. Her fondness for animals was as strong as ever. She refused to buy any cosmetics if the brands had been animal-tested. Friends remember how Lesley had once insisted on bringing Patsi, her spaniel dog—who was generally kept in Hillsborough with her parents—to stay with her for a few days in the house on University Avenue. Patsi had a great time, with Lesley letting her run wild in the nearby Botanic Gardens.

The girls had plenty of callers to No. 108, including a now friendly landlord who always got his rent on time, and would sometimes drop by for supper. Of the six housemates, it was Lesley who invariably attracted the most attention. With her gentle voice, warm smile, shiny dark hair, sparkling eyes and beautiful grasp of the English language, she could disarm most men, even the rudest. She was a hopeless romantic. She radiated warmth and personality. She could also be self-deprecating and made fun of herself all the time, once posing for a photograph wearing a set of huge green false teeth.

Late night meals often meant the dishes going unwashed, and it was left to the girl who was off the next day to clean up. Lesley wasn't slow to lift the drying cloth and did her part to make sure the kitchen was kept neat and tidy. She wasn't in the least vain, but she was particular about her appearance, especially her hair, and would spend a lot of time trying to get rid of the curls. Some of her friends remember how Lesley would go to the hairdressers for a blow dry, only to wash and dry her hair again herself as soon as she was back at home, because she deemed it hadn't been straightened enough by the session at the salon. She loved relaxing in the bath and pampering herself afterwards with rich, scented body moisturisers. She would make sure her nails were always beautifully manicured. The day she showed off her engagement ring, they were especially well done.

Lesley's first holiday with her student nursing friends was to Europe. First to Rome, and then Florence, where they fell in with a crowd who regularly went drinking. But being more or less teetotal themselves, they soon had enough of the sleazy bars, loud singing and leering men, and decided they preferred their own company. The next stop was Venice, where they stayed in an apartment and spent hours lying under a hot sun, eating melon and ice cream. They went swimming, and one day Lesley and a friend were swept away by strong currents onto some rocks. The two managed to climb to safety and pick their way back to the shore, relieved but somewhat embarrassed to be met by a reception committee of noisy Italians.

One year, Lesley and her friends went on an overland trip to Greece. On the train journey, they shared carriages with Yugoslavian soldiers and farmers carrying cages of chickens. It was Lesley's idea for them to hire couchettes as they travelled through Switzerland. By the time they arrived in Athens, they were filthy and desperate for a wash. There they stayed in a hostel, and were taken on a tour of all the city's most famous sites by a young man they met on the train, who had taken a shine to one of the girls. Then they got a boat to the island of Paxos and stayed in a little fishing village. Lesley loved the climate, but had developed what she described at the time as a 'stunted palate'. She drank only tea and coke, and could not bring herself to eat the local specialities of lasagne, moussaka and fish dishes, or the garlic, yoghurt, tomatoes and cheese. Friends remember how once, when she tried a meal of meatballs, she had pushed the plate away in disgust, declaring that they tasted horrible.

Next they moved on to Naxos and another apartment, this time on the beach and much more modern than the first. It was early May, and cold and windy. They had been joined by an American girl who complained about everything from the weather to the food to the restaurant waiters. They hired motorcycles, rode without safety helmets and got lost. Lesley's bike had faulty brakes. She read a lot and would sit with her book on the balcony, well wrapped up and with a pair of knickers on her head.

———

Lesley's first big night out with Howell was to the dentists' formal at Queen's University. Howell excitedly told friends he would be taking her to the event, but girlfriends remember how she quickly put him right on that score, telling him: 'You don't *take* me to anything. I come.' She bought an expensive evening dress for the occasion, at one of Belfast's top boutiques: Howell cringed when she told him what it cost. Before they set off from Lesley's, he presented her with a red rose.

There was no doubt that he was making all the running, and there was a time when Lesley wasn't convinced the dental student was really the man for her. In a letter to Valerie dated October 1981, she wrote: 'Every time I write to you, I think about trying to explain clearly my relationship with Colin, but then I can never make the effort. But I assure you that we have no intention of walking up the aisle together and I still think in terms of making decisions on my own. Colin is not considered.' Valerie recalls: 'Lesley told me the relationship was problematic. Colin was much hotter on her than she was on him. I don't remember the nature of their issues, but she'd write to me to say he wasn't a serious item for quite a long time.'

But things changed. In another letter to Valerie, dated August 1982, Lesley confirmed that her feelings for Colin were developing in a positive way. The couple had been together on holiday in Greece with friends, and she wrote: 'Colin didn't turn nut-brown on the beach, but I must admit I had eyes for none other than him, despite the fact he had a large, red hooter. Things are going very well between us and we have had a great time together this summer.' However, she was not afraid to poke gentle fun at her boyfriend. Another of her postcards home read: 'Dear Val, I'm sitting in the village square after enjoying a hearty breakfast. Sad to say, the heat has not impaired my appetite. Colin is beside me, looking typically Irish, wearing a white sun hat with nylon ankle socks. Most attractive!'

By November 1982, Lesley's feelings for the man in her life had strengthened further. She wrote to Valerie: 'Things are going pretty well as planned, or should I say, as dreamed . . . From the way I am talking, you can gather that I'm assuming that I have found the right one. Well, I think that I have. I am no longer lukewarm about Colin. I think the world of him. It's a good feeling. Colin and I are still getting along famously and I sometimes marvel at how funny it feels to know someone as well as I know him and yet he isn't a member of my family.'

———

And so, in spite of doubts on both sides, the marriage went ahead. After the big day in July 1983, the young couple moved as planned to the North Coast, where Colin had already secured his first job in dentistry, working for Terry Boyd and Alan Logue at their Waterside branch in Coleraine, as well as one day a week in nearby Ballycastle. When they first moved, the Howells rented a house in Portballintrae for nine months. Overlooking the harbour in one of the prettiest villages in Northern Ireland, it was an idyllic and romantic setting which seemed to bode well for the Howells' new life together.

Chapter 3

Trouble in Paradise

At first it seemed that married life was treating Colin and Lesley Howell well. Soon after they moved from their rented property in Portballintrae to a house of their own at Culmore Gardens, off the Mountsandel Road in Coleraine, Lesley joined a small Bible study and prayer group, made up of young married women, many of them with small children, from different Protestant churches in the area. They took turns to meet in each other's houses, and the newcomer was among the more outgoing. People liked her. She was thoughtful, warm-hearted and always had something to say. She was gentle and caring, and loved children. One night at a Bible group study session, the women discussed who they believed could be modelled on Christ. Lesley looked up at once and said: 'That would be Colin.' She clearly thought the world of her new husband.

But fast forward a few years, and, at the same regular gathering, some noticed that Lesley Howell had become quieter of late. As they discussed the scriptures over tea and sandwiches, she was withdrawn and at times seemed preoccupied with troubles she did not disclose to anyone. At one meeting, however, she happened to let slip the remark: 'Colin isn't all he could have been.' It seemed that the man she had married wasn't quite the saint she once made him out to be. Most of the women in the group were slightly puzzled by her comment. But one or two others knew exactly what had been going on.

———

When they first moved to the North Coast, Lesley had worked with the Marie Curie Foundation and for a time nursed in Coleraine hospital, but she felt uncomfortable on the wards and didn't enjoy it. Some of the nurses told her: 'Oh, you're from the Royal. You must have a few airs and graces.' She would have liked to have returned to Belfast, but Howell was having none of it. His professional interests came first, although he agreed to spend more time with her at weekends and go shopping, which he disliked. When their first child, Matthew, was born in October 1984, it seemed easier all round for Lesley to stop work and stay at home to look after the baby.

Howell's career, meanwhile, was flourishing. He got on well with his employers, Terry Boyd and Alan Logue, and stayed with them for five years. They were both Belfast men. Logue was the son of a Presbyterian minister from North Belfast, while Boyd, like Howell, was a Baptist at the time. They owned a number of practices, in Maghera, Belfast, Londonderry, Kilrea, Ballycastle, and three in Coleraine. They had gone into partnership in 1979 and, having started with one surgery based on the Lodge Road in Coleraine, developed the practice into one of the largest in Northern Ireland. At one stage, they had up to 35,000 patients on their books and 19 associates. Howell started off dividing his time between one of the Coleraine clinics and the Ballycastle branch, but soon he was based full-time at the Coleraine Waterside clinic.

Just after their arrival in the area, the Howells joined Coleraine Baptist Church—one of the oldest Baptist churches in Ireland. They were both very actively involved in church affairs from the beginning, and soon much of their social life centred around the church, as part of a fairly tightly-knit circle of friends. The church elders were quickly impressed by Colin Howell's obvious energy and commitment. He was appointed leader of the Youth Fellowship and helped to run their participation in the Duke of Edinburgh's Award Scheme; he drove the church mini-bus and sometimes took the children to the beach at Castlerock, where they played rounders. He also worked as an assistant with Campaigners, the church's uniformed youth section. No longer the reticent, slightly aloof young man he had been as a student, Howell had grown in confidence and was popular in church circles.

But Lesley was finding domesticity isolating and unfulfilling. She missed the challenge and the fun of working in the Royal, and the sense of worth which her nursing duties had given her. As a new mother trying to settle in an area where none of her family or old friends were close by, she sorely missed the camaraderie of her work and the shared accommodation in Belfast. Her friend Valerie Allen remembers being very much aware of the difficulties of Lesley's new circumstances: 'She was a new wife and [learning] to be a mother [too]. . . . She didn't have an outlet. She was [now just] Colin Howell's wife and had lost the place where she once shone. She had no platform for her talents.'

Always lively and resourceful, Lesley did her best not to lose her sense of humour. In a letter to Valerie just over a year after the wedding, she wrote: 'I must say, I miss work more as time goes on, although it hasn't been too bad all summer. But apart from the money and the work itself, it's amazing how much more interesting your conversation is when you have something other than the rising cost of baked beans to discuss.' By February 1985—not long after the birth of her first son, Matthew—domestic life had more or less taken over completely, as another letter to Valerie confirmed:

'I have decided to leave the house in its present chaotic state and write to you instead. I don't honestly think that I am a born housewife. I cleaned my windows for the first time in over a year yesterday. Well actually, I cleaned two of them. The others will probably get done over the next couple of months. I was due a visit from the Ma- and Pa-in-law, which has been called off, so I can revert to my usual slovenliness.

'I have been collecting all my issues of *Christian Woman* magazine for you to browse through, because I thought you might find some interesting articles on homemaking and also there are some very exciting [ones] on crocheted underpants, which have great properties of elastication, which can come in handy. Well, I know that this has hardly been a scintillating letter and now that the hubby has arrived home, I'll have to go and make some bangers and mash.'

In spite of her jesting, however, the young wife and mother struggled to cope. And it was perhaps typical of her that, even with her best friend, she often tried to hide her difficulties under a mask of humour. Howell himself recognised his wife's ability to put up a cheerful front when she thought it was required: 'Depending on who she was talking to, Lesley would have smiled and said things are great. She'd give you the great picture, and maybe she'd be more truthful to others. She was good at covering up. If we were having an argument and she was really upset and someone came to the door, she'd be turning on the charm. She'd switch to being brilliant in seconds.'

Howell liked to control all aspects of his life, but Lesley was not the subservient, compliant 'little-woman-at-home' he wanted her to be. She wasn't the tidiest of housewives and was never afraid to leave the baby with him when she wanted time on her own. Her spending habits quickly became another source of conflict: she was poor at sticking to a budget and not particularly interested in domesticity. She liked splashing out on clothes and holidays. The husband of a good friend of hers recalls: 'Lesley liked shopping. She liked clothes and style. She aspired to be like some of the other wives of dentists in the town who drove nice cars and had a nice lifestyle.'

In 1986, Lesley fell pregnant again. During the pregnancy, she went through a very stressful time: her mother suffered a series of severe setbacks in her health, before having to go into a nursing home where she died 10 weeks before the baby's birth. Lauren, the Howells' second child, was born on 14 November 1986. In the months which followed, it is likely that Lesley suffered from some form of postnatal depression, although this was never formally diagnosed. Tensions in the marriage increased dramatically from this point onwards.

Meanwhile, Howell's professional career was moving very much in the right direction. After five years working for Logue and Boyd, principally with NHS patients, he was keen to branch out and broaden his remit. He wanted to do things differently, and sounded out his employers with his new ideas—but, as Howell told police after his arrest, they weren't as receptive as he had hoped: 'I discussed changes I wanted to make within the practice, to do things better . . . They weren't willing to invest in those changes . . .' He decided to go out on his own. He offered to buy the Waterside practice, but Logue and Boyd wanted to keep it within their existing structure. He then thought for a while about opening his own practice in Portstewart, but his employers objected because they considered this part of their patient area. And so, in 1988, he paid £34,000 for a property in Ballymoney, which needed major refurbishment before it could be opened to the public.

Howell was determined that his first practice would be state-of-the-art, and that no expense would be spared in the renovation and fitting out of the premises in Queen Street. For a young man who was not yet thirty and had a very young family to think of—Lesley was already pregnant with their third child—it was an ambitious venture, with more than a small element of risk involved. But the impulsive Howell had never been afraid to take a chance. By his own admission, he liked to live on the edge. He had once been on a visit to Niagara Falls with some university friends. When they first arrived at the site of the Falls, it seemed, Howell had insisted on climbing over a safety barrier and then getting down on his hands and knees and crawling along a ledge, so that he could get a closer view of the water crashing down. He was simply oblivious to the danger he was exposing himself to at the time, as well as the obvious anxiety of his friends.

In some ways, it seemed that the young dentist's approach to business was equally devil-may-care. Howell later admitted that his business sense was not always the most grounded or circumspect: 'I was driven by what I was doing and the quality of what I wanted to do, rather than the mathematics of, can I afford to do it? I just believed it would work. It was an inspirational way of doing business, rather than a calculated way of doing it.'

It was inevitable perhaps that he quickly ran into financial difficulties in fitting out the new surgery: 'One of the mistakes I made was that I equipped and maintained [the surgery] with equipment and stuff that I couldn't afford. It stretched me further.' Once the surgery was opened, he soon had more work than he could handle alone, and he brought in a second dentist. But the profit margins didn't really improve: 'Because, as you get busier, you need to make more, buy more equipment, make more investments. You've got to pay another dentist. So the inspirational way never really worked.'

Given the financial pressures Howell faced, it probably wasn't the best time to invest in a bigger and more expensive family home. Yet this is what he did anyway, buying a large bungalow on the other side of town—Knocklayde Park—for £85,000 in November 1989. Mortgages on the new family home and the Ballymoney practice were arranged through the Northern Bank. But soon the Howells had run out of money and were living on an overdraft. And they now had a third child to think of too—Lesley had given birth to a son, Daniel, six months earlier.

The Knocklayde Park bungalow was a brand new property still needing fixtures and fittings and basic decoration, but, unable to afford to have anything substantial done, the family moved in regardless. They were so strapped for cash, in fact, that they were

unable to afford to put a carpet down. With an ill-equipped and
untidy house and now three infants to take care of, it was more
difficult than ever for Lesley to cope. A neighbour remembers once
seeing one of the children in a babygro, standing on the concrete floor
of the hallway in a pool of urine left by the family's pet cocker spaniel.
Howell found himself spending more and more time taking charge of
the children to try and take some of the domestic pressure off his wife.
He gave up playing sport so that he could spend more time with his
young family. But between making the tea, changing nappies and
helping to put the children to bed at night, he was becoming
increasingly disillusioned with the unending tensions and stresses of
his relationship with Lesley.

Soon the financial pressures were becoming intolerable. Cheques
were being returned and Lesley was unable to withdraw money from
the cash dispenser. The young dentist blamed delayed NHS payments
for the cash-flow problems. His Northern Bank manager was very
concerned about the situation, as Howell would later recount: 'I
remember getting phone calls from the bank manager, but that
happens all the time. I remember having meetings and increasing my
overdraft limit, but again, that would be normal . . . I wasn't very good
at handling money. I was my own worst enemy.' His money problems
became so critical that he discreetly tried to sell off his new home
without having to put up a 'For Sale' sign. He also approached his
former employer, Terry Boyd, and inquired if he would be interested
in taking over the Ballymoney practice where he had overspent on
equipment. He urged Lesley to ease up on her spending. She feared
her husband was going to become bankrupt.

Tania Donaghy, a nurse and receptionist at Howell's practice and a
good friend of Lesley's, found herself caught up in the deepening
domestic crisis, when Lesley phoned her one day and asked her to
remove whatever money was in the surgery's cash box. There was
£400. In a later police interview, Tania recalled that Lesley was very
upset: 'I am nearly sure she told me she wanted the cash because she
was leaving Colin there and then. However, before Lesley got there to
collect the cash, Colin instructed me to bank [it]. I felt I was piggy-in-
the-middle between both of them. But I never heard them argue or
fight. They were always pleasant to each other.'

Just before Christmas 1989, a month or so after the move to the
bungalow in Knocklayde Park, Lesley discovered she was pregnant

again, with their fourth child, Jonathan. At the 1992 inquest into Lesley's death, Howell would tell the coroner that his wife had struggled to accept that she had fallen pregnant again so quickly. Lesley loved all of her children dearly, but in the run-up to Christmas that year, the prospect of soon having to care for four young children under the age of five, one of them a new-born, in chaotic domestic circumstances and with the added stress of their dire financial straits, must have been very difficult for her.

There was another source of deep unhappiness for Lesley at the time—perhaps the one which she found most difficult to accept. Around the time of their third child Daniel's birth, in 1989, Colin had had a fling with a married woman, an old friend from his university days. Her husband was away a lot on business, and she and Howell had started a liaison which had lasted a month or so. Lesley found out what was going on and challenged him about it. She even telephoned the woman, who assured her that by that stage the affair had ended and her life had moved on.

But the discovery of her husband's infidelity, and the timing of it, devastated Lesley, and her already shaky self-esteem—badly eroded by her sense of isolation and the tensions within the marriage—plummeted to new depths. She wanted to move on and try to forget, but the affair, however fleeting, left a serious crack in the relationship. It was never the same between them again. He thought about divorce, but never seriously considered it as an option, because he was afraid of what he believed would be the stigma attached to such a course of action. And how could a man with such powerful religious convictions and so many close Baptist friends walk away from his wife and children?

By the spring of 1990, however, as things at home got worse, Howell was already actively on the look-out for another woman. Even though he was well aware of the impact his first dalliance had had on his wife, it seemed he could not stop himself from seeking gratification with the opposite sex elsewhere. It was undoubtedly a form of escapism, and he didn't seem to care what the consequences for his family might be.

———

This time, it was a young mother called Hazel Buchanan—who worked as an assistant at his daughter Lauren's nursery school—who caught his eye. She was the wife of a police officer, Trevor Buchanan, a constable and scenes-of-crime officer in the then Royal Ulster Constabulary (RUC). The couple, who had two young children, Andrew and Lisa, also lived in Coleraine and were members of the same Baptist Church as the Howells, where Hazel sometimes looked after the younger set at the children's Sunday school. She was shy, impressionable and careful about her appearance. She looked well, but those who knew of the affair at the time often wondered what the attraction was, and why the confident, demonstrative and ambitious Howell should have fallen for this particular lady, who lived on the opposite side of the town.

Hazel had a sheltered upbringing in the country. Her parents were God-fearing Baptist folks, just like Howell's. She was an excellent mother and a seemingly dutiful wife. She had little personality, but was clearly seduced by his charm and intellect. She and Howell, who had already made each other's acquaintance through church circles, would chat when he dropped off little Lauren to the Mulberry Bush Nursery School at Mountsandel, where the child would spend most weekday mornings. At one time, Hazel had also been a patient at the dentist's clinic. Gradually, the relationship began to develop.

It was in the water of the swimming pool of the Riada Leisure Centre in Ballymoney that the affair first started. It was early summer, 1990. Lesley, who was pregnant with Jonathan and resting at home, had arranged for the children to have swimming lessons, and Hazel took her two along as well. She was one of a number of mothers in attendance, but Howell was the only father there. Most of the women sat and had coffee as they watched their children in the pool, but Hazel was keen to learn how to get her breathing right while doing the front crawl. She soon found the confident and charming Howell to be a willing instructor, holding her waist high with both hands as she practised her strokes.

As the weeks passed, the two began to flirt. One afternoon in the pool, as he held her up in the water, he noticed her skin was more slippery than usual: she had been using a particularly rich body moisturiser. Before he could stop himself, he ran his hand over her upper legs, and then across her pubic area, towards her stomach and back again. Half expecting a slap on the face, he excused himself at once: 'If I'm having wrong thoughts about you, you'll have to forgive me.' But he was relieved as well as heartened when the young mother responded: 'I'm not so innocent myself,' before she gently pushed him to one side, leaving him standing as she swam away.

That day in the deep end of the pool, an invisible line had been crossed, and it was not long afterwards that the couple kissed and embraced for the first time. It happened after they had taken their children for a walk on the beach at Castlerock on an outing with other families, organised by the church's Children's Special Services Mission. On this particular day, the two had gone to his house afterwards and in his bathroom, as they were washing the sand out of their children's hair and toes, Hazel rubbed her hand on his arm. Before they knew it, they had stepped into one of the bedrooms out of sight of the children, and were kissing and touching one another.

They quickly found an excuse for Howell to call over to the Buchanan's house at certain times. He played in a church group and was handy with the guitar. Hazel said she wanted him to teach her some new chords. And so he would come to the house with sheets of music, and strum away, as she would sit at the opposite end of the sofa with her own guitar resting on her knee, trying to follow what he was doing. Her husband once arrived home unexpectedly and was not impressed. Even though the pair had always anticipated how he, and they, would react if he suddenly appeared unannounced, Trevor Buchanan realised almost at once that the music lessons were not as innocent as they looked. 'Hello Colin,' the young policeman said, as he summoned his wife to the kitchen. Hazel tried to explain that it was all very harmless and said she wondered why her husband would get into such an agitated state. Suspecting—accurately, of course—that Howell's motive for being there was not restricted to music, Trevor left the house in annoyance, driving off in his white Toyota Corolla.

The first time they had sex was early summer 1990, probably June. It was in the Buchanans' home. Trevor was out, but Howell brought his guitar with him just in case. Hazel was dressed in a denim mini-skirt and a low-cut, sleeveless blouse. The heavy scent of her perfume was an irresistible invitation which Howell did not turn down. Years later, he would identify this as the moment he got caught up in a fatal tangle that was just as much her making as it was his: 'I was walking into the spider's web . . .' Then and there, they made love, and both enjoyed it. But once it was over, Hazel went into immediate denial, feigning surprise that it had actually taken place at all: 'Did that really happen? Did that really happen?' she questioned her lover. Years later,

Howell would recount: 'I remember saying to her: "We've just had sex. Do you want me to explain it to you?"'

The affair continued, with the couple stealing moments together whenever possible. Typically, Howell was not averse to taking chances and sailing very close to the wind when it came to seeing his lover. On three occasions, he would insist on coming to the house when Trevor was there—asleep in bed, having come back from night duty. Once, Hazel had pleaded with the headstrong dentist on the telephone not to come, but he was compelled to do so anyway, and arrived in the utility room to take his nervous lover into his arms. Years later, he explained to police: 'I knew Trevor had a gun. It was just to see her. When you don't see much of each other and it's full of passion . . . You plan to see each other, then realise you can't. It was just to see her.'

Sometimes, Hazel would tell her husband she was going shopping and then rendezvous with her lover in nearby towns such as Ballymena. They would also arrange to meet while out running and cycling the roads, as part of their keep-fit routines. Sex was usually once a week—sometimes at Howell's clinic at night when all the staff had gone home, and sometimes at Hazel's house when Trevor was out. The Buchanans' garden backed onto Mountsandel Wood. Wearing his running gear, Howell would disappear from the road into the trees before emerging again to climb the perimeter fence of the forest, and sneaking in quietly through the back door. Sometimes he even slipped through the bedroom window.

The couple's movements in public were always well choreographed and nobody suspected a liaison, even when they appeared together. Friends remember meeting Colin, Lesley, Hazel and the children in the centre of Coleraine, when Lesley was on crutches after falling and breaking a bone in her foot. They thought the other woman was there to assist Lesley, but later realised it was not the only reason.

Trevor's brother, Gordon Buchanan—also a policeman— remembers how he and his wife called at the house at Charnwood Park one afternoon. The two brothers took the children for a walk to a nearby rugby pitch, leaving their wives on their own. There had been no hint of any marital discord, but by the time the men returned, Hazel had taken off on her bicycle, leaving Donna on her own. Trevor was not pleased, as Gordon recalls: 'I can only speculate now where she was going. Trevor seemed overly anxious and agitated as it was getting dark, and looking back, I think he had an inkling that Hazel was having an affair . . . For most people, it would be unthinkable to leave a visitor in the house on their own and head off on a bicycle. It was downright rude. There had to be some other reason for doing that. It left us uncertain about the relationship generally—we thought it was so bizarre.'

The Buchanans' neighbours often noticed Howell driving past the house in his Renault Savanna estate car and parking outside. It happened several times a week, mostly when Trevor was away. The couple managed to spend time together on church away days as well. On one occasion, a group of church friends and their children went on an outing to Rathlin Island, off the Antrim Coast. Trevor was on duty that day. And, preoccupied with baby Daniel no doubt, Lesley stayed at home, where she had a sign up on the kitchen wall which read: 'Boring Wife—Tidy House'. But Howell and Hazel went anyway and spent most of the afternoon on their own, apart from the main party. There were other such trips as well, one of them to a stately house in Donegal, just across the Irish border. Hazel's church duties involved helping to organise these days out, and if the proposed dates did not suit Howell because of his dental commitments, then she would see to it that the dates were changed, so that he would be able to come along too.

The lovers had quickly devised their own secret method of maintaining the lines of communication. He would tap in her number and then hang up, just before her push button telephone rang out. When she heard the faint click, she knew it was Howell wanting to talk, and would ring him back as soon as she could. If the conversation lasted more than 10 minutes, the call would automatically be registered on their itemised telephone bills, so after every nine minutes, they put the receiver down and took turns to call each other back. The discussions would often last for over an hour, and were usually late at night or in the early hours, when their children and Lesley were asleep, and Trevor was out on duty.

After the deaths, Hazel was asked why she had the affair. She said that, when she, Trevor and the two children had moved to Coleraine in March 1986, she found it difficult, living away from her wider family circle back in Omagh. It took at least two years, she claimed, before she and Trevor felt more settled in the area. She explained that she was, by nature, very quiet and did not find it easy to mix socially:

for a long time, she didn't go out much, and if she did, she was always accompanied by Trevor. Then, in January 1989, she had found the part-time job as an assistant at the nursery school, five mornings a week. It was here, she claimed, that she began to develop a more independent outlook: working with the children, meeting other young mothers and making friends—one of whom was Howell of course, whom she recognised from the church.

Recalling the impact Howell made on her life, she told police: 'Really from this time onwards, I began to [realise] there was more to life than merely being in the home. I found myself . . . not depending on Trevor as much. Trevor saw a change in my attitude which . . . he was not in favour of—he preferred me as I was before. This initially led to arguments between us and at times, a lack of communication set in. We did not huff, as it were, but felt no real closeness. I could see that Colin was a different type of person from Trevor, in that he was friendly, more outgoing and easy to talk, with plenty of chat . . .'

———

It was late summer 1990 when Hazel Buchanan slipped out of bed one very early morning, as her husband slept beside her. She dressed without making a noise, gently closed the back door, opened the garden gate and hurried through Mountsandel forest to the end of a road where Howell was parked.

The lovers were facing an unexpected crisis. Howell had quickly and quietly put in place arrangements to deal with the emergency. After all, he had found himself in this situation before and he knew who to call, and where to go. They would have to go away for a day or two, and Hazel had simply left a note to explain her absence. Later that morning, Trevor would find the note stuck on the bathroom mirror, which read: 'Going through a really hard time. Don't worry about me. Don't try and find me. I'll be back in a few days. I love you. Hazel.'

Soon afterwards, the lovers were speeding down the M2 motorway, towards Belfast International Airport. They were due to catch an early morning British Airways shuttle flight to London Heathrow. Hazel hoped that none of the other passengers would recognise either of them, as she and Howell slipped into their seats in different parts of the cabin. The tickets for the flights had been bought at a travel agent outside Coleraine, where Howell was confident nobody knew him.

Disembarking from the aircraft, making their way through Heathrow airport and boarding the tube for the city centre, they were still careful to keep their distance. They got off at Ealing and she followed him, looking over her shoulder to make sure there were no familiar faces or Northern Ireland accents in the immediate vicinity. As they walked into the reception of the clinic, a young lady in a white tunic behind the desk greeted Howell with a smile: 'Good morning, sir.' Running her pen down the list in the appointments book, she ticked off the name and accepted an envelope stuffed with banknotes. 'Would your friend like to come this way?'

That night, the couple stayed at a B&B close to the clinic, where Hazel had the procedure the following morning. The staff did not want her to leave that day because of the after-effects of the anaesthetic, but the confirmed tickets for the return journey meant that they had no choice but to go. Howell literally had to hold Hazel upright, as she staggered to a waiting taxi. On the flight back to Belfast, she felt weak and tearful, but everything had gone to plan as they had hoped. By the time they reached Coleraine, Hazel was virtually out on her feet with exhaustion, feeling guilty but still hugely relieved that an unsuspecting Trevor would never know anything about the abortion. She passed off the fairly substantial bleeding she suffered in the next few days as a particularly heavy period.

—

Just a few weeks earlier, Hazel had been sick and a pregnancy test confirmed that she was carrying a baby. But who was the child's father? She was sleeping with both her husband and her lover at this stage. Howell, as usual, hadn't cared too much about taking precautions when they made love. Around that time, when she was having sex with Trevor, the condom had burst—so in theory, it was possible that he was the father. But Trevor had brown eyes and dark hair. What if the baby had blonde hair and blue eyes, just like Howell's children? More telling still, what if the child emerged with an unusual genetic feature which ran in Howell's family—syndactyly, a fairly rare hereditary condition, whereby some of the toes or fingers are 'webbed', i.e., still fused together by 'webs' of skin. What would Trevor make of it all, if the baby was born with a rare foot defect?

Hazel told her lover she could not cope with nine months of uncertainty and the subsequent fallout if the baby was obviously his, and even though Howell had initially insisted that he would claim full parental rights if it was proved he was the father, he ultimately relented and agreed that they should arrange an abortion. In many ways, he would have been happy to keep the child, but he feared that the pregnancy might end the relationship with Hazel, which was so vital to him now as to be bordering on obsession.

Chapter 4

Buchanan–Elkin: 'She's the Right One . . .'

Hazel Elkin was born in March 1963 and brought up in the townland of Gillygooley on the Drumquin Road outside Omagh, where her parents, Jack and Peggy Elkin, had a dairy farm. The Elkins had a big family, and Hazel had five sisters: Winnie, Pauline, Jacqueline, Lorna, and Carmen—and four brothers: Raymond, Mervyn, Clarke and David. The family were well-respected in the area for their devout Baptist beliefs. Jack was a church elder and, along with his wife, devoted much of his free time to the development of the church in Omagh, where Hazel was baptised. The Elkins went to church each Sunday morning and evening without fail, with the children also attending Sunday school in the afternoon.

Unlike her five sisters, Hazel was never one for the land. She had a fear of mice and preferred to be with her mother in the kitchen and otherwise helping with the housework. Their life on the farm was a tough one, and Jack was a strict disciplinarian with a quick temper, who expected each of his children to pull their weight by helping out with the various chores whenever they had any free time. Hazel's early years were quite uneventful, apart from one or two fairly typical childhood misadventures, such as the time she was left with a large scar after a trailer ran over her foot, and then, some years later when she was at Gillygooley primary school, when she was struck by a bread van after running out from behind a school bus.

She went to Omagh High School on the Crevenagh Road, near Campsie playing fields. She wasn't academically gifted. Even at this stage, she was far more interested in style and her appearance than in Maths and English. Former staff remember her as being a bit distant and vague. She was an average pupil in the classroom, but her performance was much better in the gymnasium and sports hall, and she once captained one of the school's netball teams. She rarely fell foul of the teachers, although on a fourth year school trip to France and Holland, she and a friend had to be admonished by staff. While in Noordwijk aan Zee, a small Dutch fishing village, the two girls had invited the attentions of a couple of local boys, who were then warned to keep well clear of the hotel in which the pupils were staying.

Hazel's first serious boyfriend was killed in a motorcycle accident in 1979. Mervyn McLaughlin, 21, from Newtownstewart, was on his way to Gillygooley when he crashed. She was just 16 and was shattered by his death. She kept part of his damaged motorbike in his memory. After leaving school, she got a job as a stitcher in Desmond's shirt factory in Omagh. She also worked part-time for a short stint in Elliott's shop in the town's Campsie area, and it was there that she met her future husband, Trevor Buchanan, whose family came from the townland of Strawduff outside the village of Dromore, also near Omagh. Twenty-year-old Trevor, a young reservist in the then RUC at the time, would call into the busy grocery and confectionary shop, where local police officers would often buy their provisions, and some would get their pay cheques cashed.

Trevor met Hazel not long after his closest friend, John Wray, got married. John—also a policeman—and Trevor had been inseparable. Trevor was his friend's groomsman at his wedding in December 1979, and the following May, John and his new wife Sheila took their seats at the same restaurant table with Hazel for Trevor's 21st birthday. Hazel had bought him a watch.

Hazel was Trevor's first serious girlfriend. He was keen to know what his family thought of the new girl in his life and shortly after introducing her to his family, he asked his sister Melva for an opinion. Even though she was nine years his junior, Melva was impressed by Hazel's appearance and friendliness. 'Yeah,' she said to her brother. 'She's the right one.' She would be one of the bridesmaids at their wedding, along with Hazel's sisters, Pauline and Carmen.

Hazel and Trevor got married on 11 July 1981 at Omagh Baptist Church: the church where Hazel's devout Baptist family were loyal members of the congregation. It was a happy family occasion. All of the one hundred guests who were invited turned up on the day. The in-laws got on well, although Trevor's brother Gordon missed the ceremony, as he had accidentally locked his keys inside his car. The reception afterwards was held at the Manor House, Killadeas, County Fermanagh. One of the guests said that they had never seen Trevor happier: 'He had this funny wee laugh and he just giggled all day long.' There was no music or dancing. Once the photographs were out of the way and the meal had ended, everybody went home. Trevor's sister Melva still clearly remembers watching the Eleventh Night bonfires light up the sky—in advance of the traditional Orange Order marches of the following day—as she headed back to her brother Gordon's home in Glengormley, outside Belfast. The young couple honeymooned in Stafford in England, at the home of Trevor's Aunt Sadie, who had married a Welshman in the Royal Air Force (RAF).

―――

Even though he feared he wasn't smart enough, or as tall as he needed to be, as a teenager, Trevor Buchanan never lost hope that one day he would be able to stretch himself sufficiently—both physically and intellectually—to become a police officer. Two of his older brothers, Raymond and Victor, were already members of the RUC.

It was the mid-70s, and with the IRA and loyalist paramilitaries involved in murderous campaigns, these were dangerous times in Northern Ireland, especially for policemen. Victor, who had joined up in 1969, had been critically injured and left badly maimed in an IRA bomb attack in 1972, the deadliest year of the Troubles. And now, several years later, there was widespread sectarian strife on the streets too. It was hardly the time for young men to put their lives on the line, but Trevor was determined to follow in his brothers' footsteps.

In his quest to make himself tall enough to meet the height requirements for entry into the force—5 feet 8 inches in those days— Trevor insisted that the mattress on his bed at the family home in Dromore was replaced with wooden boards. And his parents would often find their son hanging by his legs over the door of the bedroom he shared with his brother Gordon, who was also very keen to join the then RUC. Gordon remembers the antics of his older brother: 'Trevor was . . . a few millimetres too small. In those days, they wouldn't take you. He did everything under the sun to make the height. He had wooden boards under the mattress. The hard surface you lay on would apparently help you grow. He even hung himself upside down, like a bat, with his legs over the door, or a bar, to help stretch himself. He was so determined.'

Both brothers faced another obstacle in their ambition to join the force. They had left school at an early age, to work as carpet fitters in Omagh, and neither was academic. They needed to improve on their maths skills in particular. And so once or twice a week, they were tutored by a teacher from Omagh Academy, their sister Valerie's old school. It was money and time well spent. In 1980, Trevor made the necessary height stipulation, and after both he and Gordon successfully sat the entrance exams, the two Buchanan brothers were accepted as recruits at the RUC training centre in Enniskillen. Gordon went to the depot in 1980, and Trevor a year later. Their perseverance finally paid off.

———

When they married in 1946, Trevor's father Jim and mother Lily moved to Strawduff to live on a small farm there. Lily, who was just 17 at the time, always insisted: 'And I didn't have to get married, either.' Later the couple moved to a house on Johnston Terrace in the village of Dromore, before going to live in Omagh, first at Lisanelly Heights and then Festival Park, where they bought their own home. Jim was a skilled farm worker, but he never enjoyed good health. A heart condition meant that he had to avoid too much strenuous physical exertion. He later became chief security officer at the Crown Buildings in Omagh.

The Buchanans had two daughters, Valerie and Melva, and six sons. Jackie, the eldest, became a prison officer. Robert joined the RAF and went to live in England and, as already mentioned, the other four sons—Victor, Raymond, Trevor and Gordon—all joined the Royal Ulster Constabulary.

Trevor Andrew Buchanan was born on 2 May 1959, the third youngest of the family. In his later life, many people, especially within the ranks of the police, knew him as 'Ted'. He attended the local primary school and by the time he went to secondary school—the

Duke of Westminster school in Kesh and Ballinamallard—he had already developed a work ethic outside the classroom. The young Trevor didn't particularly like school, and money in the Buchanan household was scarce, so he became an enthusiastic worker in Fred Kenwell's village hardware store at weekends and during the holidays. There he would help out in the yard, and sometimes accompany the lorry driver to deliver animal feedstuffs. He also worked on a couple of local farms, sometimes having a three-mile walk each way to his place of work.

He got a motorbike—a Honda 50—when he was 16, and soon had aspirations for one with a more powerful engine. He borrowed a gold coloured Suzuki 250 from a friend whose father owned a farm where his brother Gordon worked, but he crashed it: this would signal the end of his motorcycling career. Later cars became one of his great passions. He drove far too quickly, and crashed a couple of times— once at the wheel of a Ford Capri on his way home, when he was a policeman in Castlederg, when a senior officer gave him a dressing down for speeding. He raced a quad bike at the Elkin farm, and on land owned by a police colleague, also outside Omagh. At one stage, he had 1600 cc Ford Escort Sport with EJI 8400 on the registration plate—which was the same as his police regulation number. He had it fitted with a sun roof at a friend's garage in Sixmilecross.

Trevor was still at school when he started to drink, and occasionally make a nuisance of himself. His sister Valerie, three years older, once had to take him home from a dance in Trillick, after he was ordered out for unruly behaviour. At home, he was an untidy teenager. He would leave his room in a mess and never washed the dishes, especially after coming home late at night or in the early hours, when he would switch on the cooker to make himself some food. His little sister Melva would clear up: sometimes he paid her for doing so.

After leaving school, Trevor and Gordon worked for a while as carpet fitters for Moore and Smith, a firm in Omagh. Trevor then left to become a member of the RUC Reserve, completing his training at the age of 19. His first posting as a full-time reservist was in Omagh RUC station, just 10 miles from his home in Dromore. It was July 1978. On his first day on duty, he was asked to collect his personal issue Walther pistol. He wasn't quite sure where to go, until somebody pointed him in the direction of the armoury.

During the three years he worked in the Reserve, Trevor was based in Omagh and the neighbouring villages of Beragh and Newtownstewart. Violence in Northern Ireland was widespread at the time, and the level of civil unrest severe. In Omagh, the new recruit went out on patrol in bomb-proof cars, carrying either a submachine gun or an M1 Carbine rifle. Every morning and evening, one of his duties was to open and close the security barriers which blocked car bombs from getting into the centre of the town. But this didn't always stop the IRA, and on one occasion a bomb exploded in Bridge Street. This time, there had been a warning, however, and Trevor and his colleagues managed to evacuate the area without any loss of life.

There were also the more mundane day-to-day policing duties to be attended to, such as burglaries, assaults and car accidents. Trevor was once called out after a motorist crashed into some cattle which had strayed unto the road outside Omagh. He managed to clear the scene and then tried to calm down the farmer who owned the livestock, as he remonstrated with the shocked driver in a badly damaged car.

The young man enjoyed his early police work and, according to friends, went about his business professionally and sometimes in a very direct manner. Once he was charged with clearing the scene of a bomb alert in the town centre. People in the immediate vicinity were curious and reluctant to leave—until they heard a sharp voice over the police loudspeaker system, using the sort of language not permitted in the police code of conduct, but which they quickly understood. 'Look,' declared Constable Buchanan. 'There is a bomb up there. What are you standing around for? Can you move away!'

A former colleagues recalls Trevor's skills in dealing with the public: 'Having worked as a carpet fitter, he already knew a lot of people in Omagh. He was always able to approach them and strike up a conversation. His knowledge of the town was far, far better than officers who came from places like Belfast and Ballymena. He was a great communicator. He could sweet-talk old ladies. He was the sort of guy who would ask for a cup of tea, rather than wait to be offered one. And he got it. There wasn't anybody who could not have warmed to him, because he was so nice. There was a very, very easy way with Ted.'

Because of the times in which he lived, Trevor had to be careful about his off-duty movements. There were a couple of places in Omagh where he felt safe enough to order vodka and coke, among them McAleer's pub in Campsie, just across the road from where he first met his wife.

He was then transferred to Newtownstewart for a couple of months, and then to Beragh, where once more he opened and closed the security gates of the village every day, without being as vigilant about his own safety as he might have been. He and others like him often travelled the back roads, but didn't always vary their route or their routines, which left them vulnerable to attack. Of those days, one of Trevor's ex-colleagues recalls: 'It was sheer madness. How we escaped, I don't know. We would have parked our cars up the street, opened the big armoured barrier, unlocked the station gates and driven the cars in. Doing that, the same thing every morning, left you wide open. There were maybe three or four ways to travel to Beragh, but through time, you just took the most direct route.'

In 1980, Trevor decided to try for a place as a regular in the force. One of the things which had held him back from doing so was the difficulty with his height, as a close friend at the time remembers: 'He was told he would have a better future for himself if he went into the regular force. I had seen him operate on the ground without any training, and it was obvious he was more than capable of doing the job. He was more concerned about exam failure than he was about his height. It bothered him a lot.' As his brother Gordon also explains: '[Trevor] had a three-year contract in the full-time reserve, but he wanted a job with more security and longevity.'

After gaining entry to the regular force, and successfully completing a period of training at the RUC depot in Enniskillen, in 1981 he was posted to Castlederg—a town just a few miles from the Donegal border. It was an utterly depressing place, which had been targeted time and time again by the IRA. The police station was an old and dilapidated former doctor's surgery on the Castlefin Road. There were just two dormitories upstairs, with holes in the roof. There was no central heating. One officer from Belfast threatened to leave on his first night. The station sergeant was Raymond Cummings, who had done his training in Enniskillen at the same time as Trevor's brother, Victor.

Castlederg was one of the most bombed towns in Northern Ireland during the Troubles. Black and yellow painted 40-gallon barrels filled with concrete and connected with steel piping lined the sides of the streets, where parking was banned in a bid to thwart the bombers, who struck as many as 80 times between 1971 and 1991. When Trevor Buchanan was posted there in 1981, it was during the time of the second IRA hunger strike at the Maze Prison, where Bobby Sands and nine other republicans would die. Demonstrations and protest marches in support of the prisoners in the jail's H-Blocks were held all over Ireland. Tensions were high everywhere, but particularly in Castlederg, a small but hopelessly divided community, where many Catholics and Protestants detested each other. It was a part of west Tyrone which all but resembled a war zone. Jim Emery, a former police reservist who knew Trevor, recalls of that time: 'I well remember standing outside the cemetery gates after another colleague's funeral, wondering who was going to be next. Castlederg was not a nice place to be back then.'

Trevor was stationed in Castlederg for five years in all. The town and surrounding area had become a virtual death-trap. Every time a Ford Cortina patrol car left the station, it was followed by a second as a back-up. The car engines were never switched off, even outside the station door, when officers changing shifts swapped places. They wore body armour over their tunics and carried high-powered rifles. Nobody left the station unless it was absolutely necessary, and only provided they had the support of the military, especially along the 26 miles of border, where there was just one permanently manned security crossing. Police, and heavily armed British troops who were billeted outside the town, would be there all the time. On the Republic's side of the border, just a few miles up the road, there was a constant police presence too. The men from the two forces got on well. They would meet regularly to exchange intelligence, and sometimes the Special Branch men shared a beer, either in a bar near their own place in Castlefin, or at the back of Sammy Walls' pub in Castlederg. It was good to put a face to the voice at the other end of the telephone. Relations with the Irish Army, however, were not as good: there wasn't the same level of trust.

Trevor was out at all hours, stopping cars and checking the identities of the occupants, as well as dealing with general run-of-the-mill crime. He once investigated a spate of malicious fires at derelict buildings in and around the town, but because of the times he was living in, most of the day-to-day policing work involved matters of security. On another occasion, in March 1985, he was involved in the car chase of fleeing IRA gunmen who had opened fire on Castlederg police station. Officers protecting the home of the local resident magistrate fired on the gunmen's car as it raced along the Strabane Road, but they managed to escape.

Trevor was called upon for one special operation which few people knew about. Police had received a tip-off that Dominic McGlinchey— a dangerous and feared terrorist from south Derry and a close friend of Francis Hughes, one of the ten republicans who died on hunger strike—was planning an attack in Castlederg. McGlinchey, a ruthless gunman and an expert at making booby-trap bombs, had killed many times before and the RUC believed he was on his way to murder again. An SAS man, disguised as a police officer, was waiting for McGlinchey's arrival and stood inside the military sangar at The Diamond, gun at the ready, while Trevor was outside, stopping and examining cars before they were waved through. The two of them waited several hours, but McGlinchey never appeared and the operation was quietly called off without a word to anybody.

In Castlederg, Trevor had a close and tight circle, nearly all of them police. Personal security meant everything. It was all about self-preservation, looking out for each other, and never dropping your guard. But he had one or two good friends outside the job in the town too. One of these was a local businessman, John Doherty, a Catholic, who ran a TV rental business and later a coffee shop, and who was heavily involved in cross-community work. Trevor used to call regularly for a cup of tea at John's home. He went there one Christmas Eve with a colleague and helped the Doherty family lay out toys for the children. Doherty recalls of his friend: '[Trevor] was a very down-to-earth, special type of person. He had no trouble making friends, and we were sorry when he left for Coleraine. It would have been much quieter than Castlederg, and maybe that was a blessing. But it turned out that it wasn't.'

————

After they married in 1981, Hazel and Trevor's first home was a rented house not far from the Elkin farm at Gillygooley. Hazel had her first child, Lisa, when they lived there. After about a year or so, they moved into Omagh town, where they bought a house not far from the Gortin Road, just a few doors down from Trevor's brother Gordon, his wife

Donna and their children. Andrew, their second child, was born about 18 months after Lisa, when they were living in Omagh.

Hazel's influence on her husband became obvious fairly quickly to those who knew him. Trevor started to cut back on his drinking and stopped smoking, as one of his friends recalls: 'Hazel . . . became anti-drink . . . she was critical of him drinking. He might say: "Okay, I'll just have one or two", and she would sit there and count them.' The young policeman also became a lot more disciplined about the house: now everything was put into its proper place.

Hazel clearly held sway in spiritual matters too. Trevor joined the Baptist church she and her family went to, and quickly became a regular, as a friend of his remembers: 'The influence of her family also started to show and he became more committed to the Baptist Church. I don't think he went willingly into the Baptist Church.' If it is true that Trevor was lukewarm about the church initially, this would certainly change, and in 1985 he decided that he wanted to fully commit himself to his Christianity, by making a profession of faith in front of a gathering of fellow believers. He made the decision at his brother's home in Enniskillen, where Victor hosted a small group of people of different Protestant faiths, after he himself had committed to God two years previously.

Trevor and Hazel regularly joined the weekly gathering of church-goers at Victor's home. By this stage, as Victor confirms, Trevor's faith was something which had a real and meaningful bearing on the way he lived his life: 'He knew about God, but he wanted to commit his life in a personal way. He wanted his faith to mean something. He didn't suddenly become somebody who wasn't connected to the real world. It meant he had a personal faith which he could hang on to when times were difficult. [This] . . . created a closer bond between Trevor and me, because he was the only other one in the family who had made a personal commitment to the Lord. He was saved.'

Victor is adamant that his brother's religion was an important part of his life, not something that he felt obliged to pay lip service to for the sake of his wife and her family: 'Trevor enjoyed his faith, he didn't endure it. If something wasn't right, he would say: "Right, that's it. No more of that for me." He wasn't afraid to talk about his life as a Christian, or his faith. He was laid-back, but if an opportunity arose in conversation and he found it would be beneficial or helpful to the individual he was speaking with, then he would have had no difficulty referring to his faith. He wasn't ashamed of his faith, but he wasn't on a recruitment drive. His personality wouldn't have allowed him to do that . . . It is "life-style Christianity", when people see the change the Lord has made to your life . . . People in Coleraine wouldn't have seen the change, because he was a believer when he went there. Back in Omagh, people would have seen the difference, because he had given up his smoking and drinking days.'

Derek Ewing, a former colleague and near neighbour of Trevor's, sees things slightly differently: 'Trevor was influenced by the church in trying to please Hazel and make her happy and settled . . . Previously he was somebody who would have enjoyed a drink, and maybe on occasions taken too much drink. I remember one night he and I ended up in our company and he was tidily [inebriated]. That caused him some problems. It wasn't the accepted thing, because a couple of days later, he told us he was in the doghouse. He regretted it. I always felt there was somebody in there waiting to get out, and I believe his involvement in the church stymied him, suppressed him.'

Derek has fond memories of Trevor's diligence and attention to detail, and his great qualities as a friend: 'He was well suited to that job [as a scenes-of-crime officer] because, in my opinion, he had an eye for detail. He was a perfectionist in many ways and took pride in anything he did. He was very much into his home and his family and was big on the garden. Everybody remarked on how well he kept the house and the garden . . . It was pristine. Everything was in its proper place. He was forever keeping the place shining. He would be standing talking to you, and then he would see something in the garden, and he was away to fix it . . . He was the sort of person who would have done you a favour if he could. He would never see anybody stuck if you wanted anything. He would have given you the shirt off his back. He was very respectful: one of life's gentlemen, and I don't say that lightly. He was a man who was decent and thoughtful of other people; very proud of his family.'

One thing about which no one who knew Trevor was in any doubt was that he adored his wife. A close friend recalls: 'Trevor treated her like the Queen. The house was furnished to absolute perfection. She got anything she wanted, but she was not content. It wasn't good enough.' And Trevor's sister, Valerie Bleakley, agrees with this assessment: 'Even just watching their body language. Trevor was almost in awe of Hazel. He hung onto her very word. He was proud of her. Whatever she wanted, he provided, no matter how he got it. She kept the house perfect. The holidays came later. She always wanted nice things: nice clothes, nice furniture. That's my image of Hazel. He obviously thought she was good for him. But in hindsight, I don't think so.'

Hazel's in-laws had welcomed her into the family from the outset, and every one of them could see what a terrific mother she was to the two children. But the material demands she made on her husband meant a squeeze on their finances from the start, as Gordon Buchanan remembers: 'Hazel always liked material things, expensive things. Her needs would have been hard to meet at times. We were young police officers, starting new families, and there was a lot of expense. While our house was clean, it was often chaotic. The children had the freedom of the house and were naturally untidy. Hazel's house always seemed immaculate, despite the children. I often wondered how on earth she was able to do it. Nothing was out of place. She was always well dressed, and I know it was hard [for Trevor] to meet her demands at times. [But] she was very much accepted into the family. I had no qualms about her. We got on well. I always found her a good chatter. She was friendly and easy to talk to. '

Valerie recalls how she often despaired at her sister-in-law's spending habits. She knew Trevor worked hard to make sure his wife wore good clothes and could buy furniture of the highest quality. She remembers how, not long after Trevor and his family had moved to Omagh, Hazel was keen for her in-laws to admire a new keyboard she had insisted on having: 'Here she was, showing us this new £800 keyboard, while food on the table would not have been on her list of priorities, let's just say.'

Relatives and friends were very much aware too that Trevor was kept well under his wife's thumb. He got a call on one occasion from his best friend, John Wray, also an RUC man: John wanted to see him that night. It was 9 August 1984, the day two of John's colleagues— Malcolm White and Nigel Shackleton—had been blown up when a bomb exploded as their patrol car passed over a culvert on a road outside the village of Greencastle in County Tyrone. Malcolm, who had just been promoted to Sergeant, died the following day. John had had to travel in an army helicopter which flew the injured Nigel to the Tyrone County Hospital, where he sympathised and consoled the officer's family. It had been a very difficult and distressing day, and

John was exhausted and emotionally drained by the time he got home. He needed somebody to talk to, and so he was hoping that Trevor would come to the house and have a glass of whiskey with him.

Trevor made his way over to John's house in Omagh. Not long after he arrived, however, their conversation was interrupted, as John recalls: 'I talked the whole incident through with him. Hazel came on the phone, telling Trevor to come home. I told her what had happened and that I wanted Ted—who wasn't drinking at the time—to stay. But she was having none of it, and said: "No. He has to come home. Tell him to come home now." I had been through something terrible that afternoon, and she knew why Trevor was with me. I had plenty of work colleagues, but he was the one I turned to, because he was my mate. But as far as Hazel was concerned, she came first, no matter anybody else.'

After the Buchanans moved to Coleraine in 1986, the two men and their families kept in touch, and might have visited each other twice a year or so. John recalls a visit from the Buchanans one summer, when it had been arranged that the Wrays would show them a video recording of a family holiday in Florida. All the children were glued to the screen and according to John, his close friend and colleague sat like a child too, excited by the images of the Wray family enjoying their time in the sun at Disney World. John remembers how Trevor then turned to Hazel and said: 'Isn't it wonderful? We'll have to go there ourselves. Maybe we could go as two families?' But Hazel, who had been paying little or no interest to the video, wasn't prepared to even consider her husband's idea about going to America, or indeed anywhere else—her only response was to reply abruptly: 'Trevor, I need a new suite of furniture.'

It was August 1990, and unknown to the hosts and Trevor, she was already cheating with Colin Howell. But apparently that didn't stop her from letting everyone know who was still boss when it came to her husband and children.

Chapter 5

In Flagrante

AUTUMN 1990

Alan Topping, a church elder and very much part of the inner circle at Coleraine Baptist, was driving home for lunch in the early autumn of that year, when he saw the couple together at the entrance to Castleroe Forest Park, just outside Coleraine. They were in separate cars, but had parked side by side, with their windows open. The elder and his wife, Margaret, were friends of Lesley and Colin Howell: the families had even holidayed together on one occasion. Topping was also a good friend of Trevor Buchanan's.

After the sighting in Castleroe, Topping telephoned Howell, expressing his dismay, and challenging him to admit to the relationship with Hazel. Howell, however, refused to do so, and Topping remembers ending a terse conversation with the remark: 'If non-Christians can avoid having an affair, then you've no excuse.'

But Lesley Howell already knew that something was going on. She knew the marriage had been in trouble for some time. They were both stressed to the hilt. They had just had their fourth child. Money was scarce because of the running costs of the new home and dental practice. They were having difficulty paying bills, and the Northern Bank had been in contact a number of times. But, beyond all of this, she could sense that her husband was growing distant again, and with the sting of his admission of infidelity with the girl from his university days still fresh, Lesley was ever-vigilant for signs that he might be straying again. And the evidence was there.

Betty Bradley, who was the Howells' housekeeper at the time, remembers how Lesley once found a handful of 20 pence pieces in her husband's tracksuit bottoms and wondered why he would need such coinage when he went jogging. 'Why, Betty?' she asked her. 'Why would a married man be carrying so many 20p pieces?' The answer was that he needed them for the payphone when he rang Hazel while out running the roads. And one evening Lesley overheard her husband's hushed tones as he spoke on the phone by the kitchen wall. She felt certain he was making arrangements to meet up with another woman.

Some time after this, Howell went for a weekend away, telling his wife that he and a male friend had arranged to play golf. He claimed he needed a break because of the stresses in the marriage. He gave Lesley the name of his 'alibi'—the man he said he would be going away with. Such was her lack of trust at the time that she later questioned this man, who proceeded to assure her that everything Colin had told her was true: the two had relaxed together and played ten holes, because Colin had needed a break and to 'get his head showered'. But the young mother found it impossible to relax during that weekend, and could not shake off the intuitive feeling that her husband was being unfaithful again. Her instinct was spot-on: the 'alibi' had carefully rehearsed his lines, and it later emerged that Colin had spent a night in Bangor with Hazel.

Lesley was a proud woman, who always did her best to put on a brave face in public. Howell acknowledged her ability to find a smile when someone called at the house—but the atmosphere and the mood behind the mahogany front door was grim and unpleasant. Unable to keep her suspicions to herself any longer, she decided to confide in John Hansford, the Englishman from Bromley in Kent who had been pastor in Coleraine since the summer of 1974. Hansford had attended the Irish Baptist College in Belfast and had been planning to return to England after his studies. But he then met and married Liz Graham, an English literature teacher at Regent House Grammar School in Newtownards, County Down, and decided to settle in Northern Ireland.

It wasn't the first time Lesley had discussed matters of a highly personal nature with the pastor. She had previously revealed her distress about the three abortions she'd had before she married. As Hansford would later recall: 'She was very, very distressed. We prayed.

In James, it says: "Confess your sins to one another and pray with one another that you may be healed." I was able to assure her that having heard her do that, God had forgiven her. That seemed to bring an amazing sense of relief to her. It was now out in the open with someone else who she felt mattered.' And now, as she broke down and shared her fears that her husband was being unfaithful, Lesley Howell was once more very troubled.

The pastor decided to confront Howell immediately at his clinic, in a side room, away from the staff reception area and out of earshot of waiting patients. But any suggestions of infidelity on his part were met with a categorical denial by the dentist: 'Definitely not,' he replied.

Hansford then went to see Hazel at the Buchanans' home. His wife Liz dropped him off. Trevor was out, and once the children had been settled in another room, Hansford explained to Hazel that the purpose of his visit was pastoral. When he shared his concerns with her, however, she too denied that there was any affair—although she did speak about her disappointment at what she perceived as her husband's lack of ambition, and about her longing for more excitement in her life.

It seemed that in his quest to establish the truth, Hansford had met with another brick wall. When, however, Hazel offered to give him a lift back to the Baptist Manse, she finally admitted that she had been economical with the truth. As they sat in Trevor's car outside the big house which overlooked the school rugby pitches at Coleraine Academical Institution, her confession was a tearful one. Hansford recalls: 'She [said she] had lied. She was having an affair with Colin. She gave me the impression it had only just started, but I subsequently found out it had been going on for a little while longer.'

Within an hour, the pastor was back with Lesley again, and together they waited for Howell's return from work. The pastor confronted him at once: 'I told him he had lied before about the situation. He was very apologetic and I told him he must stand down from his responsibilities within the church, immediately. I told him he . . . was not to take communion. We would have communion every Sunday, a bit like the Brethren. It would be a step in church discipline for the Baptist denomination of churches. Because of [Colin and Hazel's] behaviour, which was considered unChristian and not consistent with the Gospel, it was a disciplinary action. It was a serious step and marked the fact that I took the matter very seriously.'

Howell's hard-won confession tallied with that of his lover in one very important respect. While both were now at last prepared to admit that the intense friendship between them was inappropriate, they were adamant that the relationship had been unconsummated. They insisted—to the pastor, and to their respective spouses—that the affair had not been a fully sexual one.

Hansford called to see the Buchanans again, and this time Trevor was at home. His wife's revelations hit the young policeman very hard, as the pastor remembers: 'It was obviously a desperately tense situation. Trevor was totally and absolutely devastated and he was really, really angry. He managed to control his temper, presumably because [I] was there. Trevor and Lesley felt a tremendous sense of embarrassment, shame and humiliation.'

The church elders were informed and disciplinary action initiated. Howell had to resign from all church organisations. Hazel also stepped back from her Sunday school duties, without explaining why to the parents. Both were banned from taking communion and, for a short period, it was arranged that the couples would not attend the same services in the church: if the Buchanans came to a morning service, the Howells would come to the evening one. As time passed, this relaxed a little, but if ever the two couples both turned up on Sunday morning, then the Howells would sit at the front, on the right hand side, and the Buchanans at the back, on the left hand side. Otherwise, it was agreed that the families would have no further contact. Lesley said to a friend at the time: 'How could Trevor Buchanan sit and look into the back of my husband's head, knowing what he had done?'

It was an awkward and delicate situation which needed careful handling. Staying away from church, however, was not an option for either couple, as Pastor Hansford explains: 'They still wanted to attend the church. Trevor and Lesley felt the church was so much part of their family and looked to me, and the church, for support. The church was their whole life.' It was decided that the congregation would not be informed. Both couples wanted their difficulties to be kept private, but they agreed to undergo counselling with Pastor Hansford. They did not want anybody else involved. This kind of discretion was very much in line with the Baptist approach to personal problems involving church members.

As far as both couples were concerned, divorce was not an option to be considered, even though it was not something which would have been ruled out by the church, according to Hansford: 'I told them it was my understanding that divorce was allowed [by the church] because of adultery. As far as my reading of the Bible was, I told them they had two options: you can divorce and I will support you through that divorce; or [you can] seek reconciliation. Both were Biblical options. The New Testament doesn't assume that because of adultery, you end the marriage. We believe in forgiveness, even forgiveness for the breaking of the marriage covenant. They had two options and I told them that whatever path they [went] down, I would support them . . . [and that] they could stay on as members of the church.'

Both couples wanted reconciliation. Or so it seemed, when the pastor called at both homes to hold initial counselling sessions. He privately felt at the time that Hazel was out of her depth in the relationship with Howell, not sufficiently streetwise and without the necessary guile to carry on an affair. As for Howell, Hansford was not convinced of the sincerity of his desire to save his marriage: 'Colin was always very cagey with me throughout the discussions, which was in total contrast to Lesley, who was always extremely open. He was an extremely charming guy, good-looking at one time and very, very plausible. Folk liked him. He was always giving time and energy to the kids [of the congregation].' But in the counselling session with Lesley, Hansford felt Howell was reluctant and evasive, and when he did speak, it was only to say what he thought they wanted to hear.

Apart from Pastor Hansford, the church elders and those directly affected, nobody was supposed to know. But Lesley revealed her distress to some close girlfriends and within their own church circle there were heightening concerns the marriage might not last.

The Howells told other friends as well. After finishing off some dental treatment one day, Howell had a quiet word in his private office with a patient, Harry Donaghy, an electrician who had worked for him to help get the practice ready in Ballymoney, and whose wife Tania was a member of staff. Meanwhile, Lesley told Tania in the surgery's kitchen, leaving her good friend and a woman who used to be their babysitter in no mood to forgive.

Tania Donaghy's professional relationship with her boss as a nurse and receptionist, which stretched back to the days when the Howells first arrived in Coleraine in 1983, was never the same again. Lesley was regularly in and out of the surgery with the children and was close to

Tania. They went to the same church and occasionally had meals out. Tania had never previously heard a bad word about Howell, but after Lesley's revelations, she refused to return to the clinic after time off on maternity leave. Harry later told police: 'I knew it was becoming difficult for Tania to look Colin in the face . . . she felt betrayed.'

To his wife, Howell expressed his remorse and regret, insisting the affair was over. At first, she was inclined to believe him. According to friends, at one stage Howell knelt down and begged her forgiveness. Lesley wanted the marriage to continue, and told him that once he had proved he was fully repentant, then she wanted them to renew their marital vows. She even bought him a new Bible as a special keepsake. Howell told friends he was deeply sorry for what had happened. He said he couldn't help himself and asked one woman: 'Have you never felt like that?'

Trevor Buchanan was also deeply hurt, but prepared to try to make a fresh start, as apparently was his wife. But he was anxious that nobody else would find out, especially his colleagues in Coleraine police station. He confided in just two people: his section leader and his brother Victor. Victor recalls: 'He didn't want anybody to know about it. He didn't want the boys in the station to know about it. He felt it could be got over, that things could get back on track and nobody would ever know it happened.'

Victor was an officer in charge of personal security arrangements for some of Northern Ireland's VIPs. His job was to put measures in place to protect these prime targets from the IRA, trying to second guess and anticipate what the gunmen and bombers might be planning, as he and his colleagues escorted senior members of the judiciary to courthouses in various parts of the country. Victor's career in the RUC had almost ended in June 1972, when a bomb exploded inside a derelict house he was searching in open countryside near Rosslea, County Fermanagh. Part of the building collapsed on top of him and another officer, leaving him critically ill and close to death, with horrific facial injuries which included the loss of his left eye. He was not expected to live but remarkably, after a series of major operations over an 18-month period, when surgeons had to rebuild one side of his face using tendons and muscle from his wrists and feet, he was fit enough to go back on duty.

In his professional life, Victor had often dealt with welfare issues— the type his brother was now sharing with him. The long hours and stress of policework at that time had taken its toll on many of his colleagues when he was in Fermanagh. Heavy drinking and marital breakdowns sometimes ended in officers taking their own lives: he had direct experience of three such cases. Although Trevor assured him he would never contemplate such drastic action, Victor was on the look-out for signs that his brother might be another potential victim.

Even though the church elders were anxious to prevent details of the affair getting out, it inevitably became the source of much gossip. It wasn't quite the talk of Coleraine, but Hazel's neighbours knew and the church was rocked by the scandal. 'It was a strange situation,' Harry Donaghy later told police. 'We knew that these other folk knew about the affair, but [they were] not necessarily [aware] that we knew. In church you could be having conversations with people, and both families came into the conversation. You had to be careful not to disclose details of the affair or to make any comments which would make people think, or ask any questions . . . Lesley and Trevor had asked us not to tell anyone.' Harry recalled once meeting Trevor at the forecourt of a petrol station: 'I spoke with him. I was straight. I told him I knew about the affair and he didn't have to put on a brave or happy face all the time, and that Hazel and him were in my thoughts and prayers, and if he ever needed to talk, I was there for him.'

Lesley started to take anti-depressants, and Howell, it seemed, was quite happy to make sure they were always available. She would have been a fairly moderate drinker, but, because of the stress of her situation, she was now developing a taste for red wine. Although she tried to share her sense of despair with close friends, she was feeling increasingly isolated, and, with her natural tendency to 'put on a brave face' in front of others, she was in some ways her own worst enemy. Years later, long after her death, Howell himself would acknowledge the depth of the despair his wife was clearly feeling, as well as her tendency to hide behind a brave face: 'I'd seen it a hundred or a thousand times before, when she was able to just flick the switch and present herself as the smiling person. She was hiding so much hurt and trauma, even to her friends. There are friends who say they knew Lesley and I don't really believe she shared her heart [with them], what she really felt. I suppose that was part of the trauma that made things more desperate and more black and [made it seem] like there was no way out.'

OCTOBER 1990

For Lesley, things would only get worse. She was still reeling from the initial discovery of the affair, still trying to believe that her husband's remorse was genuine and still hoping—despite all that her instincts were telling her—that the affair really was over, when fresh revelations about Colin and Hazel's relationship were to come to light. The effect on the young mother would be truly devastating, and the marriage—and her life—would go into free fall.

Since Howell's latest infidelity had been exposed, both he and Hazel had been adamant that the relationship had never developed into a fully sexual one. The fact that each of their betrayed spouses and, indeed, the other parties who were privy to the confessions, were willing to believe that this was actually the case might seem hopelessly naïve to many people, but this must be viewed in the context of the world in which they all moved. The belief held in fundamentalist Baptist circles is that sex outside of marriage is morally wrong, that one should marry as a virgin and remain faithful to one's spouse for the rest of one's life. In a community where the church has such influence over its followers, the guilt associated with sexual infidelity is therefore extreme—and so, in the case of Howell and Hazel, it was not unthinkable to those around them that they might have hesitated before crossing over into the perilous territory of having full sex.

Some weeks after the affair had first been exposed, however, Howell made the further admission to Hansford that he and Hazel had actually been sleeping together. The pastor anticipated that the emotional fallout for the wronged spouses—and Lesley in particular—would be very damaging. Yet again, the church intervened to manage the crisis. Arrangements were made to have the Howell children stay with friends. Pastor Hansford came over to the house in order to try to give Lesley some advance warning about her husband's imminent confession and the new bombshell which was about to hit. During this conversation, Howell waited in the bedroom, only emerging once the pastor had knocked on the door to let him know that he had done his best to prepare Lesley, who was now in the kitchen.

At first, she could not believe her ears. There was a stunned silence for 10 seconds, maybe longer. Howell and Hansford just stood there, as Lesley stared blankly in shock. Then, without warning, she lunged forward, screaming, swearing, her arms flailing and fingers jabbing at his face. Howell ducked to protect himself. There had been fierce verbal confrontations between the couple before, but nothing on this scale. This was an uncontrolled rage, and the pastor felt it best to excuse himself and leave as quickly as possible.

Lesley ran to the bathroom, locked the door and reached for a bottle of painkillers in a cabinet above the sink. She shoved them into her mouth and, in her haste to swallow as many Paracetamol as she could in one go, dropped some of the tablets into the sink while others scattered on the floor. Then she reappeared in the hallway— but this was no longer the vivacious, engaging young mother with brown eyes, dark hair and soft, mellifluous accent. She was groggy and almost incoherent as she staggered around the front living room, in search of her husband's car keys. He stood aside, as his wife left, banging the front door shut and driving off. Shaken and panic-stricken, Howell then phoned the pastor and urged him to return and help him deal with a domestic crisis which had reached a new and worrying level.

As Hansford recalls: 'Colin had the empty bottle. We were talking, trying to decide where she would have gone, which friend would she have gone to lean on, when she comes back. She wants absolutely nothing to do with Colin. She is very disturbed. We [she and I] go into the lounge, we sit together, me with my arm around her. She was really hyper, spaced out, angry with Colin. She was pouring her heart out about the problems in the marriage . . . I managed to talk her down after 20 minutes, and she then agreed that I would take her round to the Accident and Emergency department in Coleraine. I had to sign her in, because the surgeon approached me, asking if I was her husband. The social services have to be informed if somebody attempts to take their own life.'

Lesley stayed in hospital for three days. She made a full recovery, but as a young mother who had trained to be a nurse, she found the whole experience an embarrassing and chastening one. Ruth Middleton, who had once shared a house with her when they were nursing in Belfast, was one of the friends who visited her during her time in hospital. Lesley told her about taking the tablets, and then having second thoughts. Ruth would later recount to police, following Howell's arrest in 2009: 'She thought to herself: "I can't do this. I can't leave the kids." She promised me face-to-face that she would never do it again. She said it was the most humiliating thing that had ever happened to her.' Lesley would also speak to Betty Bradley, her housekeeper, about what had happened. 'I've been very silly, Betty,' she kept repeating.

The young mother later tried to have the details of the overdose removed from her medical records. Gillian Alcorn, another of her friends from nursing days and who belonged to the same mothers and toddlers group in Coleraine, recalled, when she spoke to police in later years: 'I remember Lesley being upset at the time, as there was now a written record of her overdose. I believe she asked her doctor to remove it, or re-word it, though as a nurse, Lesley would have known that the incident would have to be documented. I think it was more a cry for help at the time, and she said to me she would never do it again.'

But Lesley was badly shaken by the whole experience and still very upset when she left hospital. She tried to compose a letter to her father, but was too distraught to send it. Colin, however, was not particularly concerned, it seemed. He might have played the role of a dutiful husband and father—anxious about his wife's well-being, hoping she would make a full recovery—but deep down, he regretted that she had ever returned to the house after the incident. Even though he agreed that he would have no further contact with Hazel, as far as he was concerned, the marriage was over. He had become defensive and had lost all interest. He felt that Lesley had become irrational and neurotic. He wasn't prepared to give her the attention she demanded, and, as in the past, compensated for his lack of affection by giving her money to buy clothes, even though he could not afford it. He still yearned to be with Hazel.

Lesley went on a crash diet to lose weight. In a bid to win back her husband's full and undivided attention, she bought herself a new range of clothes, running up significant credit card bills in the process. She had regular facials, hairdressing appointments, sunbed sessions and started to attend an aerobics class. Liz Hansford remembers Lesley's efforts: 'I thought she was saying to Colin: "Look at me. This is what you rejected."'

Lesley's friend Tania Donaghy avoided Howell when she could, calling at the house to see her when he was not at home. She noticed the sadness in Lesley's eyes, as her friend grew more and more depressed. She would later tell police: 'She had changed her hairstyle and I thought she was trying to do anything to save her marriage—her whole appearance was getting like Hazel Buchanan.' But still Howell took no notice. The young mother tried hard to conceal her distress, but deep down, she was a tormented soul. One night at a restaurant, the Bushmills Inn, as Howell sat nearby, Lesley whispered into the ear of a woman friend who was also a member of her Bible study group. Lesley told her about the affair, explaining that the reason why she had lost so much weight was because she could not eat. The woman wept all the way home in her husband's car.

With further intervention from Pastor Hansford, Hazel and Howell pledged to him and their spouses that there would be no further contact between them. And for four months—between November 1990 and March 1991—this would indeed be the case. Hansford insists that all four wanted his counselling. He initiated a programme where they would first discuss problems within their marriages, and then the events which led to the adultery. Trevor, Hazel and Lesley were open and frank, but Howell was a reluctant participant. Trevor and Lesley would sometimes meet together by themselves. She was worried about him because she felt he was not coping well, although Lesley later told one of her friends: 'Maybe our conversations are not all that helpful for one another.'

While Howell might have been going through the motions of trying to repair his marriage for the benefit of the pastor and others in the church, it was obvious to Lesley when they were alone that he just wasn't interested in real reconciliation. One night when he said he was going out for a jog, he simply ignored her pleadings to stay at home. She suspected he was leaving to meet up with Hazel but he left anyway. Lesley went out for a walk to take in the air to collect her thoughts and found herself being propositioned by a kerb crawler looking for sex. By the time she got home, her husband was in bed fast asleep.

Relations between the Howells got worse and worse. There were some fierce verbal exchanges, and at times Lesley lashed out at him. She would occasionally produce family photographs of happier days, wave them in his face, and then cut them to pieces. She would snatch the telephone off him if she suspected he was talking to Hazel. One night Howell woke up to find his wife at his bedside, looking at him with clenched teeth, as she shredded his underpants with a large pair of scissors. She also kept track of his movements by following him in the car when he was out running the roads. Sometimes she questioned her husband's friends as to whether Hazel's name had been mentioned while they had been out running together.

In February 1991, Lesley and Howell joined friends at a formal ball to launch a campaign to build a new hospital in Coleraine. The event was held at the town's Jet Centre and as part of the function, guests watched a peculiarly appropriate film—*Dangerous Liaisons*, the Oscar-winning 1988 drama based on the 18th-century French novel by de Laclos about sexual conquest and scorned love. That night, Lesley looked like her old radiant self: wide-eyed and smiling confidently, in black evening dress and wearing a gold Albert neck chain, as she and Colin stood hand in hand: the picture of a contented couple who had rediscovered peace of mind. But friends in the know said she found the event distinctly uncomfortable.

Trevor Buchanan, meanwhile, was doing his best to cope with the crisis in his own way. He kept in regular contact with his brother Victor, whose job often took him to Coleraine. The brothers would meet to talk, sometimes up to three times a week in Trevor's car at the police station on the Lodge Road. Victor recalls: 'I knew there was a serious situation with Trevor and I spoke to him about it. I told him: "The middle of the night can be difficult. If you are lying awake and something is troubling you and you have nowhere to turn, a silly thought can come into your head." He told me: "I know where you are going with that. Many a night I feel like that, because you can't help going back over what happened, but you needn't have any fear about me taking my own life."' The young policeman never indicated to anyone that he was considering leaving his wife, but a close friend, Derek McAuley, remembers being with Trevor in his car as they were pulling a trailer of rubbish to the local dump. The car radio was on, and Derek remembers how they exchanged glances when the well-known Clash song, 'Should I Stay or Should I Go?' began to play.

As the weeks passed, the counselling process seemed to be having some positive effect, at least as far as the Buchanan marriage was concerned. Victor's impression was that the crisis was blowing over. Trevor told him the relationship was getting better, and while it was not fully restored, he was apparently even prepared to accept he might have been partly to blame. He called his brother and said: 'We're back in the marital bed again.' Victor remembers: 'From his disposition, it was clear his old self was returning—laid-back, affable, carefree.

There was always a serious side, but he wasn't in a state of high stress. Things were back. He told me: "Maybe there is a bit to go. I suppose I wasn't perfect either." He was trying to take the heat off Hazel.'

But for Colin Howell, there was no sense that the crisis was passing, as he would later recall in a statement to police: 'That four month period was a bit like I was choking. It wasn't going anywhere. I didn't dare tell anybody—Lesley or John Hansford—what was really going on with me, the struggles I was having, and the emotions. I was making a deliberate effort, out of duty and from my spiritual and Christian background, this was the right thing to do. That's why I did it.'

He could not bear being separated from the woman on the far side of town. He felt as if he was living in some sort of cocoon, under pressure from his wife and the church. He wanted to escape a situation he could not handle. He submitted to, but did not believe in, the counselling process. And when he was told by Pastor Hansford that Hazel was doing really well and had moved on with her life, it only made him more determined to renew the relationship. He would later tell investigating police officers: 'That was the last thing I wanted to hear. That really got me stirred up. I needed to know if she had really moved on. . . If she'd decided that, then she [could] move on and I'd need to sort myself out.'

In March 1991, after both of their birthdays that month, he decided to get in touch with Hazel once more: 'It was like holding your breath, and I remember when I phoned Hazel and she was glad to hear from me, it was like coming up for air. It was the wrong sort of air at the time, but it was the air I needed and wanted. I said: "How are things? They're terrible over here," and she said, "It's awful here [too]." So we began to identify [with] and mutually comfort each other—that life was terrible and life was black.'

Howell suspected that the pastor had tried to bluff him when he had said Hazel wanted nothing more to do with him. And when he finally spoke to her on the phone, it was clear to him that she still had feelings for him: 'It was quite obvious from the way she replied that she hadn't moved on. I was pleased, even though we were making this deliberate effort to be separate and to make our marriages work . . . I was also afraid to tell John Hansford what was really in my heart, because whether it was valid or not, I didn't trust him not to tell Lesley. I [couldn't say]: "John, my heart is breaking for Hazel and I just can't get over her." I didn't even dare say that, so I had to hide how I felt. It was really a very false time.'

The affair was back on again. Howell had been unable to withstand his fatal attraction to his mistress. Had he been able to foresee the deadly consequences which would follow, would he have tried harder in his efforts to resist her?

———

In March 1991, there was another defining moment in the Howells' marriage, and one which, in many senses, foreshadowed and indeed paved the way for the awful events to come. The balance of psychological power between husband and wife was about to shift.

When Howell and Lesley first got together, the consensus among her friends was that she was 'too good' for him—and in later years, others also wondered about the relationship. A former colleague of Howell's from his university days sums up what many thought: 'She [Lesley] was a lovely looking girl, and I often wondered what she saw in Colin. He always had a smile, but he struck me as a fairly ordinary bloke.' Lesley had always been outgoing, witty and had an engaging personality, making friends easily. She was very attractive and, as even Howell later admitted, more intelligent than him in many ways. He could be arrogant and manipulative, as well as charming when it suited him, but Lesley more than had the measure of him and had no trouble knocking him back with a cutting one-line rebuke. She never did this in public—indeed, even at the height of their marital crisis, she was never openly critical of Howell—but frequently, in the privacy of their home, she would cut him down to size with a sarcastic remark delivered to cause maximum embarrassment. Years after the deaths, Howell admitted that at times he felt belittled and humiliated by his wife, although he insisted he never lost his temper about it. This awareness that Lesley had the upper hand must have eroded his male ego, and perhaps explains why he felt so much more comfortable in the company of the prim, compliant and houseproud Hazel, who seemed to look up to him. His mistress was attractive, quiet and shy and valued what Howell told her, and no doubt he felt more at ease with this than with a wife who challenged and questioned him.

Even when the marriage—and her life—was disintegrating around her, Howell still felt that Lesley was the one in control. He found himself having to spend more time with the children and manage domestic matters, as she struggled to cope with the emotional crisis. He had effectively given up hope. He found his wife difficult and awkward. He had become defensive and sometimes felt powerless.

Six weeks before her death, Lesley rang her friend Ruth Middleton, anxious to discuss an incident which had occurred with Colin. As Ruth recalls, Lesley prefaced the disclosure in a rather unsettling way, with the words: 'I'm telling you this in case anything happens to me.' Ruth would later tell police of the conversation: 'She told me she had been lying in the bath relaxing and had taken the tape recorder into the bathroom on the extension cable. She said it was behind her on the floor, or at least that's what I understood. Colin came into the bathroom and said he needed the tape recorder. He lifted it and somehow the cable came out of it and fell into the bath. She got a shock and as a result her arm shot up and the lead went with it. The lead had landed on her arm. She did not know how this happened as it was behind her, as was Colin. He made her promise not to tell anyone, as he was embarrassed that he had done something so silly and she promised him she wouldn't tell anyone.'

Lesley did not explicitly say she believed her husband made a serious attempt to kill her, but it was clear that the young mother was very unsettled by the incident, and felt the need to communicate her fear of him to her friend. She also contacted two other close female friends—Margaret Topping, and Jen, her brother Chris's then wife—to tell them about what had happened. It was clear that Lesley's distrust of her husband had plumbed new depths.

Years later, when questioned by police, Howell emphatically denied that his wife suffered an electric shock in the bath, or that he had attempted to kill her on this occasion. But he acknowledged that it was an incident in which he felt he had seized control in the crumbling relationship. And when he appeared in court at the trial of Hazel Stewart in February 2011, he was more than happy to give a definitive account of what he believed had actually happened.

It was a Saturday in early Spring. Lesley had wanted him to put up curtains in the bathroom at the house at Knocklayde Park. Due to the financial pressure he was under at the time, he decided to do it himself. He took the children—Matthew, Lauren and Daniel—to the B&Q store in Coleraine. Lesley had bought the curtains and he purchased the rail—a pole—to hang them. There were queues at the store and it took longer than he anticipated. Howell had been meeting secretly with Hazel at the time, and, although he had not done so that day, he was late arriving back, and Lesley immediately challenged him as to why he had been away for so long. Such interrogations were part of day-to-day life for the couple by this stage.

Howell used a Black and Decker drill to bore holes in the wall in the bathroom. The drill was connected to an extension lead plugged into the hallway. The work remained unfinished by the time it came to bathe the children, make the tea, put them to bed and read them a story. He disconnected the drill and pushed it and the extension lead against the wall. Lesley was in her dressing gown and decided she wanted a bath. She emptied some Radox into the water, stepped in and lay back. She wanted to listen to music, and had brought the cassette player into the bathroom. She placed the cassette at the top end of the bath, but Howell, who feared it might fall into the water, moved it to the bottom.

At one stage he was sitting near her as they continued to argue. He was holding the extension cable, and suddenly there was a brief pause in the row. They exchanged looks. Even though he never planned to electrocute his wife, Howell suddenly realised Lesley believed at that moment he could kill her by dropping the lead into the water. He stood up with the lead in his hand and flicked it—very lightly—across her back before deliberately letting the plug fall onto the floor and walking out. There was a bang as it hit the wood, but Howell insisted Lesley suffered no electric shock.

Years later, Howell would tell the court: 'I didn't have an intent[ion] to throw it in. I saw an opportunity to get Lesley off my back . . . I was being pressurised, pressurised, pressurised and pressurised. When I held the plug and the loose cable it was to show Lesley, there's a way for me. I was saying to myself, there's a way to escape. I was showing Lesley I [couldn't] stand the control.'

Howell would later put this issue of loss of control in his life—and the terrible impact this had on his subsequent actions—in a typically Biblical context: 'King Solomon, considered to be the wisest man, said that a man who commits adultery gives up his strength to the one who is cruel. So a man who commits adultery gives up . . . his authority in the family, and therefore the control is given over to his wife, or to an adulteress. And I wouldn't like to argue with the wisest man in the world.'

Chapter 6
'Eureka'

D ressed in a black jacket and skirt, Lesley Howell wept quietly on her own, as the mourners began to drift away. Her father's coffin had been lowered from view inside the small church at Roselawn Crematorium on the outskirts of Belfast. As she looked across to the other side of the room, she caught sight of a familiar face: it was Pat Chambers, an old friend from her days growing up in Scotland, and Dublin.

Pat, who had been sitting near the front on the opposite side, was crying as well. She felt deeply for the girl she knew as Lesley Anne, who was six years her junior. She went over to say how sorry she was. Lesley threw her arms around her, rested her head on her shoulder and said: 'Pat, what am I going to do? I've lost the only man I ever loved.' 'Sure, you've got Colin. You've got the kids,' replied Pat, unaware of just how little comfort her words would offer to a woman whose marriage crisis had already passed the point of no return.

With the loss of her father, Harry Clarke, Lesley Howell's life had hit rock bottom. Harry had collapsed and died of a suspected heart attack in the Howells' kitchen just after midnight on 7 May 1991. His daughter was inconsolable.

Henry Clarke, a former Royal Marine and company director, had moved to Castlerock the previous year from his home in Hillsborough, County Down. Everybody called him 'Harry'. He wanted to be close to his only daughter and four grandchildren. He was aware of his son-in-law's financial difficulties, and even though

Lesley never discussed her problems at home, her father knew all was not well.

Grandpa Clarke used to take the grandchildren to a playground park, close to his small property high above the seaside village on the North Coast. Known locally as 'The Apostles', the twelve houses of Cliff Terrace are something of a landmark in Castlerock—six pairs of distinctive black basalt dwellings in an English vernacular style, with lattice windows, overhanging eaves supported by struts, hooded dormers and strong timber doorways inside shared arches. Built in 1888, they originally formed a terrace along the road at the west entrance to the former Downhill Estate, and were designed to house the staff of the then Earl of Londonderry, Sir Harvey Bruce.

Harry owned No. 6, a two-up, two-down. It was a tiny house, much smaller than the house he left in Hillsborough, and although it was great in the summer months, it could be a miserable and desolate place during the dark winter nights, when it was exposed to howling gales blowing in off the Atlantic. Lesley's brother Chris, who worked as an anaesthetist in England at the time, had opposed the move. Why would a man in retirement leave a fine home and some good friends in Hillsborough for such a place? His father told him he needed to get away from all that. Maybe it was because he had been spending too much time in the local pubs.

A ceremonial sword which hung from the wall in Harry's front room was a reminder of 22 years in the army. He liked his whiskey and smoked a pipe, and sometimes when the weather was good, he would sit on the front porch to take the air, as well as some magnificent views of the coastline towards Portstewart.

The Howells would call with the children to see Harry on Sunday afternoons. Matthew, Lauren and Daniel usually played at the back of the house, free from any passing traffic coming and going from a caravan park directly opposite. Mr Clarke had not been around long enough to get to know his immediate neighbours, but a few remembered him as tall with silvery hair. He had a small circle of new acquaintances in the area, including Lyle Hatrick, an insurance agent and a former captain of Castlerock Golf Club, who used to sit and have an occasional drink with Harry at the house or sometimes in the sun at the front porch. Mr Clarke would also stop off quite often at the Golf Hotel in the centre of the village for a drink—Robin Butler, the owner, was another friend. And even though it was a fair distance away from Hillsborough, old friends travelled up to see him sometimes too.

Some of Harry's neighbours recall that Lesley would often seem quiet and withdrawn when she called to see her father and a few of them thought that it was because she had been suffering from postnatal depression. Howell never acknowledged anyone. One former neighbour remembers of the dentist: 'He was cold, just cold. He never spoke to anybody.'

Towards the end of April or early May 1991, Harry had not been feeling well. Lesley always worried about him living on his own. He had stayed with the Howells from time to time in the past, and one day, after he complained of having flu-like symptoms, she prepared the spare room for her father and went to pick him up. Mr Clarke had been to his GP a few days earlier. He had been anxious and depressed. His wife had been in failing health for many years before she died, and maybe the strain and pressure of tending to her needs for so long had started to take its toll. He had been given a prescription for some moderate doses of Temazepam, Gamanil and Diazepam—sleeping tablets, sedatives and anti-depressants—as well as eye drops for glaucoma.

On the night Harry died, Lesley and Colin had gone out to the theatre, followed by dinner, and Amanda, the daughter of their housekeeper Betty Bradley, had agreed to babysit. A student at Coleraine Technical College, she had been to the house many times before. She thought Lesley was loving and kind-hearted and that Colin came across as a gentleman. She enjoyed her babysitting duties in this house because the children were always well-behaved and the Howells were never too late returning home.

The children were asleep and Amanda was doing her homework in a small family room towards the front of the house, close to the kitchen, when she heard someone shuffling up the hallway. She saw an elderly man in his dressing gown and pyjamas. Although she had never seen him before, she assumed that it was Lesley's dad. She saw Mr Clarke going into the kitchen, where he kept a bottle of whiskey and sometimes poured himself a nightcap. She heard the kettle being switched on and the door being closed.

Not long afterwards, the Howells returned. It had just gone midnight. Lesley was first into the house. She went to the kitchen and then began to scream when she found her father on the floor, lying on his side. Howell rushed in, knelt down and felt for a pulse in Mr Clarke's carotid artery. He could not detect anything.

Dr Hazel Siberry, Harry's GP, was called to the house and pronounced life extinct. Given the position of the body, it looked to be a classic case of myocardial infarction—heart failure. A distressed Lesley and her brother Chris, who had been contacted by telephone, accepted Dr Siberry's finding and agreed that a post-mortem examination was not necessary. Harry Clarke was aged 69.

At the time, nobody suspected that Harry Clarke's death was anything other than sudden and from natural causes. Why would they? But years later, after the arrests of Howell and Stewart, some people, including his son Chris, had their doubts and suspected something more sinister. Mr Clarke had collapsed just 12 days before the discovery of the bodies of his daughter and Trevor Buchanan. If Howell murdered them, then surely he would have been capable of killing his father-in-law, to get his hands on the inheritance because he was so strapped for cash?

Even though he had no definite proof, Chris Clarke certainly had his suspicions. He stayed at the Howells' home with his then wife Jennifer at the time of his father's funeral. He knew that Howell's business was in trouble and that he was cheating on Lesley, and accused him of deliberately feeding his sister sedatives at a time when he knew she was drinking. Chris told the author: 'I think it is very likely that he did murder my father. I thought initially he simply murdered him, because he might be encouraging my sister to leave. Now I think he murdered him to get his hands on money, as a prelude to murdering my sister. With hand on heart, I can't say Colin Howell murdered my dad. I just don't know for certain, but it is much more likely than not that he did.'

When questioned by police in 2009, however, Howell categorically denied killing his previous father-in-law.

His view of his relationship with Mr Clarke was that it had been good, but shallow: 'He [Harry] generally was kept in the dark about most things in our life. I never discussed with him financial difficulties or the marriage difficulties I was having . . . I think he perceived me as being a good thing for Lesley. That would be my understanding. He was kept out of all the inside details. Perhaps he didn't want to know.'

Mr Clarke had left his daughter more than £212,000 in his will, presumably as a result of the sale of his house on Monument Road in Hillsborough. She did not tell anybody just how much money she had in her account, but she did tell friends that she had become financially independent and planned to leave her husband. She was determined Howell would get nothing. Although he would later deny it, the dentist eventually did inherit the £212,000, as well as a 50/50 share of the money in Mr Clarke's personal bank account—around £12,000 — and half of the proceeds of the sale of Harry's house at Castlerock, which sold for £34,000. The other half of the proceeds from the house went to Chris, who was unaware his father had left so much money to Lesley. Howell pledged to set aside some of the money for his children's education. He also used some of it to buy a house opposite the police station on the Coleraine Road, Portstewart, which he rented out to students attending the University of Ulster.

Mr Clarke's death was a massive blow to Lesley, but Howell felt that the relationship had deteriorated so badly that he was unable to do anything to console his wife, and that deep down Lesley knew—as he did—that they were close to separation.

Shirley McPhillimy, who was first introduced to the Howell family through a friend who had been on a skiing trip with her solicitor husband Richard, who had once looked after the dentist's legal affairs, remembers calling to the Howells' house in the days after Harry's death. Lesley was preparing a shepherd's pie for dinner: she was making it early, she told Shirley, because she found it too difficult to cook in the evening. Three of the children were running around the house and it was obvious to Shirley that the young, grieving mother was finding it hard to cope: 'The bubbly personality had gone. She was sad and angry, emotional and struggling to keep herself and the family together. I knew it was a huge effort for her to keep going. She told me she was not sleeping right . . . I could tell she was stressed.'

Meanwhile Pastor Hansford had returned from a six-week speaking engagement in India, which had been arranged by a man called Shankar Sankannawar, who was living in Ballymoney, and was a Baptist heavily involved in missionary work in his home country. When Hansford had left for India, his feeling was that the counselling process was working well for the Howell and Buchanan couples. In the week before his departure, he had, in fact, been able to bring Trevor and Colin together for a meeting—and the two men had even shaken hands in a gesture of reconciliation before they parted. So, on his return to Coleraine, the pastor was reasonably hopeful that positive progress towards restoring their marriages would have been made. He did, however, continue to have his doubts about Colin—and with good reason.

In his absence, the church elders had kept the pastor informed about the death of Lesley's father, and not surprisingly, Lesley was one of the first people the pastor spoke with when he got back to Coleraine. Betty Bradley ushered him into the Howells' kitchen, where he was joined by a yawning and dishevelled-looking Lesley in her dressing gown, clearly very upset and still groggy from the sedatives she had taken. She needed two cups of coffee before she was ready to engage in a proper conversation. Surely this wasn't the same happy-go-lucky, vibrant young mother who used to walk about the house singing her heart out as she listened to music on her headset? Hansford recalls: 'I remember reading a passage from the Bible and praying with her. I didn't go away alarmed . . . I met him [her father] once, and she was very fond of him. They had a great relationship. I was about to go after an hour and a half, and I'm standing in the hallway when Lesley hugs me—really, really hugs me and doesn't let go. She thanked me most profusely for all the help I had given her and then she said her goodbyes. She was an emotional girl, but as I drove off, I kept thinking about why she thanked me and hugged me so much. I didn't smell drink off her breath.'

But when others were not around, Lesley was drinking heavily to dull the pain of the loveless marriage. At times, Howell found her incoherent and forgetful. He claimed his wife had been taking Temazepam tablets which she found in her late father's house. According to him, one afternoon in particular stands out in his mind —he remembers discovering Lesley in a drunken stupor. Lying more or less comatose on the kitchen floor, she had clearly been crying and her head was lolling in a pool of vomit and spilled red wine. Standing over her, with a broken glass in hand, was one of the children who was trying to help their mummy. The child had gone to the fridge to retrieve some milk but had dropped the bottle, the contents splashing over both of them. It was a horrible and distressing sight, and if ever there was a defining moment when Howell wanted his wife out of his life, then this was it. He just wished she would drink herself senseless, drive off in the car and kill herself.

He always believed she would kill herself eventually. He felt she had given up on the children. But he feared that if they did split up, there would be a custody battle, and that she would win. Apart from the stigma of a formal separation, that was another reason why he did not want to go through with a divorce. It would, he believed, be so much worse for the children to be with a mother who couldn't cope with them. Howell's view of the situation was that, if he left her, she would retain custody of the children—but that she was not a fit mother because of her drinking habits, which he said had started to develop after the birth of Lauren. He said she was an alcoholic, but friends and Lesley's brother Chris categorically deny this claim.

––––

13 MAY 1991

Colin Howell would later call it his 'Eureka moment'—the exact time at which he decided he was going to murder his wife and his lover's husband. It was in the early hours of 13 May—3 a.m., to be precise. Lesley had been crying all day. The tears and the recriminations had started that morning and had gone on all day, despite the fact that Chris Clarke and his then wife were staying at the house at the time. It was just after Mr Clarke's funeral. Lesley was distraught about her father; she felt betrayed by Howell. He could not comfort her. They went to bed, lying side by side, but neither could sleep.

Lesley was in a bad way. She had been drinking to try to ease her pain, which after so many months of emotional upheaval and now the loss of her father, must have seemed interminable. Suddenly she sat up in bed. She turned to her husband and told him she wished she was dead and in Heaven. She just wanted away. Then she said to Howell: 'This is going to be over soon. I am going to go to Heaven. Maybe you and Hazel are meant to be together. I'll never get over this. Trevor will never get over this.'

She turned over again, and fell into a deep sleep. Howell then hugged his wife, and found himself thinking: 'I can help you. I can help you.' For the first time in years, as he would later recount, he felt love for his wife. According to what he told one of the psychiatrists charged with assessing him in prison years later, in that moment, he didn't feel the killings would be evil or wrong: 'I believed that this would be a solution that would be good for them—that's the way I was thinking at the time.' He wanted to relieve Lesley and Trevor of their pain: it seemed to him that if he helped them to die, he would be carrying out a form of euthanasia. It would be an act of mercy; he would be doing a good thing and God would bless his actions. He was convinced too that the children would feel good as well, if their mother was no longer around. He felt in that moment that Lesley had actually given him permission to kill her: 'It was a way out of this prison for her, the children and me.'

Fired up by this insight—as he saw it—Howell then got out of bed, and made his way over to Hazel's house straight away. Chris Clarke, who was sleeping in the spare room, remembers hearing his brother-in-law leaving in the early hours, and remarking to his wife Jennifer: 'You would think he would cut that out while Lesley needs support.'

This was perhaps the first time the murder plan was discussed between Howell and Hazel. Her initial reaction to her lover's germinating plan was one of disbelief. But over the next few days Howell began formulating his plan in earnest. The more he thought about the idea, the more it seemed to make sense to him. He remembered how, during a particularly heated row not long beforehand, Lesley had screamed at him: 'You'd probably be better off if Trevor and I were killed in a car crash.' It was a throwaway remark, uttered in anger and despair, but now it seemed to reinforce Howell's feeling that arranging their deaths was the right thing to do. Finally, he could do something good for his wife, he could help her.

The lovers arranged to meet at the Barmouth Road to discuss the plan a second time. Howell told her: 'I have a plan for Trevor and Lesley that can look as if they committed suicide, but I need your help.' He explained that they would die of carbon monoxide fumes. Hazel's first reaction, according to Howell, was to express fear about the consequences for them if they were found out. She told him: 'If we get caught, I'll slit my wrists. If I see them coming to get me, I'll have my wrists slit.' She insisted that it was a crazy idea which would not work. But she knew he needed her on board and although he didn't go into all the details, Howell was clearly determined to go ahead. It had been on his mind—albeit subliminally—for weeks, if not months, possibly as far back as the previous October, when his wife had to have to her stomach pumped after the overdose.

Howell told Hazel he wanted the deaths to be painless. He was afraid Trevor might wake up and shoot him. And so, part of his plan was that both victims would be well sedated. As they sat side by side in Trevor's car, Howell took out the tablets he had brought with him—Lorazepam, an anti-anxiety drug. He told Hazel these belonged to his mother, who sometimes stayed at Knocklayde Park and took them when she had trouble sleeping in a different bed. He instructed her to use two spoons to crush them, and then to put the powder into Trevor's food.

He tried to make the plan sound as straightforward as possible, as Hazel's retentive powers had never been very good. In the run-up to the murders, he refrained from using words like 'dead' or 'killing', talking instead about when he had 'finished' with Lesley, and so on: 'Our communications were always sanitised to avoid the horror, the real horror of what we were doing . . .'

In his mind, Howell visualised a future with Hazel and her children. They could all be one big, happy family. Yet even though Hazel had professed her love to him, he was never convinced beyond a reasonable doubt that this kind of future was what she wanted. Howell murdered for love, yet without a guarantee that the new woman in his life was ready to commit herself.

But his tunnel-vision take on reality at the time was such that he didn't stop to consider any of this for very long. His emotions, his thinking processes, his decision-making: all of these had been warped and distorted by months of domestic conflict, financial pressure and the relentless emotional distress of his wife. It was too intense and he just couldn't handle it any more. As far as Colin Howell was concerned, he was left with only one option.

Chapter 7
Till Death Us Do Part

18 MAY 1991

Lesley Howell fell asleep around 11 p.m. on the couch in the living room that night. She had changed into her nightie and lit a fire, so that she could sit up and watch television. She just wanted to be by herself and have a few drinks from the box of red wine she had bought earlier in the day. Howell was quite happy to leave her alone. As he would later admit when recalling the events of that night, he was not the nurturing type: 'That was one of the harsh things about me.' It was surely an understatement.

Earlier, Howell made sure the children had been to the toilet before putting them to bed and then blocking their door with a hockey stick. He had deliberately kept them up later than usual to tire them out. They normally went to bed around 8 p.m., but he had not put them down until 10 p.m. They had all celebrated Daniel's second birthday that afternoon and the children were in high spirits and somewhat overexcited, and so they had been quite happy to stay up past their normal bedtime.

That afternoon, as he busied himself in the garage, assembling the plastic slide he intended to give his son as a present from Mummy and Daddy, Howell set aside the child's toy for a few minutes to attend to something else. Picking up a baby's feeding bottle he had brought with him from the house, he cut it in half, and then squeezed the neck of it—the narrowest part of the top half—into the end of a garden hose. This was the 'dry' hose, as he called it—an extension hose he used when watering the grass and the garden flowers. The other hose he had was kept permanently connected to a water tap near the house. For his current purposes, the dry hose was best: free of any water or moisture, it would ensure the steady, uninterrupted flow of deadly carbon monoxide fumes from the exhaust of his car.

As he stood in the garage looking at his handiwork, he went over some of the details of the murder plan again in his mind. For it all to work, it was important that Lesley should be sleeping on the sofa. Had she been in bed, the extension hose would not reach the bedroom and the plan would have to be aborted. He had calculated the distance previously, carefully counting out the number of paces from the garage to the living room. But it was fairly certain that this detail would fall into place that night—after all, it had become a habit of his wife's in recent times to sleep on her own.

Lesley had been out of the house for a good part of that day. She had forgotten to buy Daniel a card for his birthday, and had gone to do this and some other shopping in Coleraine. She went to the hairdresser where she got her hair coloured, with red lowlights. Then she stopped for a quick coffee in Couples café nearby—a customer who was there that day remembers of the young mother: 'She had bought her kids lot of presents. She was a lovely woman . . .' In the café, Lesley saw her next door neighbour, Rosemary Legge. Although the Legges and the Howells were not particularly close as neighbours, they were on good speaking terms. Rosemary commiserated with Lesley over her dad's death, and would later tell police: 'I gathered from her [that] she was just mechanically going through the motions of doing general domestic things, but had no real interest in what she was doing.'

The young mother returned to the house and then left again some time later, because she had an appointment for a sunbed session at Dorothy Moody's Green Acre Studio on the Green Road, a few miles outside Coleraine. She thought the session was scheduled for 6 p.m., but later realised it was for 7 p.m. Afterwards, she had a brief chat with Dorothy's daughter about the fact that she had fallen asleep on the sunbed, and booked another half hour session for the following Monday. During the hour she had to wait for the sunbed, Lesley had turned up at Knockintern garage on the Ballymoney Road to buy petrol. Gillian Hunter, whose husband Uel owned the garage, was behind the till that evening. She was concerned to see that Lesley, a regular customer, seemed to be unsteady as she dismounted from her

Renault 5 car and struggled to insert the nozzle properly into the petrol tank. Lesley came in to sign for the purchase before Gillian saw her driving off towards Ballymoney. Howell had an account at the garage, and Gillian knew him well. She was so struck by Lesley's appearance and demeanour that evening in fact that she decided to ring Howell to let him know she was worried about his wife. It was a detail which would come in very handy for the dentist later and would help to corroborate his claims that Lesley had been in a suicidal frame of mind that evening.

Meanwhile, Howell had been trying to contact Hazel throughout the afternoon. He was unaware she had been to Lisburn with Trevor and their two children, to do some shopping and just to get out of the house. The family outing hadn't been a success, though. The atmosphere between Hazel and Trevor had been very tense because of the rekindled affair. They had argued for most of the afternoon and returned home around tea-time.

Howell was getting more and more alarmed. He kept dialling Hazel's number, waiting to hear the click, and then putting the receiver down. But she failed to call him back. He didn't know where Hazel was, and he needed to make sure she was ready for what was going to happen later that night. After Gillian Hunter's call, it occurred to him that Lesley might be planning to leave him, and that she might end up crashing the car somewhere. Then again, maybe she had arranged to meet somebody. As he would say in court in later years, he did not feel that he was in a position to question his wife's movements at this stage in the relationship. She was basically free to come and go as she pleased, without being answerable to him: 'I had lost all my dignity and leadership in the family at that stage.'

Eventually, Hazel called him. It was a hurried, surreptitious call and she kept breaking off to look over her shoulder. Trevor was outside in the garden. Howell whispered urgently: 'Tonight's on. We're going to do it.' Again he went through the key things she would have to take care of. He told her she would have to make sure Trevor's car was parked away from the garage. He reminded her about the tablets and that she would need to make sure Trevor was asleep. He concluded the call by saying to his lover: 'If I don't turn up, it's because something's wrong at this end.'

Early that Saturday evening, Trevor called to see his neighbours, Liz and Bertie Johnston. Liz Johnston, who later went on to become the Ulster Unionist Mayor of Coleraine Borough Council, knew of the Buchanans' marital problems and quickly picked up that Trevor was upset when he turned up in his tracksuit bottoms, sweatshirt and trainers. He asked her husband Bertie, an engineer, if he could repair a bicycle wheel belonging to his son Andrew. Liz, who knew Trevor through her work as a British Telecom supervisor before she entered politics, would be one of the last people to see him alive.

Liz invited Trevor and Andrew in for a cup of tea, but the young policeman said it was too close to dinner time and that they could not stay. Bertie was unable to carry out the repair work until the following Monday because he didn't have the necessary equipment available at the house, and he handed the wheel back to Trevor. Liz remembers: 'I noticed the vacant look when he came to the door, and I said to Bertie afterwards that they must have had a row, because I knew what was going on in the background. It was known within church circles, not just among the Baptists . . . Trevor had lovely dark brown eyes, but they were really glassy and he was shaking. You knew he was irritated and agitated about something. He had the wheel in his hand and he was playing about with it. Trevor just took Andrew by the hand and walked away, and that was the last we saw of him.'

Trevor later called with another neighbour, Derek McAuley. He stayed talking for an hour and then returned home. He seemed in good form. Derek was friendly with both Trevor and Howell. He went jogging with the dentist. His wife Hilary was one of Hazel's closest friends.

Later that night, once the house fell silent, Howell slipped out to the garage again to finish his preparations. Donning a pair of surgical gloves he had brought from the surgery, he pushed the wider part of the child's feeding bottle over the mouth of the exhaust pipe of his car. The bottle was made out of a hard plastic, and he knew it would not melt. No tape was needed to complete the adaptation. Sometime before midnight, he checked on Lesley again. She was fast asleep. He noticed that she had been listening to music on her headset before falling asleep. Now Howell pulled the hose through the kitchen to where his wife was lying—a distance of 25 or so paces, as he had previously calculated. He stretched it to its full length, then returned to the garage to switch on the car ignition. Back in the house, he leaned over his wife on the sofa, and pointed the hose nozzle in the direction of her face. He then tucked it under the quilt she had pulled over herself, and positioned it to within six or eight inches of Lesley's mouth. He then backed outside into the hallway, so he could watch from a safe distance. The door could not be completely shut because of the hose, so he was able to peep into the room every 30 seconds or so.

Howell stood in the hallway for a few minutes, maybe five, as Lesley began to inhale the deadly fumes now filling the room. He felt himself getting stressed, as the smell got stronger and stronger. His wife started to become restless and he feared she was about to waken up. He moved towards her again. She began to turn unto her side, her head resting on a pillow. Howell then swiftly pulled the quilt up over her head. His wife suddenly stirred and called out the name of their eldest child, Matthew. He knew that she realised that her life was in peril. He panicked. Howell was never to forget his dying wife's weak, plaintive cry for their young son. They were the last words she uttered. Years later, he would recall: 'That is one of the memories that haunts me. She called his name. I didn't expect her to be awake. I hadn't imagined [this] would happen.'

It was dark, and in what little light there was from the living room fire, he could see what he had to do—and that was to physically restrain his dying wife. She struggled slightly, but clearly hadn't the energy to fight back. He recalled: 'I had a reality check of what was happening. It was almost disbelief.' As her head lay on the pillow, face up, Howell sat on top of her. He couldn't see her eyes because of the blanket covering her face, but as he straddled her in the final moments of her life, he believed that she was aware of what was happening.

Lesley's arms were now trapped by the quilt, and he held the hose pipe under it with his right hand, leaning down hard on her head with his left, until she stopped breathing. By this stage, he was feeling unwell. The fumes were making him dizzy and light-headed, and he feared he would be overcome. He went into the hallway again, took a few deep breaths to compose himself, and then returned, this time holding his breath. He wanted to make sure that Lesley was dead. He pressed her chest a number of times, to check if she was breathing. He didn't bother to feel for a pulse.

In that moment, Howell couldn't believe what he had done.

Gathering himself, he pulled the hose back out of the room and went out to the garage. He disconnected it from the exhaust, rolled it up and put it into the back of the car. Back in the house, he removed the nightdress Lesley was wearing. He dressed her in dark leggings and a blue tee shirt, and carried her body to the boot. He had pushed the backs of the rear seats forward to create more room. Howell knew he had to move quickly now—it was essential that he complete the second killing as soon as possible, so that post-mortem results might not reveal too much of a time lapse between the deaths. Covering Lesley's body with a blanket, he set his bicycle on top of her. Years later, he would say of his wife's murder: 'It was like a surgical procedure.'

Before leaving, he made one final check of the house. He went inside again and cocked his ear to the children's bedroom door. Everything was quiet. He gathered up some family photographs from a cabinet and from the wall, as well as Lesley's Sony Walkman and headset.

He called Hazel to signal that he was on his way. She was in bed with Trevor, but heard the click of the phone and got up at once to call him back. 'I'm finished with Lesley,' he told her breathlessly. 'Is everything ready? I'm coming round.' He asked if Trevor was sleeping and if their car was outside the garage. Hazel confirmed that her husband was asleep and that the car would be parked as instructed by the time he arrived. She did not ask the question: 'Is she dead?' because they were not using such bald words.

Telephone contact with Hazel was vital, as Howell would tell the court in later years: 'There has to be constant confirmation. Anyone who has tracked, for example, terrorist activity [around] to a bomb, [knows] there are probably 100 mobile phone calls. So when you are planning something as devious and as complex as this, you have to have regular contact. I couldn't just have turned up, because I needed . . . to be prepared emotionally and practically.'

Howell locked up the house at Knocklayde Drive. After putting Lesley's body in the boot, he freewheeled the car onto the road. In the Legges' house next door, there was still activity. There may have been a house party, he surmised, and he did not want to attract attention.

Howell took a direct route to Hazel's house. He drove into the town's Waterside area, along Railway Road and through the town centre unto the Lodge Road. He passed the police station and veered left at the Lodge Road roundabout, which took him to the Mountsandel Road. Nervous that he might run into a police checkpoint, he took a right and then a left at a T-junction, into

Charnwood Park. He had made this journey so many times before. The Buchanans lived at No. 34, a bungalow on the right. It had taken him 10 minutes to get there, and it was already well into the early hours of Sunday morning. It was all taking longer than he had anticipated. He reversed the car into the drive. There was nothing there to block his way.

Trevor's white Toyota Corolla was sitting at the front of the house. Howell waited for about 30 seconds. He opened the car door and put one foot outside. He looked for Hazel's silhouette at the kitchen window. Just then, the garage door flipped open. Howell wound down his window on the driver's side, put his head out and reversed in. There was no light in the garage, but he saw Hazel run and disappear into the adjoining utility room. He reversed over something on the floor. He was not sure what it was: he thought it might have been a puncture repair kit or even a bicycle. He was worried the crunching noise might waken Trevor.

There was not much room inside the garage because of shelving. Howell pulled the door closed and waited inside. Hazel came back and told him that Trevor was still asleep. She disappeared again, and when she returned 30 seconds later, she asked, nodding toward the car: 'Is that Lesley?' In other words—was Lesley's body in the boot? Howell said it was. Hazel was standing on the steps at the entrance to the utility room at this stage. Howell then started to connect the hose pipe to the car exhaust, as before. Once finished, he went into the utility room. Hazel went to check again that Trevor was asleep. She returned to say that he was. All of their exchanges were spoken in whispers.

Howell then moved into the kitchen and waited. According to his later account, he noticed a plate on a worktop. On it sat a bread roll which had been sliced open and filled with tuna fish. The crumbs of what must have been a second roll were also visible on the same plate. Mixed into the tuna of the uneaten roll, Howell could see what he presumed to be little blue flecks of the Lorazepam tablets he had given Hazel. In court, he would later say: 'I was horrified and shocked and probably annoyed that my accomplice had been clumsy and not crushed [the pills] up finely enough, that they still would be visible.' But he would never mention it to her at the time, or in later years: 'I wasn't there to be annoyed at something she hadn't done properly in terms of the preparation. But it was just striking and clumsy that she had made a tuna sandwich that you could actually still see the blue flecks of the tablets in.'

While Hazel checked on Trevor again, Howell went into the lounge. The fire was not lit. The grate had been cleared. He then went quietly up the hallway. The main bedroom was at the top end of the hall, on the left-hand side. He looked into the room. Trevor was asleep in bed. The door was slightly ajar, but he pushed it open a little bit more to get a good look. The young policeman was lying face down on the far side of the double bed, wearing his boxer shorts.

Howell went back to his car and started to unroll the hose. This house was smaller than his, and he knew he did not need the same length of hose. There was a lot of excess coiling, and he considered getting a knife and shortening the hose, but decided it would take too much time. So he kept moving. Hazel was behind him somewhere and every now and again, she would disappear. He later recalled: 'She was more of a shadow than a person.'

He brought the hose up to the bedroom door. He opened the door and brought two or three coils into the bedroom. He placed the tip of the hosepipe on the pillow on Hazel's side of the bed. He then went back to the car and switched on the engine. By the time he returned to the bedroom, however, the coiling had fallen off the bed. He lifted it back on again and waited outside the door.

After what had happened with Lesley and how she had woken up, Howell feared the same might happen with Trevor. And sure enough, Trevor must have heard something, for he stirred. Howell saw his victim lifting his head. Immediately, he rushed into the room, grabbed the nozzle and pulled the duvet over Trevor.

So much for the sedatives Hazel was supposed to have given her husband. But, as Howell told police later, he had now 'crossed the Rubicon', and there was no going back. Andrew and Lisa were fast asleep in an adjoining room. In a frenzied whisper, Hazel expressed her concern that fumes from the car might seep in under the children's bedroom door, but Howell told her not to worry, that it would not happen.

He then jumped on top of Trevor, in an attempt to try and wrap him in the bedcover. What happened next was not entirely clear to Howell: Trevor may have grabbed him by the wrist, and then the two men wrestled and rolled onto the floor. The struggle might have lasted 15 to 20 seconds. Howell bumped his head. He remembers them being on their knees together, and at one stage, looking into each other's eyes. Neither of them spoke, as he recalled. In an adjoining room, Hazel could hear the sounds of a struggle. She would later find her husband's watch on the floor.

By this stage, Howell had the hose in his right hand and, desperate for a quick kill, he shoved the nozzle between Trevor's teeth, while pulling the blanket over his head, enfolding his body completely, and trapping his arms. He then listened as his victim gasped for breath and finally stopped breathing altogether.

Howell felt nauseous from the fumes. He was dizzy as well, but not so dizzy that he could not walk. He knew he needed fresh air quickly. He went outside, switched off the engine of the car, and then ran out into the back garden to a small path leading into Mountsandel forest. He thought he was going to be sick into a hedge, and doubled over, holding his stomach. He didn't vomit because, as he would later claim, he was afraid of leaving forensic evidence.

Meanwhile Hazel had dropped a pair of denim jeans, a blue sweatshirt, socks and some laced shoes on the floor of the hallway for Howell to put onto her dead husband in the spare bedroom. Howell carried him in one movement there from the main bedroom, and dressed him. Then he put his victim's body over his shoulder and made his way to the car. He opened the boot, lifted away the bicycle and set Trevor down, to the right of Lesley's body. He swiftly covered both bodies with the sheet and placed the bicycle on top again.

Hazel already had a fire blazing in the living room, and was in the process of getting rid of some of the incriminating evidence. Howell gave her the rolled up hose to destroy—he didn't want to dump it somewhere and risk it being found. She cut and hacked it into pieces and threw it onto the fire.

Hazel then went into the bedroom, pulled away the bed covers and pushed them into the washing machine. Years later, Howell recalled: 'I don't even remember seeing her face. I just remember her presence rather, and reading how she was. I know I was particularly shocked that I had this physical struggle with Trevor and that he had fought back and that I'd overcome him and had to hold the pipe in his mouth. So there had to be panic. It was one of those things that when you started, you've got to finish it. I just pushed through . . . I wasn't particularly looking to see how Hazel was reacting, one way or the other. So it would be unfair of me to say she was distraught. I don't think relief would be the right word [either].' He also revealed: 'I never had to confront her, so there was never any eye-to-eye contact or face-to-face. I don't need to look at her because she's there to be the perfect accomplice.'

At this point, Howell noticed that he had a bump on his head. He didn't think Trevor had managed to strike out at him, but assumed now that he had. He would never discuss with his lover subsequently how her husband had fought for his life. For now, however, he was seized with the urgency of the next step in his plan.

He was worried that forensic evidence might be discovered in the bedroom. Perhaps a piece of skin belonging to him or Trevor—and which had been detached during their struggle—might be found in the fibres of the carpet? Howell had spent time in the forensic science laboratory at Queen's during his year out studying anatomy, and regarded himself as being forensically aware. And so he instructed Hazel as he left: 'Make sure you hoover the floor.' He did not tell her where he was going, because he was not even sure himself.

The Buchanans' next door neighbour, Ronnie Gray, then a primary school headmaster, had been in the bathroom of his house in the early hours. He opened the window and heard footsteps. He suspected it might have been a prowler and in order to get a better view, he went to the lounge window at the front of his bungalow and looked out again. He saw a car reversing out under the amber street lights, and he guessed it was probably Trevor on his way out on some kind of police-related matter. It was approximately 3.40 a.m.

Chapter 8

'Let This Be Our Secret'

Colin Howell put his foot down on the accelerator and drove towards the village of Castlerock, some four-and-a-half miles away. In the boot of the car lay the two lifeless bodies of his wife and his lover's husband. He couldn't quite believe what he had done. When he reached the outskirts of Coleraine, he turned right off the main road and onto the Cranagh Road, reducing the chances of someone spotting his car, or even worse, being waved to the side of the road by police—not an uncommon occurrence in Northern Ireland at the time.

Howell had another reason for taking this slightly circuitous route. About a mile outside Castlerock village, he changed down a gear, enabling him to negotiate a narrow stone bridge. He then turned right into Barmouth Road. He knew this area well: it was where he and Hazel used to rendezvous, near a bird sanctuary on the banks of the River Bann. There would be few people about, especially after dark. Just courting couples in cars with the headlights switched off. It was here that he and Hazel sometimes had sex. It was here that he had discussed the plan for the murders with his lover.

He passed over the level crossing of the Coleraine–Londonderry railway line, which skirts a stretch of Castlerock golf links. He pulled in by the side of the road, lifted his bicycle from the boot and left it hidden in deep grass on a verge, outside the boundary fence, between the fifth green and the sixth tee box. He then drove to the entrance to the beach at Castlerock. The next part of his plan was not clearly formulated as yet—he had never been able to get too much beyond the point at which he had carried out the two killings. He now needed to find a credible venue for the staging of the double suicide, and the thought had just occurred to him that the beach might be a good place. But almost as quickly, just before he reached the sand, he changed his mind. Daybreak was approaching fast, and he feared he might meet people out for early morning walks. He would be seen. He was also worried his footprints would be found in the sand.

So he turned the car and kept driving, through the village, up a steep hill and then on to the row of tiny cottages, The Apostles, sitting high above the town. He went round to the back of the houses and to a brick garage at the rear of No. 6, until so recently the home of Harry Clarke, Lesley's father. Howell pulled on another pair of the rubber surgical gloves which he had taken from the surgery. He was careful to wear gloves throughout what he would later refer to as 'the procedures'.

Once he had pushed open the up-and-over door of Harry's garage, he reversed in, leaving just enough room to enable him to open the boot. The garage was narrow and he had to manoeuvre the car tight to one side. The place was cluttered and untidy. There were old kitchen worktops and shelving up to the ceiling. An artificial Christmas tree was lying on one of the ledges. A wooden chair sat on top of a bench in front of the window. There was an empty grey plastic bin underneath, close to an old radiator. Lengths of electric cable wire dangled from a couple of hooks and below these was a foldaway orange and white coloured summer chair.

He removed the sheet covering the bodies and, still trembling with adrenalin, carried Trevor's body from the boot and down the side of the car, heaving it onto the driver's seat. Trevor's body was now lying low, his head slumped to the right at the same level as the dashboard, his backside off the seat. Howell could not manage to close the door because his victim's right knee jammed in the hinge of the open door. He then placed Trevor's right hand on the steering wheel.

Howell's next task was to get Lesley's body into position. He laid her out on her back—so that she was stretched out the full width of the boot, with her right arm raised towards her head and her left across part of her stomach. Her legs lay sideways. He pushed an old lampshade to the one side and then tried to fit her bare feet into a pair of white training shoes. Now he was in too much of a hurry to lace them up, and so didn't bother. Lesley's knees rested on a rolled-up red, yellow and green striped golfing brolly which Howell would have used to shield himself from the rain when he played a few rounds with friends.

His work was not quite finished yet. He set out three family photographs beside where his wife lay. One was of her with her brother Chris and their father Harry: in it, she had a shorter hairstyle, Chris sported a beard and their father stood between the two of them. The second picture, framed in brown wood, was of Lesley in her Royal Victoria Hospital uniform with her mother, on the day she graduated as a State Registered Nurse. And the third photo captured happier times too—it showed Lesley and Howell, just before they left her rented house in Belfast for a dinner dance at the School of Dentistry: Lesley was in formal evening wear, clutching a red rose, and Howell was in a dinner suit with a red carnation in his button hole, his hands behind his back. The oval-shaped photograph of the seemingly perfect couple was framed in silver.

Howell had noticed some days previously that a vacuum hose, which once belonged to an old hoover in need of repair, had been lying in the boot of the hatchback for weeks, and he had known it would come in handy. He pushed one end into the exhaust pipe and placed the other just inches away from Lesley's head, beside one of the unfastened safety belts. The narrow hose kept falling out, but he knew that once he pulled the tailgate closed, it would stay in place.

Everything had more or less gone to plan thus far, but there was one final thing he had to do. His wife had always enjoyed listening to gospel music on her Sony Walkman, especially when the children were asleep or occupying themselves. She could get on with the housework and retreat into her own little world, tidying up as she danced from room to room, singing to herself. Howell switched on the ignition and, as the engine started to tick over and release more noxious fumes, he inserted a tape into the Walkman, positioned the earphones in Lesley's ears, pushed the play button and then pulled down the tailgate.

He had a moment of slight panic when he first turned on the ignition without firing up the engine—he had forgotten to open the driver's side window, which would enable him to get out of the car, since the door was now blocked by Trevor's body. Once he had opened the window wide, he switched the car engine on fully. He then climbed onto the roof and slid down over the bonnet. He took one final look back as he closed the garage door. All he could hear was the faint voice of Adrian Snell—the English-born religious singer who was his wife's favourite, and who she had once heard live in Belfast's Ulster Hall—coming from Lesley's earphones.

Howell took off, picking up his pace quickly into a run. In his hand was a plastic carrier bag, inside it the blanket he had used to cover the bodies in the boot, and the used surgical gloves. But he needn't have worried. There was no one around. The deathly silence was broken only by the sound of the waves of the incoming tide and the chimes of the clock in the tower of Christ Church Parish Church, which sounded every 15 minutes. Castlerock was asleep.

The people next door to Harry Clarke's never heard a thing. Moore and Ann Adair from Londonderry had been out the night before at the Golf Hotel. Their small dog, a Yorkshire terrier called Lucy, was in the kitchen and slept undisturbed. The first the Adairs would know of the deaths was later that day, when Moore went to get a newspaper and found a police officer standing in his doorway.

Howell made the first part of his escape on foot. By the time he jogged down the steep hill of Tunnel Brae, jumped onto the sand and turned right, he had the beach at Castlerock to himself. He was wearing jeans, trainers and a jumper. He ran towards the mouth of the River Bann, where it collided with the sea—known locally as the Bar Mouth.

Howell had always kept himself fit. He was competitive and had once cycled through France. To his right, he could now see the lights of some houses and the Golf Hotel. He was the only sinner around and soon he was by the water's edge. He turned right again and made his way up along the side of the river. Then he moved inland, and, head down, pushed his way through the heavy undergrowth, and the thick and choking buckthorn bushes by the side of Castlerock golf course. The first signs of daybreak were beginning to emerge. He could have cut through the golf course and been confident enough that he wouldn't have encountered anybody out on the fairways at this ungodly hour, by making his way towards the seventh hole and then the sixth. That would have been the most direct route, but he decided to stay off the course and stuck to the river's edge.

Eventually he made his way back to the Barmouth Road where he had left his bicycle, close to a few occupied cottages on the edge of the nature reserve. All was still and there were no signs of life. He didn't take long to retrieve the bike from its hiding place. Soon he was on his way again, this time peddling frantically towards Coleraine. The steep hills on the road of the three-mile return journey did not present such a huge challenge to Howell: he had cycled many mountainous roads before. Although the enormity of what he had done had perhaps yet to sink in, his heart was racing with the physical and mental strain of the last hours. But he was a man on a mission and still very much in control.

It might have been around 5 or 5.30 a.m. by the time he got home. It was now light and he worried that somebody in the neighbouring houses might have seen him. He checked that the children were still asleep and then he called Hazel using the click system. Although there was clearly no need now to worry about Trevor hearing anything, he did not want to disturb her two children. Hazel called him straight back and he told her he was home and asked if she'd done as instructed: 'Have you cleaned up? Have you burned the hosepipe?' Hazel assured him she had. He then briefed her on what she was to tell the police later that day, once the bodies were found: 'You have to say that you heard Lesley and Trevor speaking in the early hours of the morning . . .'

Howell went to the living room, where he had left the windows open to get rid of the fumes. He raked out the ashes in the grate from the night before. With firelighters, wood and coal from a bucket sitting on the hearth, he lit a new fire and, using a pair of scissors, he cut up the jeans and long sleeved sweatshirt he had been wearing. The surgical gloves were also thrown into the flames, along with the plastic bag.

Howell did not go to bed. He knew he would have to call the church elders later and report Lesley missing, claiming she had left the house with Trevor in the middle of the night and had failed to return. He would tell them too that he had been involved in an altercation with Trevor: this would explain the bump on his head, in case anyone noticed.

But there was one more detail which needed his attention now, one which would help convince everyone that the deaths had been suicides. While Howell had never been one for keeping a diary himself or for writing letters now that his student days were over, Lesley had always been more inclined to put pen to paper. She would have exchanged letters all the time with her old friends from school, and the girls she had met while nursing. Not so long beforehand, when Howell had been rummaging through some old papers and documents in the house, quite by accident he had found a note Lesley had obviously written when her spirits had been very low. Normally her writing was small and tidy, but the way this note had been written was not as neat, and it was obvious that these were the words of a woman in deep distress, who might have been contemplating suicide.

The note read: 'Dear Colin, I'm just trying to go to sleep now, [for] how long I don't know. Thank you for your help over the past few days and for the good times in our marriage. I don't know what to say to you because I don't know how I feel, but I have seen that life goes on after a few weeks of pain, and, let's face it Colin, I am nothing in comparison to what you lost in the one you loved awhile back. If I wake up in the morning, just let this be our secret. Lesley.'

Maybe she had had second thoughts about the note even as she wrote it, because it appeared to have been crumpled up. In any case, Howell had set it carefully aside. Because it did not look fresh in fact, he hesitated initially as to whether he should use it at all. Yet something which appeared so clearly to reflect a depressive and suicidal state of mind was too good to pass up, as a handy extra 'prop' when it came to executing the next part of his plan—to convince everyone that the deaths had been suicide rather than murder. The note was perfect after all. He set it down on the kitchen floor and waited.

Chapter 9
Getting Away with Murder

Robin Hastings was relaxing with a glass of pink gin in the men's bar at Castlerock Golf Club with a couple of pals when his pager buzzed with an urgent message to call Coleraine police station. It was late Sunday afternoon on another gloriously warm May day on the North Coast. From its vantage point, the club house afforded a spectacular view over the entrance to Lough Foyle and the fishing village of Greencastle in County Donegal on the far side, where a few hours later the sun would set, and then dip to leave a stretch of the Inishowen Peninsula with a brilliant orange skyline.

The Coroner for north Antrim, who played off a six handicap, had been in excellent form as he held court with his regular golfing partner, Bill Yea from Dungannon. The two were delighted at having just relieved two friends of some money which had been wagered over 18 holes on the great championship links. Now, however, Hastings had to break off the conversation, before going to make a call on the public telephone outside the secretary's office. A police officer on the other end of the line wasted no time in telling him the grim news: 'We've found two bodies in a garage at the back of The Apostles. Looks like suicide.'

In cases of sudden and unexplained deaths, whose circumstances can include anything from road fatalities to murder, a coroner must be informed immediately, as part of the investigative process which will eventually lead to a public inquest over which he, or she, must preside to examine and determine the possible causes. Suicides are not uncommon—but two together is highly unusual. Hastings, a highly experienced coroner by this time, asked to be kept informed of developments, returned to his chair in the lounge upstairs and beckoned the bar steward for another round. He needed a stiff drink.

———

The bodies of Lesley and Trevor were discovered after two separate earlier attempts had failed to trace them. The first person to look for them was Jim Flanagan, one of the elders of the Howells' church. Colin Howell had telephoned Jim, a language teacher at Coleraine Academical Institution, that morning, telling him Lesley was missing. He asked his church friend if he would be good enough to go to the village of Castlerock and check No. 6, The Apostles, the house of Lesley's recently deceased father. Howell told Jim that, given her distressed and emotional state, it was likely that his wife might have gone there to grieve. He explained that he would have gone himself but that he had no one to keep an eye on his children in the meantime.

Flanagan duly drove out to The Apostles. He checked the outside of No. 6 and the locked garage at the back, but could see nothing unusual and returned to Howell's house straight away. An agitated Howell asked him if he would call the ferry companies to ask about Lesley's possible whereabouts: he told Jim that he had already been on to the police and hospitals to inquire if there had been any car accidents or emergency admissions. 'Maybe she and Trevor have boarded a boat for Scotland,' Howell thought out loud, explaining that Lesley had been drinking the night before and had driven off. She could very well have gone to see Trevor, as the two had been confiding in each other about their spouses' affair. Jim was well aware of the marital difficulties in the Howell and Buchanan households.

Before Flanagan left Knocklayde Park to go to a Sunday morning service at Coleraine Baptist, Howell showed him a letter, purportedly written by Lesley. Flanagan would tell the police in the investigation after the deaths: 'I've been asked since if I thought it was a suicide note. There was no hint of that in the letter as far as I could see, although I wouldn't be experienced in these things. But there was an indication suggesting that she was going away and there was a sort of a farewell in it. She expressed her love both to her husband and to her family. I read that, but I have no clear memory of the phraseology. But those sentiments were in it.'

Howell then got in touch with another church friend to ask if he too would come to see him. Derek McAuley said he found Howell, dressed in a sweatshirt and tracksuit bottoms, looking anxious and agitated. He was now saying that Trevor had come to the house during the night and that he and the young policeman had been involved in a brief struggle. Then Trevor had driven off with Lesley, who had the keys to her late father's house. McAuley also remembered being shown a suicide note, which he read quickly without paying too much attention to the contents. 'I do recall that I could see no marks or injury on Colin Howell, so obviously the two of them had not been battering the daylights out of each other,' he would later tell police.

The last time McAuley had been to The Apostles, it had been a social call to see Mr Clarke—a civilised and pleasant visit. But now, McAuley feared for his life. He was terrified that Trevor Buchanan had become deranged because of the marital strife and, thinking that he, McAuley, was the man he'd been fighting with the previous night, might shoot him. The front door was closed, but unlocked. He was concerned about going inside because he knew Trevor was a policeman who had access to a gun. He told the police later: 'It had crossed my mind before that if Trevor had taken the "head staggers", he could possibly have killed Hazel and Colin with his firearm. I even on occasion had told him, or rather asked him, to keep his gun at the police station.'

In his account to police, McAuley remembered pushing the front door open and shouting: 'Trevor, you know the drama is over now, it's Derek here. It's me, Derek, not Colin.' He climbed the narrow stairs towards the bedrooms, with visions of Trevor sitting with his gun ready to shoot the first person to walk through the door. If not, he feared, then Trevor and Lesley might be lying dead in one of the rooms. He shouted out again: 'It's me, Derek, not Colin,' and checked the rest of the house. Then he made his way to the back, walking over towards the garage. It was a sunny day, and he had to shade his eyes with a hand as he squinted into a back window. He saw Howell's Renault car and noticed how dirty it was. He didn't see anybody inside, but could smell what he believed to be gas. He then moved along the side of the garage towards the front again, where he could have sworn he glimpsed someone peering out from behind a curtain window in the house he had just left. He went into the house again but found no one, and then decided that it was time to leave.

Back at the Howells' house, the dentist had looked at McAuley in astonishment when he assured him there had been no one at No. 6, and that all he had detected was a strange smell of gas. 'They were there,' Howell had shouted in disbelief. 'They were there, they were there.'

It was Jim Flanagan who eventually found the bodies, when he returned to the house a second time at Howell's request. It must have been a harrowing experience for a father whose daughter had died the previous year. Howell had called him again, this time as Jim was leaving the church in Coleraine, where Pastor Hansford had conducted an adult baptism as part of a service which had lasted longer than usual. David Green, an off-duty police detective who had been at the church service also, agreed to go with the elder. It was around lunchtime.

After failing to get a response to knocking on the front door and windows, the two men went into the house. The back door was lying open, and Green noticed the kitchen ceiling light had been switched on. They shouted out and searched the upstairs as well. Flanagan then went to the garage, not expecting to find anybody there either, but when he lifted the up-and-over door, he saw the car, with Trevor Buchanan's body lying slumped well down in the driver's seat, his right knee stuck in the joint of the open door. The car had been reversed into the garage. Flanagan called out, and then discovered Lesley Howell's body in the boot. She was wearing the headset of her personal stereo, and some family photographs lay beside her. 'I'll never forget the smile that appeared to be on her face,' Flanagan would later tell police.

As he hurried over to the garage to join his friend, David Green could smell exhaust fumes. The car engine was not running. There was a little smoke in the air. He checked Trevor's pulse and then Lesley's, after opening the boot. Then he noticed a hose attached to the exhaust pipe.

———

Family and friends of the couple were stunned, but Howell appeared to take his wife's death remarkably well. Some put his composed reaction down to the shock of it all. Three of the four children were up and running around when Pastor Hansford called to tell Howell that his wife was dead. Howell went to the patio door which opened onto the garden, where Matthew, Lauren and Daniel were playing on the slide Daniel had been given for his birthday the previous day. Calling the children in, their father told them their mother was dead and in heaven. They began to weep and hug each other, and when one of them asked him when she would be coming back, he replied: 'Never.'

The pastor had been stunned by the news, and would later tell police: 'Trevor Buchanan was such a steady fellow, and I believed he was not the type to take his own life.' But Howell, he noticed, showed little or no emotion: 'I felt that maybe he was holding back and would eventually explode emotionally.' Jim Flanagan, present at the time too, was also taken aback by Howell's reaction to the deaths: 'He seemed to take the news reasonably well, but that may have been through shock or disbelief or whatever.'

Howell telephoned his parents, Sam and Sarah, at their home in Portadown, County Armagh. But he made no mention of his relationship with the wife of the man who had also died. He left that to his minister who had to fill Sam and Sarah in on the full background when they arrived at the Howells' house later that evening. The pastor recalls: 'They were very distressed.'

Hazel was at her neighbour and best friend, Hilary McAuley's house, when Liz Hansford called in to break the news. Standing in the hallway and just hours after he had checked for himself, Derek McAuley said he couldn't believe there had been such a tragedy. Hazel came out of the lounge. She hardly spoke. The pastor's wife recalls: 'She held her face in her hands and bent over. She must have rehearsed that: the moment somebody comes and tells her. The best way is to cover up the face. We were dealing with an affair, which happens in church life—not very often, but it happens. We were dealing with suicide and a wife who must feel responsible for driving her husband to do this. I would have said she looked guilty at that point—guilt for having driven her husband to suicide. You are not remotely thinking of anybody else and you are not acting as a police officer to these people. You are a minister dealing with folk who have had an affair and a tragic suicide of people who felt humiliation, shame and rejection.'

Hilary McAuley put the kettle on and made some tea, but Hazel said little, and according to Liz Hansford, there was no emotion. The tears didn't come until later, and that was in front of her two children. Liz Hansford feels this had its own explanation: 'You don't always cry when you are in shock . . . I was looking at a woman whose husband had just taken his life.'

Liz Johnston and her husband Bertie were just about to begin lunch when she heard a radio news bulletin which reported that two people, a man and a woman, had been found dead in Castlerock. The names were withheld, but Liz immediately suspected that Trevor could be one of them. Gut instinct told her that the man who used to smile and wave, as he drove past in his white Toyota car with a spoiler on the back, would not be calling again. She recalled looking up at Bertie, saying: 'I hope that is not what I'm thinking.' They speculated as to the identity of the bodies: 'We were putting two and two together because there was so much talk at the time about the affair: how the church had intervened, and was working away in the background to try and get everything sorted.'

As she had been a local politician with an extensive network of contacts, it wasn't long before Liz got a call which confirmed that those in question were indeed Trevor and Lesley: 'When somebody told me the names, I couldn't believe it.' Liz had many fond memories of Trevor Buchanan, and before she died of cancer in October 2009, she wept in the study of her home as she spoke of one of her biggest regrets, saying: 'I should have told the police to have him shifted, transferred to somewhere else. If something had been done, it would not have happened. I blame the church for that. If we had told the police privately, and told them what was going on, they could have moved Trevor further away.'

The day after the awful news had broken, Liz was one of the first of the neighbours at Hazel's door to offer her sandwiches and cakes as well as some of her china cups and plates, in preparation for the days to follow, when there would be many people calling. She didn't know Hazel as well as she had known Trevor. She held out her hand to the young mother, but there was no firm grip and it felt, or so she thought, as if it wasn't really a handshake at all. Her impression was that Hazel was in shock: 'She was cold and to me, she really wasn't in mourning. I thought her grief was going to come later. That's what can happen to some people. They withdraw into themselves, keep it there; they don't talk and then maybe in a few weeks, sometimes months it all comes out . . . She was very controlled and, in the kitchen, she just left it to the rest of us to attend to everybody. She just stood back. I remember being in the garden, asking her about her memories of Trevor, their holidays together and so on, and she never replied. I found that strange, that she didn't say anything. She just said: "Look. Look where the wheel is lying." And sure enough, there it was at the bottom of the garden where Trevor had thrown it. It was the wheel he had brought to our house.'

There was soon talk that Trevor might have been having second thoughts about suicide, and was trying to get out of the door, when he was overcome by the fumes. It made his death all the more poignant.

Shirley McPhillimy, the friend who had been with Lesley just days earlier, was devastated. She told police: 'I kept thinking: was there anything I could have said or done to stop it? When I saw her on the Tuesday, she was still coping, still holding a routine, still happy to save her marriage, still loved Colin and most importantly, she still absolutely adored her children. She did not give me any cause to think that perhaps she was suicidal . . . I found the circumstances of her death very strange . . . I recall the attempted overdose and also on the Tuesday before her death, her [saying]: "Maybe they'd be better off without me—why not just let them have each other?" But never did I actually think that she would consider suicide. I never thought she would be capable.'

The Howells' housekeeper, Betty Bradley was distraught but puzzled too: 'I did wonder why she had decided to leave her devoted children, whom she loved dearly.' Lesley's friend, Tania Donaghy, had her own theory, which she shared with police: 'It was my belief at the time that Lesley had done Colin a favour by taking her own life, and that she must have talked Trevor into helping her to do it, and that he had got caught up in the car, causing him to lose his life as well. I just couldn't understand it [though], because Trevor was always known as a very steady fellow.' Tania's husband Harry, who called at both the Howell and Buchanan homes on the night of the deaths, found Colin coping well: it struck him that there were no tears or signs of emotion, and that Howell was calm, controlled, and gave the impression he was putting on a brave face: 'As far as I was concerned, you couldn't lose your wife and not be emotional. I thought he must be devastated, but was holding back his grief.'

It was Howell who contacted Ruth Middleton, Lesley's friend from her nursing days, to tell her that his wife was dead. Ruth remembers screaming down the telephone: 'It can't be. It can't be.' But she was also thinking: 'What have you done? Did you force her to do it?' She later told police: 'I had big, big doubts, but because it was a double [suicide], I couldn't understand it. If it had just been Lesley, I would have been very suspicious.'

Howell also phoned Valerie Allen to break the news to her, telling her he was sorry. Valerie, a university lecturer at the time, was living in Stirling with her boyfriend, Ares Axiotis, a philosopher and an American naturally blessed with a jaundiced view of human nature. He had never met the Howells, but when she told him her friend and a man had been found dead in a car at Castlerock, he replied: 'Mark my words, he's bumped them off.' Valerie was heartbroken to hear of Lesley's death. She remembers of that time: 'I had lots of dreams about her. It just felt we had been chatting on the phone and I would always feel good. The dreams were good. I never cried. I just felt very angry about the whole thing.'

Trevor's family, including his mother and father, Jim and Lily, travelled up from Omagh that day. Gordon Buchanan, not long home after a break with his wife, Donna, in Belfast, had been in the garden playing with his two children, when she had called him into the kitchen. He burst into tears as she told him that a former neighbour who moved to Portstewart had called with the news: 'Trevor has been found dead in a car in Castlerock. A woman's body was there as well.'

It was a Sunday afternoon, and the roads in and around the part of the town where Gordon lived were heavily congested with long tailbacks of traffic. Thousands of Gaelic Athletic Association football fans were on their way to a first round Ulster championship game between Derry and Tyrone at nearby Healy Park, further up the Gortin Road. With Gordon sitting weeping in the front passenger seat, it seemed an eternity before his wife was able to negotiate her way through the chaos. Eventually they reached his sister Valerie's bungalow at Clanabogan, a few miles outside the town, where their parents had been having lunch. But by the time they pulled into the driveway, Victor, who was already there with his wife Lorna, and a police colleague, Ken Balfour, had broken the news to Lily and Jim.

Gordon's mind immediately drifted back to the last time he had spoken with Trevor and he wished they had been on their own the day he had seen his brother at his home in Coleraine, a couple of months earlier. Gordon recalls of that meeting: 'We had a general conversation and it was good to catch up with him again. I had a friend with me. There was certainly nothing obvious and maybe if it had just been the two of us, he would have talked. Suicide leaves you with so many questions. Was there anything I could have done? Why didn't I notice?'

The journey from Omagh to Coleraine can take the best part of two hours. There are some fast stretches on the road north, but it can be painfully slow at times, especially the last leg outside Limavady, where the road climbs high before dipping downhill towards the River Bann and the town centre. It was a miserable and depressing trip. When they finally pulled up outside Hazel's house, the place was already filling up with her extended family, also from Omagh, and some senior police officers. Trevor's sister Melva and her husband Syd had also just arrived. They had been with their two boys to the park at Castle Archdale in County Fermanagh that afternoon when they had heard the news. They were met at the door of Hazel's house by Pastor Hansford. And then Hazel appeared. She was embraced in the hallway by her in-laws.

But not everybody was in a forgiving mood, and tensions already started to emerge as friends and neighbours fussed around the kitchen preparing tea and sandwiches. Trevor's sister Valerie recalls: 'Hazel came into the room and cried. She said she was really sorry. It was her fault. We knew then she had the affair. I actually felt sorry for her. I said: "It's okay." But at the time, I also remember thinking: "What am I doing here? It's not okay. Trevor is dead and it's her fault."'

Gordon's recollection of Hazel's attitude is a bit different: 'I don't recall hearing the word "sorry". I never witnessed any remorse. I put it down to grief and shock on Hazel's part. We were convinced by the minister, and the police, that it was suicide. I was a policeman. Trevor was a policeman. My two older brothers were policemen, and we took as sacrosanct anything the police told us. In my heart of hearts, I could not accept that Trevor would take his own life. He loved Hazel too much. He loved his children too much. He was a genuine

Christian man who had become very involved in the church, taking part in the services. He definitely would not have sat in a car waiting for somebody else to die alongside him. It was just not him. But we were told by people we trusted impeccably—the police and the clergy —that sadly, it had been suicide. There was no other answer for it. We were left to reconcile with that, but we never did.'

Victor Buchanan was equally bewildered. It was the Baptist minister, Jim Garrett, from his church in Comber and a police colleague who had told him. His first thought was that the death of his brother might be terrorist-related, because of the high IRA threat level in the Coleraine area at the time. He remembers disbelief at the idea that it had been suicide: 'I could not understand why Trevor had suddenly committed suicide, knowing the conversations we had and knowing it was the last thing that would have entered his mind. That was from his lips. He always felt he didn't have the guts to do it anyway. He told me: "You needn't worry. It is the last thing I would even consider." We knew how much he loved the children. Trevor had three loves— the Lord, his wife and children, and his work. All in that order. The affection was apparent. It wasn't switched on, or switched off. There was no question about his love for Hazel. If he hadn't loved her, he would not have stayed with her. There is absolutely no doubt about that. He wouldn't have endured it one step longer. It was only the love he had for her, that he could see beyond all that had gone on. He was prepared to take her back and make a go of it again.'

Melva, the youngest in the Buchanan family and just 23 at the time, remembers that everybody else was given an explanation about the affair, but that she was told nothing until she overheard the pastor talking about it. She was warned to remain dignified, and respect Trevor's memory. She recalls: 'I must have gone with the flow and did what everybody else told me to do. At that stage, you went through so many phases of emotions. I was only the wee girl and it wasn't up to me. I remember saying to Valerie: "If this was Syd [Melva's husband], his sisters would have me over the coals, asking questions." But nobody was asking any questions [of Hazel]. We believed what we were told. I don't even recall Hazel speaking to me. We didn't see much of her. Any time she answered the door [over those few days], she had a different shell suit on. It was the shell suit era, and if it wasn't white, it was pink, or lilac, maybe green . . .'

Hazel's dress code wasn't the only issue which bothered her young sister-in-law at the time. In front of people who gathered at the house that day, Hazel wondered out loud how she was now going to mow the grass. Neither was she familiar with the workings of the oil central heating system, and who would be around the house to help her? Melva was angry: 'How could she think of such things when her husband had just died? What is she talking about? Who cares about cutting the lawn or worrying about keeping the house warm? You could have cut the atmosphere with a knife. We were outside most of the time, in the front garden, hanging around. I was angry with her for quite a while, and then I realised it wasn't really her fault. Trevor chose to take his life. Affairs can happen. I remember feeling at the time really sorry for Trevor and what he must have gone through. He was such a proud person and this was how he had to deal with it. And then I would probably have been very angry with him as well. I would have thought he had been silly and it was a stupid thing to do.'

It would be many years of course before Trevor and Lesley's families would learn the truth about their deaths. In the meantime, they were tortured by the terrible unanswered questions which an unexplained suicide always leaves behind.

Chapter 10

'Why Didn't You Come to Me, Son?'

Colin Howell held his son Matthew by the hand as he made his way through the crowded congregation. Before he took his seat for Lesley's funeral, he paused briefly, pointed at his wife's coffin and then whispered in the child's ear: 'Your mummy is in there.'

Coleraine Baptist Church was packed for the first of the two funerals to be held that day, Tuesday, 21 May. Howell's parents, Sam and Sarah, his brothers, Jim and Gordon and his sisters, Maud and Pauline, were all there. Lesley's brother Chris, his then wife Jen, and many of Lesley's friends, especially those with whom she had nursed, were among those who took up most of pews towards the front. Some of her old girlfriends stood over the coffin and wept. Pastor Hansford, wearing a clerical collar, stood waiting until everybody had found their place, before delivering his words of welcome. Extra seats had to be brought in to accommodate all the mourners.

Valerie Allen and Hilary Scargill came to see Lesley off together. The night before they had stayed at the Golf Hotel in Castlerock, where they met up with Chris Clarke and were able to regale him with some stories of Lesley's exploits. Toasting the life of their dear and well-loved friend, they reminisced about the charming young mother who had a wicked wit, a fine taste for melodrama and who told a great story. Chris really hadn't had the chance to see as much of that side of his sister as Valerie and Hilary had, and he enjoyed listening to their fond memories of Lesley.

Of the funeral service itself, Valerie recalls: 'Nobody said anything about the reasons why Lesley took her life, but then there were little children there. It seemed to me that they tiptoed around the awkward issues. It felt hollow.' Lesley's friend was no more than cordial towards Howell and once the day's formalities ended, she wanted nothing more to do with him. His demeanour at the funeral and attitude to Lesley's death somehow left Valerie cold: 'Colin apologised prettily enough for me at the funeral, and he seemed sad and sombre. He sounded distressed when he called. He wasn't crying and was obviously embarrassed talking to me . . . I felt angry at him. He took away my friend. I felt sad about the whole system . . .' Another friend of Lesley's, Pat Chambers, who travelled up from Dublin, refused to shake Howell's hand. She clearly blamed him for driving his wife to take her own life: 'Lesley would not have harmed a mouse . . . She adored her children. She would never have left them. She was such a bubbly girl, so full of life . . .'

But if some members of the congregation at the service for Lesley felt nervous and uneasy, and maybe a touch awkward because of the circumstances surrounding her death, the atmosphere was nothing compared to the behind-the-scenes tensions, resentment and acrimony which threatened to overshadow the funeral of Trevor Buchanan later that afternoon.

Nobody dared say a word at the time, but the ill-feeling probably began to simmer from the moment the tearful and apologetic Hazel opened her front door to acknowledge and embrace the first wave of sympathy of her friends and neighbours. Even then, the Elkin and Buchanan families had kept their distance from one another, with Trevor's family quickly settling in one room, and Hazel's in another.

Trevor's family members were hurt and disappointed by the way in which Hazel had decided to handle the funeral arrangements: it was very far from the typical country wake they would have expected and had been hoping for. Trevor's coffin was not kept for a period in the Buchanan house, as would have been the custom, which meant that there could be no official mourning in the family home. Instead, Hazel had decided that, once the post-mortem examination was complete, her husband's body would be transferred directly to Wade's funeral parlour at the corner of Abbey Street, just across from Coleraine Baptist Church, and would remain there in one of the three small viewing rooms, next to where Lesley Howell's body rested. Trevor's family was disappointed about this, not least Trevor's father,

Jim, for it meant that the first time they would see Trevor's body would also be the time they would have to say their final goodbyes.

Gordon Buchanan recalls that moment with devastating clarity: 'At the funeral parlour, I can remember dad, mum and our immediate family. Donna, my wife was in the hallway. The room was very small. There [were] quite a lot of people and some from the Elkin family. I can't recall if Hazel was there ... This scene is indelibly imprinted in my mind. Trevor was in the coffin. I noticed bruising on his face. It was explained away that there had been some alleged scuffle between him and Colin Howell at Howell's house. It was said that Trevor had gone to confront him. When Dad entered the funeral parlour to see Trevor for the first time since his death, he paused briefly and then went straight to the coffin and lifted Trevor's head and upper body out of the coffin. He held him in his arms and said to him: "Why did you do it, son? Why didn't you come to me?" It was horrendous, an unbelievable scenario. Dad basically died [himself] that day. He lived a lot of years after that, but he retreated to his house, sat in the corner and lost the will to live ... He was still a great man and a caring father, but he had lost his spark ... That pain and hurt was always there. He never got a release from it.'

Jim Buchanan would have preferred his son to have been buried in the graveyard of the Holy Trinity Church of Ireland in Dromore, the family's spiritual home. It was the church where he and the rest of the family were once regular attendees. But the family did not insist, out of respect for Hazel's wishes, as Trevor's sister Valerie explains: 'Dad wanted Trevor's body back in Dromore ... to be buried there. Again, being the dignified people that we are and with Lisa and Andrew in mind, we thought it would not be fair. Trevor stayed at the funeral parlour, but it was nothing to do with procedures, or post-mortems. Hazel just didn't want him at the house.'

While the Buchanans were prepared to let the issue of the funeral parlour go, they could not agree to Hazel's proposition—endorsed, it seemed, by those in charge at the Baptist Church—that there should be no church service for Trevor, but that the ceremony should take place in the funeral home. Gordon explains: 'The funeral was going to take place from the funeral parlour. I've no idea why. We assumed it was something Hazel, Colin Howell and the church had decided. We insisted there was a funeral from the church. Trevor was part of that church. He was a member taking part in Christian services and was entitled to be buried from that church.' Valerie confirms her brother's impression: 'They didn't want a church service, because it was suicide. Pastor Hansford definitely said that to Victor at Trevor's house, the day after he died . . . At the time I felt the church was trying to distance itself. I could understand why at the same time, because this was an awful situation for any church . . . I felt they wanted it over and done with and out of the way. [But] I would never say they did anything deliberately underhand.'

When the Buchanans insisted that there should be a proper church service for Trevor, Pastor Hansford agreed to accommodate their wishes, as Gordon recounts: 'Once we brought it up, there was no real resistance to it. But if we hadn't brought it up, Trevor would have been buried from the funeral parlour. If anything, I think we were too dignified.' Pastor Hansford's recollections differ from those of the Buchanans, and he denies that there was any resistance to a church service: 'It is wrong to say the church did not want the funerals to take place from the church. I never thought of not doing the funerals from the church. The church was not embarrassed. That was not the case. There were huge congregations at both funerals. There was no debate about the funerals not being in the church. Nobody raised any objection to that at all.'

The pastor is also adamant that a Union flag had been draped over Trevor's coffin, which he asked to be removed: 'Symbolism may mean everything in Northern Ireland, but historically Baptists believe in the separation of the Church and the State . . . I felt the situation in Northern Ireland was best helped by the separation of Church and State, not bringing the two together . . . It was purely the symbolism on the coffin in the church. The flag was taken off the coffin, and then put back, in the foyer, as it left.' But, as Trevor's relatives can confirm, there was at no point a flag on the coffin—his was a private, family funeral, without any police or other trappings.

Hazel's questionable dress sense at the service was also a source of disquiet, as Trevor's sister Valerie recalls: 'She definitely wasn't a grieving widow, the way she was dressed at the funeral. She wore a black skirt which was quite short for that time, and a red jacket. I don't recall what she had under it, but you could see her cleavage. It wasn't appropriate at all for your husband's funeral.' Gordon concurs: 'She came dressed completely inappropriately . . . It was not fitting for a funeral. I just felt, this woman clearly is not thinking straight.' And as far as his family were concerned, it seemed that Trevor's widow showed no obvious signs of grief, as Valerie recalls: 'Hazel didn't have a reaction. I think women are more perceptive, but you could see she didn't care. No doubt it was a relief to her that he was gone. That's how she behaved, as if it was almost relief to her. She didn't behave like someone who [was] grieving and hurting.'

Valerie also found the way the church service was handled irksome and insensitive: 'I remember during the service, Pastor Hansford talking about the loving wife and mother Hazel was. I was getting angrier, angrier and angrier and thinking: "If he doesn't shut up, I'm going to shout at him." He didn't mention Trevor's mum and dad, or his family, who really loved him. It's very clear Hazel didn't love him, or she wouldn't have had an affair. And here he [the pastor] is, talking about this loving wife and mother, but no mention of those who really loved him . . . he didn't acknowledge us as a family—even mum and dad—when we were grieving. He could see that they were broken and he didn't acknowledge that.'

Valerie was so annoyed by what she felt was the pastor's lack of recognition, that once the service ended, she hurriedly ushered her parents from their seats to stand in front of Hazel, as her brother's coffin was carried out of the church. And she asked that the procession wait at the cemetery gates until her Church of Ireland clergyman, the Rev. Brendan McCarthy from St Columba's Parish Church in Omagh, emerged from the back of the queue of mourners, to take his place by the graveside to say a prayer on behalf of the family. It was a wet and miserable afternoon.

Even some of Trevor's police colleagues in 'B' section, who attended the funeral in civilian clothes, felt that there was a strange atmosphere. They had contributed to a collection, but decided against joining the family afterwards. Derek Ewing, then a police crime prevention officer and near neighbour of Trevor's, remembers: 'There was a lot of talk about the Church, verging on a conspiracy. It was very much a closed shop. I got the impression—as did a lot of people who were there—the funeral was something the church had to have, but might have preferred there wasn't as many people present . . . You just got the impression you were somewhere where you were not really wanted. I felt intrusive . . . Hazel was very composed. It was a strange affair, not like a normal, standard funeral—[it was] a strained event with a strange atmosphere.'

Trevor's family and some of his friends and colleagues felt strongly that the church had not handled the affair and its aftermath very well. Derek Ewing sums it up: 'It was beginning to emerge the church had been involved in the counselling process and hadn't done Trevor, or Lesley, any favours. It seemed as if it was a crowd of well-meaning amateurs trying to reconcile a problem who did not have the expertise to do it. There were problems on both sides and they were trying to bring them back together. If they had kept their noses out of it and left it to the professionals . . .' Valerie was very much of the same opinion at the time: 'I just thought Hansford handled it really badly, from start to finish. He told us he had been counselling both couples, which seemed very unusual. Then he went away, just before Trevor and Lesley died . . . They were left with nobody to counsel them while he was away. He should have referred them to professional help. Obviously he did care for them, and thought he was doing his best. I met him at a conference in Belfast a few years later, because he recognised Brendan [the Church of Ireland clergyman who spoke at Trevor's graveside on the family's behalf]. I can't remember exactly what he said. But he admitted that he had handled things badly at the time. I went over to him, shook hands with him, told him who I was and that I had become a Christian and said that if anything good came out of Trevor's death that was one thing . . . He was very pleased about that.'

Pastor Hansford defended himself, however. He said: 'People looked back and said: "Why wasn't that done? Why wasn't this done?" They were trying to find some reason why the event had happened. It took its toll on me. But the elders were all united, all of one mind. There was no cover-up. I don't feel a responsibility that I messed things up, or that the church did.'

The Buchanans wish that they—and the police—had asked more questions of Hazel at the time. But they felt that Trevor's widow had enough to cope with already, as Gordon explains: 'As far as we were concerned, an affair had happened and as a result of it, Lesley and Trevor had taken their lives; Hazel could not have anticipated that and would not have wanted to see him dead. In many ways, we looked at her—albeit she had played a part in his Trevor's death—that she hadn't sought it and that in many ways she was a grieving widow with children who had a massive burden to carry . . . Through our own decency, we didn't question her. We didn't quiz her. We were convinced the police had done a good job . . . In retrospect, I wish we had asked more questions. I wish the police had asked more questions. But I have to emphasise how much faith we had in the police, believing what they told us was accurate. In my wildest dreams, I would not have predicted murder.'

The deaths left his congregation shattered, according to the pastor: 'I assumed a lot of people would not come to church because they couldn't cope with being there. And yet, the church on the Sunday afterwards was full. They wanted to make a rhyme or reason why this happened, and why it happened to us . . .'

Jim Buchanan would never recover from his grief. Gordon suffered a deep depression. Lily, Trevor's mother, appeared to be coping in the immediate aftermath, as Valerie recalls: 'Poor Mum was there, but she wasn't there. Mentally she appeared to cope very well at the time, but the reality wasn't hitting her.' Three months later, however, Mrs Buchanan was admitted with a nervous breakdown to the Tyrone and Fermanagh psychiatric hospital in Omagh.

One of Gordon's most abiding memories will be the day of his brother's funeral: 'I remember standing in the rain . . . I remember standing at the hearse outside Wade's. I was completely in another world . . . I remember standing, staring at the coffin and thinking that this cannot really be happening . . . All these years we have been asking ourselves: "Why? Why? Why? What could we have done? Why did we not recognise what was going on?" Trevor had no choice. If Trevor had taken his life, at least it would have been his choice. Now we know he was given no choice . . . Trevor's death was murder. It was so cruel, so calculated and so unnecessary.'

Chapter 11
'I Have Taken a Mother from my Children'

His wife wasn't even buried when Colin Howell sat down and penned his lover an extraordinary and impassioned letter, imploring her not to walk away, and to ignore Pastor Hansford's strong recommendation to dissociate herself from him altogether. Fearful of being seen by others to be initiating contact with Hazel so soon after the deaths, Howell didn't hand the letter to her himself. Instead, he folded the three foolscap pages, placed them into a sealed white envelope with Hazel's name on the front, and gave it to her close friends and near neighbours, Derek and Hilary McAuley. It was just hours before he would take his place beside his wife's grieving friends and family at the cemetery, where they would watch her coffin being slowly lowered into the ground.

These were the killer's words to his lover:

'Hazel —

The pastor has given me the message from you that, although with your heart, you want you and me, you now realise with your mind that it is best that we never get together again. Is that true? I must know, because if it is, you must ring me and only to say: "It is true". Don't allow me to think there is hope, if there is none. You will kill me. I can accept it now if you say it, but I can't allow myself to progress to find out later . . . And you must decide now about our future, and not wait and see. I will not ever try and change your mind, no matter how lonely I get.

Read the rest only if you want to know why I disagree about certain things . . . the pastor said to you. First. He told me he will do everything in his power to stop us getting together. That, I believe, is not his thinking mind, but his very strong emotional reaction of anger and guilt at their deaths. He is a very clever man and is capable of convincing you that our marriage would be a disaster and will, in the days to come, continue to convince you if you remain uncertain. If, with your mind (not your feelings) you accept what I think, then we will both go to the pastor and tell him that in the long term (maybe one to two years), we have decided now to get together later, but we will give him certain reassurances, so that he can accept for the sake of the church what we would say to him. I will set out my proposals at the end. I will deal with the three [sic] things he used to convince you our marriage would be a disaster:

Lisa and Andrew: I heard Lisa twice said that she didn't like me. That is hard. But I believe she is talking about a time eight months ago, when I was with you more than you were with Trevor. That is what she didn't like. Trevor is gone, so when I come back on the scene in a year's time, if you haven't got someone else, then she will be needing a father figure, and the threat I used to be will be replaced by a need. I will talk to her and Andrew about Trevor and what they did with him, and tell them I understand that they miss him. I will allow Andrew to cut the grass and do manly things, to copy what his dad did. They will be so loved by me that difficulties (which there will be) will be overcome and sorted out. If I understand and talk to them: they are not a reason for disaster.

Your grief for Trevor: I agree that we might have underestimated this response in our hearts. The length of time it takes to get over this will determine when we get together. During this time, we must not see or talk to each other. When we miss each other, we must look at Trevor and Lesley's things and photos to concentrate our feelings on their grief. I miss Lesley and am so sorry that I didn't love her enough, and for all the sins I have done to her. I need time to sorrow [sic] for that before we can be together. But once it's done (although maybe never completely gone), we can give ourselves to each other without looking back. The pastor says you would go to pieces a few months after we

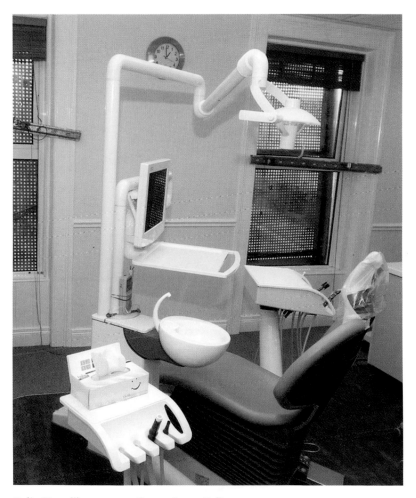

Colin Howell's surgery at Queen Street, Ballymoney.

Photographs of his children on the shelves of Colin Howell's office in Ballymoney.

The Renault Savanna car in the garage behind the row of houses in Castlerock known as The Apostles, where the bodies of Lesley Howell and Trevor Buchanan were found.

Colin Howell's solicitor, Adrian Harvey of Trevor Smyth and Co., Belfast.

John Hansford, the former Pastor of Coleraine Baptist Church, defended his handling of the counselling process involving the two couples: 'Colin was always cagey with me. Hazel portrayed herself to be innocent, but I don't think she is.'

Colin Howell on a night out with his second wife, Kyle. She urged him to confess to the church elders, telling him: 'The truth will set you free. It's the truth. You must get it out.'

Colin and Lesley Howell on the day they married at Windsor
Baptist Church, Belfast in July 1983, before a reception at the
Conway Hotel, Dunmurry, where the two families reached a
compromise over the serving of alcohol. Lesley's brother Chris
said: 'It was bizarre and slightly uncomfortable.'

Lesley Howell joking with two of her bridesmaids. Lesley got a bikini wax and the girls thought it hilarious. They were in high spirits, yelping and laughing.

Colin and Lesley Howell photographed together for the last time in February 1991, just months before he murdered her. Lesley's friend Shirley McPhillimy told police: 'They appeared to be a normal happy couple. They put on a good show.'

Lesley Howell on the day she graduated as a State Registered Nurse at the Royal Victoria Hospital, Belfast, where she once won a silver medal for being a top student. A junior doctor remembers her treating an elderly woman in the haematology ward: 'She was extremely good to that lady, but then all patients liked her.'

Constable Trevor Buchanan. He stretched himself physically and academically to become a regular member of the Royal Ulster Constabulary. His brother Gordon said: 'He did everything under the sun to make the height. He was so determined.'

Matthew Howell, who died after falling down a stairwell in St Petersburg, Russia. Friends recall how he resisted pressure from his father to pursue a career in dentistry. One said: 'Matthew hated his dad.'

David and Hazel Stewart with her two children, Andrew and Lisa. David, a former police Chief Superintendent who was once a staff officer to the ex-RUC Chief Constable Sir Hugh Annesley, told police: 'She is a kind and trusting person with a soft nature. At times she can be too trusting.'

Melva Alexander, Trevor Buchanan's younger sister: 'The biggest problem at the time was being told Trevor was in the back of a car with another woman. I have spent eighteen years correcting that statement.'

Victor Buchanan, Trevor Buchanan's older brother: 'Trevor's faith was something which had a real and meaningful bearing on the way he lived his life.'

Gordon Buchanan, Trevor Buchanan's brother: 'What Hazel did amounts to the ultimate betrayal. Howell is clearly cruel and calculating and I will be forever haunted by the knowledge Trevor was aware of what was being done to him—in his own bed, the safest place one could imagine.'

Valerie Bleakley, Trevor Buchanan's sister: 'I just couldn't believe that Hazel was involved. Surely she couldn't have been that stupid? How could she do such a thing and deprive her children of a father who loved them passionately?'

Daniel Howell: 'My father remains a danger to society.' With Lauren Bradford, Colin Howell's daughter: 'I feel like he has finally restored their honour, albeit almost twenty years later. He could have gone to his grave with it.'

Former RUC Detective Inspector David Green, a member of Coleraine Baptist Church, who became suspicious after finding the bodies. He told police in 2009: 'I wanted to help the investigation, but I didn't want to stand on anyone's toes, or make a nuisance of myself. I was concerned something had happened.'

Trevor McAuley, who shared eight years of his life with Hazel Stewart before she left him for another man, David Stewart: 'She was a total grabber of opportunities. Nothing was ever good enough. She was materialistic to the hilt. Cold-hearted.'

Lesley's aunt, Alice Berry, and her brother, Chris Clarke. Howell asked Mrs Berry, a teacher from Lurgan, County Armagh, not to come to their home after Lesley's father, Harry Clarke, died. Chris Clarke suspects Howell murdered Harry as well. Howell denies it.

Derek McAuley, a Coleraine Baptist, who steamed open and then photocopied Colin Howell's 1991 letter to his lover, told police who questioned him in February 2009: 'People shouldn't be opening other people's mail. It's lousy.'

Harold Burke, a paedophile Howell once tried to help when they were members of the Barn Christian Fellowship. They ended up sharing a cell at Maghaberry Prison. Burke told police: 'He was frequently rambling and talked a lot about judgement and hell.'

Dr Alan Topping, who holidayed with the Howells in Tenerife in 1986, shared David Green's suspicions. He told police in February 2009: 'We discussed the possibility of Colin being responsible for the deaths and how he may have managed to kill Lesley and Trevor and then return from Castlerock.'

Valerie Allen, one of Lesley's bridesmaids, now living in New York: 'Before they married, she told me the relationship was problematic. Colin was hotter on her than she was on him.'

Trevor Buchanan's parents, Jim and Lily. Jim died in July 2007.

Robin Hastings, the coroner who presided over the 1992 inquest, where Howell and Stewart lied and lied again as part of the cover-up pact: 'Colin Howell wasn't a nice man. He was a chancy fellow, a smart arse. Hazel had to be devious as well because she went with the cover-up.'

Superintendent Raymond Murray (*left*) and Inspector Ian Magee, who headed up the new police investigation. They decided not to have the bodies exhumed. At one stage Adrian West, one of the UK's leading criminal psychologists, was consulted as part of their inquiries.

The landmark row of houses in Castlerock, known as The Apostles. Harry Clarke lived at No. 6 and it was in his garage behind—just days after he died—that the bodies of his daughter and Trevor Buchanan were discovered. The garage was demolished after new owners bought the house.

Just yards apart in Coleraine Cemetery: the graves of Trevor Buchanan and Lesley Howell.

were married. Do you agree? I think I know you better than he does and believe he is wrong, if you have time alone now to sorrow for your guilt and loss.

Your family: I was so glad when you told me your dad hugged you for the first time. I know how important that is to you, and we will do nothing to set that back. If enough time passes, and when they see how much I care for you and will look after you, they will accept both of us. All they are worried about now, and will ever be worried about, is that you are happy and that you will have someone who really loves you. They see how bad things went for Winifred [Hazel's sister] and they are scared for you. The reason I disagree this is a reason, is that they don't know me. To them, I am the one who made the daft phone call which caused so much trouble. I also am the one who got you to this position. So obviously all their advice will be against me. I have talked for hours to my Dad and my sister Maud about whether there would be acceptance for you and me in our family, and they have said (even in these early days) that the most important thing would be how well you cared for me, and they would accept you with a great welcome if you loved me. So don't be scared of families. The most important thing is that we must wait a long time. But I will wait for you if you decide, and are convinced in your mind that these things are correct.

Coleraine and the Church: For the sake of the Church, we must not [make] contact while we are both in Coleraine. Here I am going to say the hardest thing to take. If you decide the pastor is right, then you will probably always stay in Coleraine. If you decide that we can one day be together, then we both must leave Coleraine eventually. I will probably leave the Church immediately but I may also leave Coleraine, even if you decide our future is together. I will definitely leave by September if you are still convinced by the pastor. Consider this seriously. If you decide that you and I will be together one day, then I think that by September (new school term), I should move away to Portadown and you should move to Omagh. Lisa and Andrew will be surrounded by the security of family, and so will my children. The main reason for saying that is this: when we get together, you would be making the children move because of me if they stayed now in Coleraine, and there is a chance they would blame me for

the move. If you say yes to me about our future, we will talk a lot
more about this. So don't feel any pressure about it. There may be
more important reasons for staying.

If in your heart Hazel, you really think it is over for us, then
you must say it. If you can say without doubt that we can
overcome these problems given by the pastor, then say yes to me
and don't look back. We will meet with the pastor and tell him
our plans—we will ask him to council [sic] us if he agrees. We will
be honest and open and not secretive. We will lose many friends
who won't accept us, but we can walk down the street together,
proud of each other, because from now on, we are forgiven and
will be disciplined and will honour God. And we won't lose all our
friends, if we take our time.

I have taken a mother from my children, but God will provide
for them and I only hope and pray it can be you. But only if you
can accept in your mind, as well as your heart.

Love, Colin'

Derek McAuley, however, did not pass on the letter to Hazel straight
away, most likely because of all that was going on with the two
funerals. Before he handed it over a few days later, he decided to steam
open the envelope. Once he had read Howell's letter, he made a
photocopy of it, then gave Hazel the original, without telling her what
he had done. McAuley showed the copy to his wife and also to Pastor
Hansford: he was convinced that the minister was being misled by the
duplicitous Howell. McAuley then filed the photocopy away with
other papers.

Howell's letter wasn't seen again until 18 years later, in 2009, when
McAuley handed the copy over to detectives who had reopened the
investigation into the deaths after the dentist's confession to the
murders. When questioned, McAuley told police: 'I remember when I
read the letter, thinking Colin Howell was crazy—talking about him
and Hazel, and blaming Pastor John Hansford for their problems,
despite the fact that Pastor Hansford was involved in counselling the
two couples . . .' When he was asked to give his interpretation of the
last paragraph of the letter (which began with the words: 'I have taken
the mother from my children . . .'), McAuley replied: 'I can only say
that I thought Howell was referring to his affair with Hazel Buchanan

and [how] this affair had led to his wife, their children's mother, committing suicide. I just couldn't believe that, after all that had happened, Colin Howell was still pursuing Hazel Buchanan. I never mentioned the content of the letter to Hazel Buchanan. I have thought over this matter a lot since Colin Howell's arrest, and can say I honestly believed that Colin and Hazel discontinued their relationship after the deaths of Lesley and Trevor.' Sometime after the deaths, McAuley met the dentist by chance in Portstewart and he took the opportunity to challenge him about the affair, telling him: 'You overstepped the mark. Hazel's a good-looking woman, but she was Trevor's.'

In the weeks following the funerals, Howell spoke with friends and apologised for what had happened. Some believed he felt genuine remorse about Lesley's death and the fact that his infidelity might have pushed her to suicide. Others, however, suspected a PR offensive on Howell's part, in a bid to regain some credibility and support. One of these later told police: 'Everybody was crying and distraught at the funeral. Colin didn't appear sad at the time. I felt he was putting on an act. I felt he wasn't sorry she was dead.' Another, who also spoke to police, recalled having an instinctive feeling that something was amiss: 'We called with him at the house and he gave me a hug. I had this awful feeling, down the back of my neck. I felt very uncomfortable, it was horrible. Colin was talking about starting a new life, that it was an opportunity for us all to start again. Lesley was just dead and I couldn't believe he was saying this.'

Howell asked Ruth Middleton and Carolyn Younge, another friend of Lesley's from her nursing days, to help go through his wife's belongings. He offered them some of his wife's jewellery. Ruth accepted a locket and she took some other small items as keepsakes to give to Lesley's old Belfast housemates, Ann Kempton and Linda Patterson. Ruth recalled that Howell's mother and two sisters, Pauline and Maud, were in the house at the time. She also remembered clearly how, when she remarked on how awful it was that Trevor had also died, Howell had replied loudly: 'He took my wife away.' As she would later comment to police: 'It was said over his shoulder and was inappropriate. It seemed to be said for the benefit of the rest of the house.' Howell gave Margaret Topping one of Lesley's watches, and to Linda Brockbank, another friend, he presented one of his wife's neck chains. Before the deaths, Linda had known that he and Hazel

Buchanan were very much in love, and she would later tell police: 'I think everyone would have known that at the time. Hazel would have told me that she knew it was wrong, but she had a strong love for Colin.'

Ruth Middleton wasn't the only one who felt Howell's actions and words in the immediate aftermath of the deaths were inappropriate and at times bizarre. Chris Clarke was angered and disconcerted when his brother-in-law offered to give him the Adrian Snell tape which Lesley had supposedly been listening to as she waited to die. Howell was insistent that Chris should have the tape as a memento of his sister. But Chris, who did not share his sister's religious convictions, felt it was a rather ghoulish gesture: 'Firmly and increasingly impolitely, I said "No". I didn't particularly want a tape of religious music, and actually it was something which was fairly horrific for me. I wasn't going to have fond memories. I thought it was hugely inappropriate and very strange.'

Howell, it seemed, wanted nothing more to do with any reminders of his late wife—not even the shared memories of her former girlfriends. One of them later penned a collection of reminiscences about Lesley, which she wanted Lauren to have, as a cherished reminder of her mother, and how much they all thought of her. The hardback notebook which was given to Colin was never passed on to the child, it seems. One of the friends in question speculated: 'I don't think he ever gave it to her. I believe he kept it in the safe at his surgery.'

Howell's infidelity to his late wife had become a hot topic of conversation in Coleraine circles. There was sympathy for him in some homes, but none in others, where people blamed him for driving his wife first to drink and then to suicide. In the weeks which followed the deaths, it seemed that the grieving widower's focus was much more firmly fixed upon himself and his efforts to garner support from those around him, than on his grief. One couple, who also belonged to Coleraine Baptist Church at the time, were stunned when he called unannounced to see them one night to defend himself and his reputation. The woman of the house recalls: 'Colin wanted to explain himself. He didn't come to unburden himself or seek emotional support. He just wanted to set out the facts as he saw them . . . I detested him because of the affair and what he did to Lesley. She was devastated, an emotional wreck. Before the deaths, I could take him or leave him. I would never have said he was a nice man. Nobody actually said anything at the time, but I actually guessed he had been having an affair. The pastor tried hard to manage the situation, and under the circumstances, he did as best he could. It was extremely difficult to handle.'

Another member of the congregation remembers that Howell did manage to win over some people in their church community: 'One of the elders felt Colin had been badly treated. Colin would have convinced him of that, and the elder berated John Hansford and accused him of not being fair. Anyway, Colin came back to John Hansford and apologised. I was there that night and Colin was unemotional, cold and detached. He never showed a sign of remorse. He wasn't a broken man. His father Sam was there. He understood Lesley had been having an affair with Trevor, which was nonsense, and he said the church had been a tower of strength to Colin . . . The tensions and ill-feelings were all suppressed. Nobody openly talked, or was seen to be judgemental of Colin. But there were a lot of feelings at the time.'

———

A few days after the funeral, two of Hazel's friends stayed with her for a night. As they sat up into the early hours, the telephone rang. The two women went out of the room to give Hazel some privacy. Afterwards she told them that it had been Howell, but did not go into any detail about the conversation.

The women of the Bible study group rallied to help both families, inviting them for lunch, and in Howell's case, arranging to look after his children. But, as one of Hazel's friends at the time recalls, Trevor's widow was finding it very difficult to cope, and felt isolated and shunned in the streets by people she knew. Parents whose children attended the same school as Lisa and Andrew were aware that the young mother found it embarrassing and awkward when any of them tried to engage her in conversation outside the school gates. One of these parents recalls: 'She would have little eye contact with me. It was as if she didn't want to speak to you.' Another mother, one of whose children was in the same class as Lisa at the Irish Society Primary School, remembers getting little response when she tried to commiserate: 'I remember the first time I tried to talk to her. I went up to say how sorry I was. She just hung her head. I could never get over that. She just snubbed me and everyone else. She didn't have any social graces . . . I was friendly with a completely different crowd. I might meet her from time to time down town, but she would never have acknowledged you . . . She was the talk of the town. People felt sorry for her, but as they say: "The bigger the Bible, the bigger the rogue." She was walking about as if she was innocence personified, but yet she had been having an affair . . . Here she was professing to be a great Baptist, walking up and down the Mountsandel Road, hardly able to look you in the face. We all knew she had something about her looks. She was a very vain girl and she knew she had this power over men . . . Everybody thought she was good-looking.'

Meanwhile, there was a crisis brewing within Coleraine Baptist Church. Although the fallout from the deaths was certainly not the only factor, the first signs of a rift within the congregation started to emerge around about this time, as John Hansford came under increasing pressure from the elders who were not happy with the way he had handled the situation, according to some members.

Howell and Hazel were shamed into leaving the church. She started to attend Limavady Baptist Church, which was 16 miles away and where Jim Smyth, who had previously been based in Omagh, was pastor. Howell found a place in The Barn Fellowship, a small independent church near Ballymoney.

But even though the controversial couple had gone, repercussions continued to be felt by the congregation they left behind. One member recalls: 'Relations between Hansford and the elders broke down. Everybody knew there were all sorts of ill-feeling which divided the church . . . The elders were not helpful, because they had either lost faith in Hansford, or were trying to oust him. They had another agenda going on in the background. Perhaps it was convenient. It was a bit of a mess, because it gave them more leverage and an opportunity to beat him over the head . . . Hansford went off with stress. There was a meeting of members which was conducted by one of the elders. All sorts of bland terms were being used, like everybody was working hard to resolve issues. They had meeting after meeting in the church. The elders were not happy . . . with the direction the church was going in. The divisions which happened in the church didn't begin until the following year, or 1993, although the suicides may have been a contributory factor. Hansford resigned and went to Belfast. No one really knew why.'

But this version of events is challenged by Willis McCloskey, a businessman and also an elder at the time, who had been easing himself out of church affairs because his wife Daphne was terminally ill. McCloskey explains how he saw things: 'It was a new situation for the church. We were knocked back, stunned. There wasn't a question of hiding anything or keeping anything under wraps. People did think there had been a pact between Lesley and Trevor. This situation was new to everyone and it was difficult to handle. At the time, everyone was so sad and grieving. I wouldn't say the church would, or should, have handled it any differently. There was positive intervention by Pastor Hansford. The church took action when the whole thing surfaced, but the matter wasn't swept under the carpet. There was a lot of sympathy towards the families. A lot of people were hurting. There was concern for the children, but the church responded sympathetically and responsibly.'

Incredibly, even in the days and weeks which followed the deaths, and throughout everything else which was happening, Howell and Hazel were still maintaining contact. It seemed that the fervent appeal Howell had penned in his letter so soon after his wife's death had not missed its mark. They had sex within six weeks of the murders, when Howell cycled across the town to the Buchanans' house and climbed in through a bedroom window to join his lover under the duvet. Despite their attempts to keep the continuing liaison secret, to those who lived nearby, the tell-tale signs were there. Howell could be seen parking his car off the Mountsandel Road and then walking the short distance to the Buchanan house, hoping none of the neighbours would notice. But they did. Howell was strongly challenged once by Alan Topping, but he emphatically rejected claims that he was still seeing Hazel. Topping was so angry, however, he told the dentist that he hoped he would at least see fit to move away from Coleraine. Some years later, Howell wrote to him, telling him that God had forgiven him, and that he too had forgiven Topping and his wife.

Towards the end of 1991—not much more than six months after the tragedy—the undoubted friendship was there in full view, for all to see. The American singer-songwriter Don Francisco, who specialises in contemporary Christian music, was giving a concert at Belfast's Maysfield Leisure Centre, and sitting in the audience, four or five seats apart, on the ground floor, were Howell and Hazel. They shared an interest in guitar music, but on this particular night they were only interested in each other. Observers sitting in the balcony spotted the lovers exchanging notes on pieces of paper. Again, Howell denied there had been any contact, and later, when she was questioned back in Coleraine, an angry Hazel had insisted: 'It wasn't paper. It was sweets.'

Yet, in the months after the deaths, the couple continued to put on a good show of grief and general devastation for their families and social circle. Friends who called at Howell's house for Sunday lunch a few months after the deaths found him in a distraught state. He detailed how Lesley had killed herself, relating how he had been in bed, but hadn't heard her getting up. How he had assumed she didn't want to waken him and, rather than cause any noise by starting the engine of the Renault Savanna, she had pushed the car out of the garage and onto the road. One of the women who was there that day remembers: 'His eyes were watery and we felt really sorry for him. He hugged me and said: "What am I going to do?"'

Perhaps not all of it was play-acting. Two months after Lesley's death, Howell found two-year-old Daniel crying out for his mother and pointing to her photograph on the wall. As he recounted in later years, he took his young son in his arms and thought to himself: 'What have I done? What have I done?' And Hazel told friends more than once that she used to have a certain dream about Trevor. There was one scene in particular in the dream which troubled her greatly: the one where she found herself walking along a corridor and holding out her arms to her late husband. But Trevor just turned and walked away.

Chapter 12

Deviance and Denial: Colin Howell and Sex

Whatever hopes Colin Howell might have harboured, the murders didn't quite pave the way to blissful happiness with the woman with whom he had become increasingly obsessed. In spite of his declared willingness—in his letter to his lover immediately after the deaths—to play the long game when it came to their relationship, and wait until an acceptable length of time had passed before going public again, there was one thing over which he had no control, and that was the impact of the murders on his and Hazel's sex life. He couldn't have predicted how things would become increasingly dysfunctional between them after May 1991. Even though sexual dysfunction was something with which Colin Howell had been well-acquainted for most of his adult life.

Despite their best endeavours, the toxic couple would find that penetrative sex was never quite the same after the murders. Hazel had a deeply troubled conscience, and her guilt over the deaths of her husband and Lesley meant that she found it increasingly difficult to relax when they were having sex. She soon became filled with the conviction that if they did not have intercourse, then they were not sinning. And that if they were not sinning, then God would protect them from discovery. Howell later described this strangely distorted thinking as a 'twisted Christian, spiritual logic', whereby God would not only protect them if they desisted from sex, but actually forgive them too: 'There was this twisted logic . . . that if we don't have full sex, then maybe God will forgive us and we won't get caught . . .'

A strong element of denial had always been part of Hazel's modus operandi, it seemed, when it came to sex with Howell. It was evident from their very first sexual encounter, when she expressed surprise after the event that it had happened at all. And after the deaths, this lack of honesty continued, with the couple refusing to acknowledge even to themselves that they were having sex, particularly in the run-up to the 1992 inquest, as Howell would later confirm in police interviews: 'So this myth began to develop and that became a pattern from then on . . .' Even when they did not have full intercourse but reached orgasm they were still in denial: 'But both of us denied to ourselves and each other that we were having sex, and the climax was always followed up by extreme guilt . . .'

Eventually, full sex stopped altogether, although the relationship continued for another four years after the murders. One can only imagine the level of frustration which must have been experienced by Howell, a man with, by his own admission, a particularly voracious sexual appetite. It is not surprising then, that he did not give up their sex life without a fight. He had a solution, just like he had a solution for everything.

Hazel liked being under the influence of gas and air. She had had it when she called as a patient before the affair started: it made her feel relaxed and quietly euphoric. But it was only after the murders that she discovered that the laughing gas combination could raise her libido and make her feel pleasantly detached, thereby lowering her sexual inhibitions. The discovery was made by the couple one night on the way home from a meal at a Chinese restaurant, when they had called into Howell's surgery so that Hazel could have her teeth scaled and polished.

Obsessive about her appearance, Hazel was very particular about her teeth and had had some cosmetic work done for her by Howell, which she was keen to show off. She didn't like to go to Howell during daytime hours, however, for fear of being seen—thus the afterhours visit to the surgery after the restaurant on this occasion. Before starting the cleaning process, Howell had given her the nitrous oxide combination he would usually administer to patients who suffered from some anxiety during treatment, as Hazel did. Although by mutual agreement, they had effectively stopped having intercourse by this stage, that night, they ended up having sex on his dentist's chair. Howell was able to act out his fantasy, for a short time anyway, and

Hazel felt no sense of shame. Under the influence of the laughing gas, she had no trouble in climaxing. It would be the first of many out-of-hours encounters when the couple would have the clinic all to themselves.

Their use of drugs to heighten—or, in Hazel's case, to simply enable—sexual enjoyment was cranked up a notch, however, on the occasion when, at the Buchanan home, Howell produced a needle and sedated her intravenously, injecting her in the right arm with Hypnovel (a trade name for midazolam), a powerful valium derivative often used as a precursor to general anaesthetic before surgery. The couple proceeded to have sex, although Hazel was barely conscious throughout, and for a while afterwards. It seems hard to reconcile the dentist's actions with the man who many years previously had sacked a member of his staff caught inhaling laughing gas during lunch hour. But then again, double standards and hypocrisy were behaviours which Howell had been comfortable with for much of his life.

A friend from that time remembers an exchange with Howell shortly after his 34th birthday in 1993—some two years or so after the deaths. He had been given a card by an acquaintance, in which was written a verse, from James 1:15: 'Then, after desire has conceived, it gives birth to sin; and sin, when it is full-grown, gives birth to death.' Colin asked his friend what she believed the verse meant, and why it might have been chosen by the person who gave him the card. Talking to police in later years, she remembered that the conversation with Howell as a calm and civilised one, but also that she felt distinctly uncomfortable when he moved to hug her afterwards: 'There was always something hidden in Colin's eyes. There was a stillness about him. I talked to [him] about the verse and its true meaning. I then clearly remember him saying: "It's not like I'm into pornography."'

Yet again, Howell was deep in denial. The truth is that he was very much into pornography—so much so that, at more than one point in his life, he had despaired of ever being able to free himself of what had become an all-consuming obsession. He began reading top-shelf magazines when he was a student in Belfast. Over the years, Howell developed a formidable sex drive, and there were days when he thought about nothing else. Naked women looking out from the pages of porn magazines did wonders for his sexual vanity, and he once told someone that he felt as if he was some sort of Adonis.

Pornography—particularly the online variety—later became a

very real and serious problem for him, taking up much of his spare time and threatening to overshadow his real relationships. And the fact that this type of sexual gratification was considered wicked and immoral within the very strict Christian code of ethics he prided himself on living by, made Howell's torment at being unable to stop all the more agonising. He would liken his addiction to that of an alcoholic always thirsting for the next drink. Describing on one occasion his often futile efforts to walk past sex shops without going in, he told police: 'It is as if you are in the AA, walking past a pub and gasping for a drink. You can smell the Guinness and just want to go in.'

It had all started with the magazines. He read them voraciously. Just months after he married Lesley and while they were holidaying in Fuengirola, Spain, he produced one at their hotel room, telling her he had found it in the wardrobe, and insisting his wife act out a sexual fantasy with him. Other times, he would try to spice up their sex life by hiring pornographic movies. Lesley was never comfortable with it, however. Years later, there would be a weekend in the Lake District with Hazel. They booked separate rooms for the trip: at that stage, due to Hazel's guilt about the murders, they had agreed a non-penetrative sex pact. But Howell managed to charm his way into her bed anyway, opening a porn magazine and proceeding to pleasure them both. Hazel was filled with self-loathing afterwards, for breaking her self-imposed vow of celibacy, and that brief act would overshadow the rest of their time away from Coleraine.

Howell never used prostitutes, although he was obviously tempted, especially when he was in London on business. When he was there, he would look at massage parlours, but he refused to enter, for fear of catching an infection. He would often find himself standing outside sex shops, fighting an overwhelming desire to go inside and see what was available. Sometimes he would call a friend in a panic, try to calm himself and then walk on. Other times he didn't bother struggling with his conscience, and just slipped in anyway to have a look and make a purchase. But it was when the internet became an essential part of his working life that his addiction really took hold. Soon he found himself availing of any opportunity he could to sit at his computer screen, log on to X-rated websites and masturbate: in the surgery office after hours, and at home when everyone else in the house was asleep.

Before he confided in anyone about his growing problem, Howell found himself, along with some of the church elders, offering to lend his help to another member of The Barn Fellowship who was struggling with sexual difficulties. Harry Burke's particular weakness was downloading pornographic images of young children. By some strange quirk of fate, many years later, after his confession to the murders and his subsequent incarceration in Maghaberry prison, Howell would find himself sharing a cell with Burke, by then a convicted paedophile.

Howell had known Burke since 1992, during the time his relationship with Hazel was still ongoing. He was one of the dentist's patients at the surgery and they shared the same religious beliefs. They played football, went clay pigeon shooting at a club near Castlerock owned by Burke's father, and once went on a fishing trip together. Burke was single at the time and had few friends. Some years later, he went to South America to help with an organisation called Youth with a Mission, working with street children in Bolivia. He was hardly the type of individual who could be trusted in the company of those who were so young and vulnerable. But nobody knew of his secret proclivities then, not even the local woman he met and went on to marry, before bringing her back to Northern Ireland, where they would have four children of their own. His sordid compulsion to download as well as make indecent child images never left him, however. Eventually his Spanish-speaking wife discovered the dark side of her husband. Her suspicions were aroused when she realised that any time she went unannounced into his room while he was working on his laptop, he would slam down the lid before she could see what he was up to. Finally she challenged him and learned the unsavoury truth.

Howell and Burke were both members of the small independent local church known as The Barn Fellowship. With Burke's marriage now in crisis, the elders of the Fellowship became privy to the fact that one of their members had a serious problem. Howell and a few others in the close circle of the church started to counsel him, even taking him to a one-day conference on addiction in Belfast. Howell, of course, found the day particularly enlightening, given his own compulsions. But he had yet to share his problem with his friends from the Fellowship and, to them, he was just a fellow believer keen to help out a troubled member of the flock.

Burke's difficulties were intractable, however, and the best efforts of his friends were to no avail. Howell visited him at his home on one further occasion, before deciding it was time for him to step back and let others try to help. Later, the elders found they had no choice but to bar Burke from the Fellowship altogether.

Burke was subsequently charged with downloading illegal images of children, and he has been in and out of prison several times since. He was angry with the men who threw him out of the Church and felt he had been unfairly treated by one of the elders in particular. Some years later, he turned up on Howell's doorstep, as the family were about to sit down for dinner. A difficult few moments ensued. With children of his own in the house, the dentist had no intention of allowing a convicted paedophile access to the family home, and quickly turned Burke away with a fairly direct refusal: 'Harry, I can't invite you in. I have young children here and we know your background. You really have to sort things out before I can re-establish our friendship.'

Imagine the look of disbelief on Howell's face then, in early 2009, when Burke put his head around the door of his cell in Maghaberry Prison, where the dentist was being held after his arrest. They even found themselves having to share a cell for few days. Burke was back in custody, facing new charges of breaching a sexual offences order, having allegedly sent an indecent message from his mobile phone. Howell was suffering extreme paranoia at the time and believed that Burke had been sent to spy on him.

Although he had maintained his silence regarding his own problems when they had first tried to help Burke, Howell was soon compelled to confide in trusted members of The Barn Fellowship, as his obsession with porn became ever more powerful. By the time he was married to Kyle, his second wife—whom he met not long after his relationship with Hazel had finally ended—his online compulsion was causing serious problems in his life.

Unlike Burke of course, Howell restricted himself to 'soft' adult pornography—information he would later volunteer during police interviews: 'Anything I looked at was no worse than me buying a top-shelf magazine in any garage or petrol station. The worst you could see [there] was the worst that I was looking at on the internet. I never got into fetishes like rubber or sadomasochism, or anything I would call a deeper level and the need for something more satisfying . . . If I actually came across "fetish" things, then I would just leave it. Two men or two women with sex toys—that would have been the worst I would have looked at. I would have used a keyword like "secretary" ... That would have been an area I would have targeted.'

Howell's second wife Kyle soon knew about her husband's questionable use of the internet, and she wanted him to do something to sort the issue out once and for all. How could she feel special and the only woman in his life if he was browsing porn sites online all the time? But the screen at night was an irresistible lure. Every now and again, he promised to stop, but couldn't help himself. The more he tried, the worse it got, and so he decided to confide in some of the elders at his church.

Two good friends, who breakfasted and prayed with him every Thursday morning at one of their homes, tried to help. They suggested a method which had the approval of many Christian-based organisations in the United States, and which they felt Howell would be comfortable with. And so he signed up to a software company specialising in 'accountability' and filtering programmes which monitor the sexual content of web pages. Covenant Eyes, the firm in question, was founded in 2000 by Ronald DeHaas, and took inspiration for its name from a passage the Bible—Job 31:1: 'I made a covenant with my eyes not to look lustfully at a young woman.' At $60 for a year's subscription, it seemed a relatively inexpensive way for Howell to try to break his destructive habit.

As recommended by the manufacturers, the dentist's next step, after purchasing and installing the software, was to elect an 'accountability partner'—in his case, a church friend—who could monitor the web pages Howell looked at on his own computer. The partner would be alerted on a weekly basis by e-mail and provided with a detailed report of the sites the dentist visited when he powered up his Apple laptop, which he also used for business and for PowerPoint presentations for patients. Each website address would appear on the report, along with a rating, which could vary from 'E' (Everyone) to 'HM' (Highly Mature), the HM classification denoting anything containing nudity, erotica or pornography. For example, the sites accessed to consult the couple's online bank account, or by Kyle when ordering food for delivery from the local supermarket, would be classified as 'E', and scored at the lowest level, around 20 points or so. But if Howell accessed a site of an explicit sexual nature after he keyed words like 'Babe' or 'Hot Secretary' into Google, then the score would soar to somewhere between 200 and 300 points, and the 'HM' rating would appear. If anything unsuitable appeared on the reports, it was the partner's task to phone Howell to discuss the lapses with him.

Howell had the programme on his laptop for four years, and during that time, his friend, whom he referred to as his 'watchdog', would be called upon more than once. Sometimes he could go for up to three months, maybe six, without looking at anything out of bounds, but the self-imposed ban was never indefinite. When he wanted to, he simply used his office computer which didn't have the software installed on it. Once the surgery emptied and his staff left for home, Howell would close the door to watch porn and pleasure himself. As he would later tell police, he was cheating on his 'watchdog' too: 'I bypassed my own guards.' Finally, in mid-2008, he had the Covenant Eyes software removed from his laptop, claiming it was playing havoc with the other content on his hard drive which he needed for his work.

———

And Howell's sexual compulsions extended to his chair in the surgery also. While the devout dentist would, according to former staff, sometimes read his Bible and pray with like-minded patients who called for treatment, every now and again he also took advantage of heavily sedated and vulnerable women to satisfy his predatory instincts.

At the height of his career, Colin Howell was notching up between 2,500 and 3,000 appointments each year, the majority of these for women who, he claimed, tended to look after their teeth better than men. When he first began to specialise in implantology in 1999, most of his patients were in their 50s, but as the years passed, he began to notice more and more younger people coming to him for cosmetic work. Most were women who wanted sparkling white teeth and a brilliant smile to brighten their appearance and boost their self-confidence.

Howell's approach in the surgery was generally business-like and professional, and most of the women who came to see him were impressed by his quiet manner. He dressed casually in chinos and open-necked shirt and he often arrived at the clinic carrying a small shoulder bag. Howell was always in a hurry. He might say a quick hello to the girls at the reception desk, gather up his mail and sprint upstairs for the first appointment. He was efficient with his paperwork and his appointments book was nearly always full. The initial consultations and assessments were normally carried out on Thursdays, and once he decided what treatment a particular patient needed, they were sent well-tabulated letters outlining various options and the costs involved. Patients came from all over and for different reasons. He was prepared to accommodate them, no matter the hour and sometimes was called upon to work at weekends to facilitate patients with Monday to Friday jobs.

Howell was clearly the boss in the surgery, as one former patient recalls: 'He came across as a really powerful and influential man. If he said to jump, the staff would have asked: "How high?" All the staff ran around him. It was as if he was this God-like figure, this God-like man. Everybody bowed to him and did whatever he wanted them to do . . . The nurses were lovely and made you feel at ease. They would not have said very much. They would have been very quiet . . . He would have dominated the whole conversation.' Regular patients noticed that there were few glossy-style magazines of the type which are generally to be found, well-fingered and out-of-date, in dentists' waiting rooms. Howell did not approve of such reading material, it seems—he much preferred travel brochures, or books with a strong Christian message.

But the dentist did not treat all his patients the same. With some, particularly women, he could be charming and reassuring and, if they worked in a profession which excited his interest, then he was keen to know how they were getting on and where their job took them. Others found him less engaging, uncommunicative at times, and occasionally downright rude. He would stand with his back to them as they entered his surgery and, without turning his head simply say: 'Why don't you just pop yourself into the chair?' He might not speak again throughout the treatment, not even to explain what he was doing.

And maybe the signs were there that Colin Howell was not entirely what he first appeared to be. One female patient recalls: 'The one thing I remember about him is his smile. Obviously being a dentist, he had teeth that were perfect, but he had this huge smile. He was always smiling, this big, white, grinning smile.' He might compliment young women patients on their hairstyles, their clothes or ask what part of the world they had been to, to get such a fantastic tan. On one occasion, he questioned one particularly well-endowed young lady as to whether she had her belly button pierced. Body piercing, he told her, made him feel a bit squeamish, but when she raised her tee-shirt ever so slightly, to reveal her midriff and the piercing, he said admiringly: 'That's lovely.' Another female former patient remembers: 'He would've been very charming sometimes, a bit over-the-top. Sometimes he was sleazy, not . . . like you'd expect from a dentist or a doctor. He would have been over-friendly, a bit smarmy.'

One patient who was treated by Howell around the same time as her closest girlfriend claimed that, while he was escorting her out of the surgery, he made what she believed to be a risqué remark: 'It was lovely, doing two friends together.' If it was not intended as a double entendre, then she felt the observation was, at the very least, highly suggestive. Of course, she was not to know that Howell spent so much of his idle time leering at late night internet pornography, especially at women acting out lesbian scenes. This patient refused to respond and thought to herself: 'You are a stupid man and I am not going to let on that I caught what you are getting at.' Howell later claimed that he had been completely misunderstood, telling police: 'I thought it was very nice that two friends had been buddies enough to go to a dentist [together]. It was a really buddy thing to do.'

Howell's inappropriate behaviour in the surgery, however, went far beyond the occasional sexual innuendo. Before being sedated for any procedure, his patients had to complete a consent form and give a telephone number in case of an emergency. They were advised not to drive for 12 to 24 hours after treatment and not to fill in any legal documents. An escort also had to be available to collect them once their treatment had finished. A nurse had to be with him at all times when a patient was in the chair. But his staff were totally unaware of what he got up to when he was left on his own with patients.

Like all dentists, Howell used a range of sedative drugs of varying strengths, the doses depending on the nature of the procedure. Gas and air—nitrous oxide and oxygen—was used to calm particularly nervous patients. For more complex and potentially painful procedures, Howell's drug of choice, and that of many dentists, was Hypnovel, or midazolam, which is usually administered with a needle in the arm or back of the hand. This drug can produce varying degrees of short-term amnesia very quickly after it is given, for up to 24 hours. Many patients will feel quite tired for the rest of the day. The recommended dose of Hypnovel for routine treatment is 5 to 10 mg. Some of the procedures carried out by Howell on a number of his patients, however, were complex and lengthy—they might last the best part of an afternoon—and therefore doses of between 10 and 20 mg could be justified. In some cases, he would administer as much as 25 mg, which would still have been within the therapeutic range.

The immediate effects of midazolam usually begin to wear off after about 45 minutes, and like all dentists, Howell had to keep a detailed record of all dosages. Some of his patients had a clear recollection of the time they were being treated, some only partial memories, and some none at all for several hours afterwards. They could only be discharged when they were able to stand and walk safely and none was allowed to leave for at least an hour after the last dose. The hygienists' room next to Howell's surgery was often used as the 'recovery room' for his patients, but some of the women who left Howell's clinic hardly knew where they were. He would help them walk across the room and physically support them as they descended the stairs where their relatives or partners would be waiting. Howell tended to escort most of the women from the surgery, claiming that if they fell, the nurses were not strong enough to catch them and he wasn't prepared to trust anybody—including their relatives—to help them outside. Between the periods of time when he was left alone with a patient in the chair of his surgery, post treatment, and the occasions on which he would insist on escorting them outside, Howell found he had ample opportunity to force himself on some of his defenceless patients. And, like the predator that he was, he took his chances whenever he could get them.

It was only in 2009, after Howell had made his extraordinary confession to the elders and subsequently surrendered himself to the police, that his abuse of patients was exposed. After his arrest, police asked all his female patients to get in contact, as part of their investigation. They feared abuse on a wide scale, possibly going back decades.

Twenty-eight women came forward to be interviewed. Most said they had no complaints about Howell's treatment of them. Others, who had been given sedation during their treatment, said they had no recollection of any abuse. Some of the women who came forward said they had no memory at all, primarily because of the length of time which had elapsed since they had had the treatment. It is believed, however, that there may well have been some patients who had refused to confirm that they had been in Howell's chair, largely because they dreaded the prospect of being traumatised by police questioning, or of having to relive the experience of being indecently assaulted. Eventually, officers narrowed their investigation down to five women, whose abuse by Howell would become the subject of court proceedings. None of these women can be identified for legal reasons. Allegations by a sixth woman remain on police files.

___

18 MAY 2011

Howell did not look, but he was close enough to hear her distress. At first she tried to wipe away the tears with her right forefinger, and then she reached into the brown leather handbag at her feet for a white handkerchief. Wearing a slim beige dress and with jewellery on her wrist, she was an attractive woman with blonde hair and a slight tan—just the sort of patient the dentist liked to take on when they presented themselves at the surgery for cosmetic treatment. Women who feared the needle and the invasive drill cried all the time, and he was used to it. He would calm them down, offer words of reassurance and tell them not to worry, that everything would be just fine.

Only this time, he and the lady weeping quietly over to his left were not inside his surgery in Ballymoney where she had been heavily sedated before her treatment started in studio one. Now she was free to maintain a respectable distance—well away from him and his gloved and groping hands . . .

Colin Howell cut a sad and sorry sight at Antrim Crown Court as a small group of his former patients sat in the public gallery and listened to the explicit details of how they had been shamelessly violated by the man in the dock.

The anaesthetic had left them groggy and unsteady. He helped them to their feet—and then acted in a salacious manner as he walked them to the door and then one step at a time, slowly down the back stairs to the street outside. He got two of the semi-conscious women to rub his groin as he held their outstretched arms. He stroked the skin of two more and cupped the breasts of others. One woman who challenged him afterwards was told that she had just imagined it. It was because of the sedation—sexual fantasy is recognised as a potential side effect of midazolam, although not a common one.

On a scale of one to ten, the indecent assaults apparently fell into the low-end category. But that was probably little consolation to the women who felt that they had been violated and their trust abused. One said the memories had flooded back after Howell's arrest: 'I felt ill. I felt sick to the pit of my stomach. Because the first thing that came back into my head was: "Did he touch me? Did he do that? Maybe this is real?" After all these years, I felt really uncomfortable with him and had this underlying feeling something wasn't right. I was battling with myself in the head as to whether this really happened or not, and convinced myself that no, it was the twilight sleep.' Another woman, who was groped under her padded coat by the lecherous Howell, did not want to tell anybody at the time: 'I didn't say anything to him because you're mortified. I was embarrassed. But it was very clear that it happened. I wasn't thinking to myself: "Did I dream it?" I'm not a touchy-feely person and I thought to myself: "Why didn't I just elbow him or say something?"'

Howell eventually admitted abusing five women at different times over a period of four years, between March 2004 and December 2008. All of them had been heavily sedated, although it was concluded that none had been deliberately drugged to facilitate his sexual gratification. The dosages he administered intravenously were all within the therapeutic range, the court was told. Judge Corinne Philpott handed him down a sentence of five-and-a-half years, and also ordered that he be added to the sex offenders' register.

Chapter 13
The Inquest

14 MAY 1992

For months, Hazel Buchanan had been dreading the prospect of her husband's inquest. And now—just a few days before the first anniversary of the deaths—the day she had been so afraid of was upon her. She and Howell had managed to fool the police so far, it seemed, but this public examination of the circumstances surrounding the demise of Trevor and Lesley was another huge hurdle to be overcome.

If Hazel was terrified, Howell was fairly calm. Years later, he told police: 'I wasn't sure how afraid I should be. I felt relatively confident in what had happened, in the way I had done it and the way I covered it up, and that I would never be caught. I also had a fear, but not as much as Hazel. My role was keeping her calmed down . . .'

Now, as she sat in the courtroom at Coleraine Courthouse flanked by her sisters, Winnie and Lorna, Hazel bowed her head and wept. One of her legs began to shake uncontrollably, and the state of unbearable tension she was in, as she waited to take the stand was there for all to see. Winnie gently placed her hand on her sister's knee, to try to stop the shaking. As she glanced around the courtroom, she recognised the face of the man she'd met one day when she had called to see Hazel at Charnwood Park after Trevor's death. It was Colin Howell, the husband of the dead girl, Lesley. Winnie was shocked to see how composed and detached he appeared to be.

Sitting on his own, back straight and with his head held high, Howell's stomach was, however, churning as well. He knew that this was the day that he and his lover would have to tell the hearing their version of events on that night almost a year previously. He and Hazel had given detailed statements to police in the immediate aftermath of the deaths—but the moment had come for them to stand up in a public court and confirm their accuracy. It would have been a nerve-wracking prospect for anyone, but how much more so for two people who had been lying from the outset? And, like Hazel, Howell had been suffering from nightmares, which began to plague him about six months after the deaths. He would often see Lesley's face coming towards him. Each time, she was smiling and saying in that lovely voice of hers: 'Colin, I forgive you.'

The coroner presiding over the hearing was Robin Hastings, one of the first officials to be alerted on the day the bodies had been found. Hastings had been the Coroner for North Antrim for nineteen years. Having qualified as a solicitor in 1949 and worked for a short time in his father's legal practice in Magherafelt, he lived in New Zealand for some years before returning to his native Northern Ireland. Although he once kept a herd of cattle and reared chickens near Moneymore, he had soon returned to a job in the law, working for the Director of Public Prosecutions in Derry before taking up his present position. Hastings was a rather eccentric-looking individual: tall, with a ruddy complexion and a shock of hair, he walked with a slight limp and his appearance was often rather dishevelled and untidy. He was known for his love of golf, but also for his propensity to wear Moses sandals with no socks, even in the snow. Hastings had overseen scores of inquests—but never a double suicide.

The police officer in charge of the investigation was Detective Inspector Jack Hutchinson, who had been appointed to the case by his superior officer, Superintendent Hamilton 'Hammy' Houston. The post-mortem examinations of the bodies of Trevor Andrew Buchanan and Lesley Anne Elizabeth Howell had been carried out on the night of the deaths by Dr John Press, the assistant State Pathologist. He would retire in 1998, having carried out around 13,000 autopsies.

According to Press's report, death in both cases had been as a result of poisoning by carbon monoxide. External and internal examinations on Trevor confirmed that everything was normal and intact, although there was an abrasion, 1 cm in diameter, on the front of his right knee and two abrasions, 2 cm and 0.5 cm in diameter, on the front of his left knee, as well as a cut on his lip. Analysis of a blood sample revealed a relatively low Temazepam concentration of 0.13 micrograms per ml and a carboxyhaemoglobin concentration of 71%. No traces of alcohol were detected. The report confirmed that Trevor had always enjoyed good health.

External and internal body examinations of Lesley Howell confirmed that everything was normal and intact. There were no marks of violence, but blood samples revealed an alcohol concentration of 117 mg per 100 ml and three different types of drugs: Diazepam (0.35 micrograms per ml), Nordiazepam (0.54 micrograms per ml) and Temazepam (0.24 micrograms per ml), as well as a carboxyhaemoglobin concentration of 61%. The pathologist's commentary offered some interpretation of these results: 'Death was from poisoning by carbon monoxide, a poisonous constituent of the fumes emitted by internal combustion engines. The proportion of the haemoglobin of the blood inactivated by this poison, 61%, was high and was within levels previously detected in cases of fatal poisoning. There were no marks of violence . . . An analysis carried out by the forensic science laboratory revealed that at the time of her death . . . the alcohol concentration of 117 mg per 100 ml was not high and the drug levels were within the therapeutic range. In view of this, it is unlikely that the alcohol and drugs accelerated death to any material extent.'

After the reports had been read out to the court, it was the turn of various individuals to give testimonies. Among these were Gillian Hunter, the owner of the Knockintern filling station Lesley had visited on the evening of her death, and Pastor Hansford. But by far the most crucial of these testimonies were of course those of Colin Howell and Hazel Buchanan, the bereft spouses of the deceased.

Howell told the inquest that there had been stress and division in his marriage after the birth of their daughter Lauren. Their first child, Matthew, was born on 21 October 1984. While Lesley was pregnant with her second child, her mother had gone through a succession of serious illnesses. She had died in a nursing home, 10 weeks before Lauren was born, on 14 November 1986. His wife, Howell claimed, had suffered postnatal depression. Their third child, Daniel, was born on 18 May 1989. The following month, Lesley fell pregnant again and he said that initially she found this hard to accept. The situation in their marriage then worsened between April 1989 and January 1990 and things broke down completely after the discovery of his affair with Hazel Buchanan.

Howell then spoke about Lesley's overdose in October 1990 and claimed the marriage was subsequently marred by frequent displays of anger and sometimes physical violence by his wife, who often referred back to the attempted suicide. He confirmed that Lesley and Trevor Buchanan had stayed in touch since the revelation of the affair: 'She seemed to be in regular contact with Trevor and on an occasion I know Trevor rang our home.' It became obvious, Howell continued, that Trevor also shared Lesley's mistrust that the affair would start again. He described his wife's response to her father's death as being of disproportionate magnitude and claimed that her attitude to the stability of the marriage changed for the worse after the bereavement. She suggested separating and on one occasion said that he would only be happy if she and Trevor cleared off to leave him and Hazel with the children.

Next Howell gave his detailed version of the events of the night of the deaths. He claimed that on the Saturday evening, Lesley had returned home at 7.50 p.m. with a three-litre case of red wine and had begun to drink. For the previous two weeks, he said, she had been drinking excessively and taking tablets. He left the house for 10 minutes and when he got back at 10 p.m., he said she was finishing off a telephone conversation. When he asked her, she denied that Trevor had been on the line. She became irritable and made accusations towards him about his affair with Hazel. Now in her pyjamas, she told her husband he couldn't realise the depth of pain he had caused her and Trevor. He also got dressed for bed but stayed up to watch TV. However, the atmosphere in the room, he said, was uncomfortable and Lesley told him to go to bed. Later, he said, he heard Trevor in the house.

Howell's account of Trevor's alleged visit to their home on the night of the murders was nothing if not convincing: 'I assumed he had entered by the rear door, as the front door bell hadn't rung. I went to the family room and saw Trevor and Lesley standing there. When he saw me, he referred directly to my relationship with Hazel in strong language. At the same time, he stepped towards me as if to grab me, but I grabbed hold of him and restrained him. He immediately responded by regretting what he had just said and offered no more resistance . . . Lesley, in equally strong language, rebuked [sic] his apology to me and abruptly made me aware they wanted to talk alone and I left the room. He was gone in less than 10 minutes and when I entered the room afterwards, Lesley was lying on the settee in the same room.'

It was now about 11.40 p.m., according to Howell. He tried to reconcile with Lesley but she wanted to be left alone. She seemed drowsy and calm and he went back to bed at about 10 minutes after midnight. He awoke at 8.20 a.m. and assumed his wife was still asleep on the settee. He saw that the garage door was open and his Renault was gone. He then entered the kitchen and found a few pages of a notepad normally kept beside the telephone, with Lesley's handwriting. It was difficult to read. This was the alleged 'suicide note', Howell explained to the court: 'I read the note several times to understand that there was an implication of suicide stated. My immediate thoughts went to the missing Temazepam tablets and my first action was to contact the police to enquire if she had been in an accident, being aware of the amount of alcohol and tablets taken the previous night.'

Howell then identified for the hearing Lesley's handwriting on a calendar which was kept by the kitchen phone. On it, she had recorded her father's death on Tuesday, 7 May—which was of course the date Harry Clarke had died. But she had noted his death again in an entry for Thursday, 9 May. On Friday, 10 May, she recorded her father's funeral, but had written the wrong time—1 p.m., rather than 11 a.m. Her confusion seemed to suggest that she was a woman in the throes of disintegration, who had lost track of herself.

When her turn came to speak, Hazel was nervous and nowhere near as self-assured and confident as her lover. She managed nonetheless to confirm the main facts of her statement. After giving a short account of how she and Trevor had first met and what their marriage had been like, she went on to describe the impact her affair with Howell had had on her husband: 'Trevor during this time was made aware of the affair, and found it most difficult to reconcile with. He was generally unable to accept what had happened and could not genuinely forgive me or Colin for both of our infidelity.'

Hazel claimed that her husband did not respond favourably to the counselling with Pastor Hansford. Life in the house became very difficult, with many arguments, some of much greater intensity than others: 'Trevor, up until the end, could not come to terms with what had happened in our marriage. Trevor always feared any of his friends at work would get to hear of the affair. He didn't want anyone at the station to know of it, including his supervisors. It was always a big issue with him to keep the affair a secret . . . Some weeks before the end, Trevor was meeting Lesley to discuss the problem. After Lesley's father died, our marriage situation got worse generally.'

Hazel then recounted how she had spent the final day with her husband. They spent a few hours in Lisburn on the afternoon of Saturday, 18 May, but had returned home at around 5 p.m., much earlier than had been planned because of the general unpleasantness. Sometime after 9.15 p.m., she had made supper and watched TV in the same room as Trevor. With the exception of a few sharp outbursts of annoyance with each other, she said they were uncommunicative. She had gone to bed at 10.15 p.m., but Trevor had stayed up, she claimed.

The next part of Hazel's testimony to the court must have been the most difficult to deliver, because she knew that it was a tissue of lies: the story that Howell had concocted to convince everyone that the deaths had been the result of suicide. But she managed to continue: 'I fell asleep and sometime later heard voices in the house. I knew it was Trevor's voice and I recognised the other as being that of Lesley Howell. I don't recall what they were saying, and both were talking at a normal level. I can't be sure of the time, but it was certainly the early hours of the morning, maybe 3 a.m. or 4 a.m. I only heard them briefly. I didn't intervene, as I did not want to confront Lesley, as we just hadn't talked of late.'

Hazel then recounted how she had fallen asleep and woken up some one-and-a-half hours later, at 5 a.m. Trevor was not in bed. She had looked outside and had seen the family car parked at the front of the house. Trevor normally kept it in the garage. She said she couldn't settle. She tidied the house and didn't want to telephone anyone to alarm them, especially the police. Jim Flanagan called after 9 a.m. to enquire if Trevor was at home and she told him he had been away part of the night. At lunchtime, she was then informed that bodies of her husband and Lesley Howell had been found in Castlerock.

The court then heard from Pastor Hansford, David Green (who had been accompanying Jim Flanagan when he had found the bodies), and Una Fitzpatrick, a police scenes-of-crime officer attached to the CID in Coleraine. There were testimonies also from Dr Hazel Siberry, the local GP who had formally pronounced Trevor and Lesley dead, and Inspector Hutchinson, whose report for his sub-divisional commander concluded with the statement: 'It is believed the deaths were brought about as the result of an affair by the spouses of the victims, initially over the period of March–October 1990 and indeed afterwards, even up until the time of the incident. Neither of the suicide victims, despite reconciliation attempts by the church being made principally by Reverend Hansford, could come to terms with their spouse's infidelity. Lesley Howell had made previous suicide attempts. This was most likely the motivating factor in both of them taking their lives.'

The inquest verdict recorded that both Lesley and Trevor died of poisoning by carbon monoxide fumes. In the case of Lesley, the court's findings read: 'The deceased was emotionally upset by difficulties which had arisen in her marriage and by the recent death of her father. She was found dead in the back of her car at 6 Cliff Terrace, Castlerock, which had a hosepipe from the exhaust into the car. Another person was dead in the front seat of the car.' The wording of the verdict for Trevor's case was almost identical: 'The deceased was emotionally upset by difficulties that had arisen in his marriage and he was found dead in the front seat of a car in a garage at 6 Cliff Terrace, Castlerock, which had a hosepipe from the exhaust into the car. There was another person dead in the rear of the car.'

The coroner signed off the verdict with his signature, RR Hastings, dated Thursday, 14 May 1992. This effectively signalled the closure of the investigative process into what appeared to have been a terrible tragedy. For Colin Howell and Hazel Buchanan, however, it signalled that they had successfully negotiated another giant hurdle in their bid to get away with murder. Or so they thought.

———

After the arrests of Howell and Hazel in relation to the murders in 2009, Mr Hastings, who retired as a coroner in 1997, spoke about the inquest tribunal and the police investigation at the time. He remembered querying the pathologist's report, in relation to the traces of drugs which had been identified. But he insisted all the procedures had been correctly followed and that he did not believe that the integrity of the police investigation or of his judgement at the time could have been called into question. He was adamant that all possible avenues had been explored, and that the police could not have done any more.

At his home in Portrush, Mr Hastings said that he had clearly believed the evidence of Hazel and Howell at the time, but now accepted he had been duped. He recalled of Hazel: 'She was a pleasant sort of woman, but obviously she had to be devious as well, because she certainly knew what had happened, and went with the cover-up.' Of Colin Howell, he said: 'He wasn't a nice man. He was just a chancy fellow, a smart arse. That is the impression I got of him.' The couple's evidence at the inquest had been convincing, he admitted: 'I had no hesitation in believing them, but we didn't get the full story then. I suppose if you want to kill someone and you don't want to be caught, then, as murderers go, they had to be smart murderers. When they were charged, I was shocked. I've known quite a few murderers in my day . . . but this was just cold-blooded. It was nasty. It was shocking.'

The former coroner was very clear about one more thing: that the Baptist Church did not welcome the publicity that the affair attracted: 'I have a strong memory of the time, and I'm quite confident about this. The Baptist Church wanted this kept quiet.'

David Green, however, who, along with Jim Flanagan, made the discovery of the bodies in the garage, has admitted that he always had his suspicions about the circumstances of the deaths. A church elder and police detective who was stationed in another locality at the time, Green did not disclose his doubts at the inquest in May 1992. It was not, in fact, until he made a statement to police just before Christmas 2009—almost a year after Howell and Hazel were arrested—that it emerged just how deep his misgivings had been.

Green told the first hearing that he had checked the bodies for signs of life before alerting police. He had the impression Lesley and Trevor, whom he knew, had been dead for some time. Privately, the detective was far from convinced about Howell's version of what actually happened that night, but, as he later insisted, his first statement was factually correct. His second, however, was considerably more detailed, and gave some insight into why he had decided to stand back from the original police investigation.

Green twice refused requests for an interview with the author of this book. But this is what he told police in 2009: 'I have always been suspicious of the circumstances of this case, maybe because of my background as an investigator, but I'm not aware of anybody else having similar suspicions. Obviously I wanted to help the investigation, but because I was stationed in a different police division, I didn't want to stand on anyone's toes or make a nuisance of myself. But I was really very concerned that something bad had happened. In my own mind, I did not accept what happened at face value.'

Ex-colleagues described Green, who opened an art gallery after retiring from the force, as a first-class officer who was thorough in his work. He knew the Howell and Buchanan couples, and had been aware of the marital difficulties. Green recalled that the feeling within the church at the time was one of sadness—sadness for the families and the children left behind. He said he spoke with the pastor in the aftermath: 'After the deaths I had discussions with Pastor Hansford about the whole scenario and that I was concerned that something bad had happened.'

Eight days after the bodies were discovered, the church elders held a meeting. It appears that the letter which Howell had written to Hazel and handed over for delivery to Derek McAuley was discussed, and it is clear that Hansford and Green were not the only members who had their suspicions that all was not as it had appeared. Alan Topping had doubts as well.

In his 2009 statement, Green said that he had expressed his concerns to the 1991 investigators on a number of occasions, hoping and assuming their inquiry would be robust and thorough. He kept rough personal jottings on his theories and thoughts, as well as notes about possible inconsistencies, but he realised that he had to step back: 'After a period I tried to sort of keep a loose hold of the whole thing, but because I wasn't the investigator or part of the investigation team, it was all I could do.' But his doubts lingered and kept niggling at him. He held on to a copy of an article which appeared in the *Police Review* magazine of August 1993, entitled 'Making Murder Look Like Suicide'.

The article focused on the case of a heavily pregnant woman, Mrs Paula Gilfoyle, who was found dead in Merseyside in June 1992, hanging from a roof beam in the garage of her home in the Wirral. The deceased had left a lengthy note telling her husband Eddie that he was not the father of the child she was carrying, and that she could no longer live with the lie. Even though her neighbours and friends said they could not believe that such a lively, happy and popular woman, who was looking forward to having her first child, could have taken such drastic action, Birkenhead detectives had considered it an open-

and-shut case of suicide. That was until they discovered that Mr Gilfoyle, a theatre technician at a private hospital, had told his wife he was attending a course on the causes and effects of suicide. To help him with the project, he asked her to write suicide notes. He even took her to the garage to show how a suicidal person would put up a noose. It turned out to be part of a well-rehearsed ploy.

Gilfoyle had been cheating on his wife with a female work colleague who ended the relationship after Mrs Gilfoyle found out and warned her to stay away from her husband. An embittered Gilfoyle had murdered his wife and then made it look like a suicide. He had used one of his wife's handwritten letters which suggested he was not the child's father to try and convince the police the death was as a result of her own actions. The inquiry team consulted a psychologist who specialised in psycholinguistics, which applies psychology to the use of language. He was able to confirm that the note was a fake. Police reconstructions also showed that Mrs Gilfoyle, who was 5 ft 8 in tall and eight months pregnant, could not possibly have reached the 10 ft 2 in beam to secure the rope. In addition to this, the position of her feet on a small set of stepladders was also inconsistent with her having carried out the 'suicide'.

So, Green wondered, was the so-called suicide note which turned up in Howell's house on the day Lesley's body was found authentic? Could it have fitted in with the timing of her overdose, months previously? Had Howell been conditioning his wife with drugs? That might explain her apparently poor memory, which Green said he had once discussed with his wife. He noted how quickly Howell had Lesley's effects cleared from the house. The sudden death of Harry Clarke just days earlier concerned him as well. Was a post-mortem examination carried out, he wondered?

When the bodies had been found, why, Green asked himself, was the rear light of the vehicle on and one of the wing mirrors pushed back? Did the police check Howell's financial affairs? Green said he remembered that Lesley had informed her husband he was not getting any of the money which had been left to her by her father. Was the dentist in debt? Howell had an injury on his forehead—how did he sustain it? Why had the dentist not heard his wife leaving their home and how could she have done so, if she had been drugged up? He noted that Lesley had told Margaret Topping that Howell was in charge of the drugs, and had informed Pastor Hansford that her husband was giving her drugs to help her sleep, so that he could go and see Hazel while Trevor was on night duty.

The questions in Green's mind multiplied. Trevor Buchanan had booked a family holiday. He had invited a police colleague, Leslie Clyde to join him at church on the day he had died. Surely those were not the actions of a man contemplating suicide? And why was Trevor, a man who was always immaculately dressed both on and off duty, dressed in only jeans and a tee-shirt when he had been found?

Green's statement concluded: 'I had very serious doubts about Colin Howell and his possible involvement in something very nasty in relation to Lesley, Trevor and Lesley's father. I passed on these concerns, and even my gut feelings, to Detective Inspector Hutchinson and Detective Superintendent Houston. I passed on everything I knew, even though I realised that my thoughts and concerns about this tragic case could be considered bizarre, and insensitive beyond belief, given the apparent tragic circumstances.'

Hamilton Houston, who appointed Hutchinson to take charge of the 1991 investigation, insists, however, he has no recall of Green raising his concerns. He is adamant that if officers had been aware of the letter which Howell wrote to Hazel, and which contained the comment about 'taking a mother from her children', then they would have launched a murder investigation: 'Had this letter been made available in 1991, the police investigation, on behalf of the Coroner, would have become a murder investigation. I have no doubt the letter contained the key which could have unlocked the truth, and most likely the Buchanan and Howell families would have been spared a cruel ordeal.'

According to Houston, it was not until October 2010 that he became aware of David Green's misgivings. During the initial inquiry, he insists, he maintained an open-minded approach and had no reason to suspect a crime had been committed: 'What I can say is that if David Green had told me anything that would have raised concerns with me, I would not have needed any encouragement to ensure relevant further inquiries would have been carried out.'

Chapter 14
'A Sad Adulteress'

Jonny Howell was just eight months old when his mum died. In later years, whenever he or his siblings asked their father what had happened, Howell would always reply: 'It looks like suicide, but no one was really ever sure.' Some of the Howell children remember seeing their father cry once in the weeks after their mother's death, when Matthew was aged six, Lauren, four and Daniel, two. The only other time they recalled him ever getting emotional about Lesley's death was a few months later, when little Daniel had pointed towards a photograph of his mother and started to weep. Otherwise, Howell seemed to adjust quite quickly to single parenthood, reading the children stories from the Bible at bedtime, or reaching for his guitar to sing them a song. As time went by, Lesley's name was rarely mentioned in the family home, with Howell actively discouraging the children from discussing their mother even amongst themselves. Visits to her grave stopped. Soon it was as if—as far as Howell was concerned anyway—his wife and the mother of his four children had never existed.

But while to friends and even to his own children, it seemed as if Howell was taking Lesley's death remarkably well and coping admirably, every so often he would react to situations in bizarre ways, which suggested that underneath his façade was a deep unease.

In March 1992—almost one year after Lesley's death—some of the widower's friends decided to hold a surprise 33rd birthday party for him at the family home. It had been arranged that a doctor friend and an old pal from his time at university would take him out for a time, while the house was set up. Everybody hid in the kitchen and waited.

When Howell returned to the house and switched on the lights in the kitchen, he gasped in astonishment, as they all broke into song, wishing him a happy birthday. He couldn't believe it. One of the guests there that night remembers: 'The look on his face was sheer fear. He was like a cornered rabbit. His eyes were staring and he didn't look at all comfortable.'

Then there was the time in early 1993 when he had contacted David Hussey—a former acquaintance from his student days—completely out of the blue, to commiserate with him over the death of his brother. David, who had also studied dentistry, went on to become a senior lecturer and consultant in restorative dentistry at the School of Dentistry at Royal Victoria Hospital in Belfast. His brother, Harold, had been a serving officer in the RUC. On Christmas Eve 1992, Harold had attended a family party with David at their mother's house in Omagh. It had been a great family get-together, with a sing-song in one room and karaoke in another. But just days later, on 27 December, Harold Hussey was found dead in his car.

The young policeman had been staying with his in-laws on the outskirts of the town, at Gillygooley, where Hazel was raised. He had spent the day driving around Northern Ireland to look at various police stations where he had served in the past, before he pulled in by the road side, a few miles outside Omagh, attached a hosepipe to the exhaust of his car, and switched on the ignition. He died from carbon monoxide poisoning. The large attendance at his funeral service at Trinity Presbyterian Church in Omagh on New Year's Eve was a very public acknowledgement of the 39-year-old sergeant's popularity. Friends, especially his police colleagues, were stunned.

Howell and David Hussey had not spoken for several years and they were never particularly close friends. Hussey knew Hazel Buchanan's family quite well: her brother, Raymond Elkin, was also a dentist, who had studied at Queen's as well and had been in the year below David. Howell, however, telephoned Hussey, saying he had just wanted to get in touch to pass on his sympathy and telling him: 'I know what you are going through. You know, I have been through something similar myself in the past few years. I'm thinking about you.' But the gesture left Hussey bewildered. He would later tell friends that the call had made him feel uncomfortable. As one friend said: 'It put him in the position of having to discuss a very personal and sensitive family issue with a man he hadn't seen in ages.'

Hazel Buchanan, meanwhile, rarely discussed the death of her husband with anybody outside her immediate family. Even those close to her never heard her utter the word 'suicide'. About a year after the deaths, Hazel had turned to one of her sisters and said: 'Wouldn't it be lovely if Trevor walked through the door now, to see the joy in Lisa and Andrew's faces?'

One former colleague of Hazel's, who knew her when she had worked part-time in the office at a fertiliser and seed merchants, recalls of her: 'I always got the impression that she was holding something back, and that she didn't feel comfortable talking about her husband's death. I felt that I knew her, but on the other hand, I didn't . . . You knew as much as she wanted you to know. Her personal life was a closed book. Hazel had low self-esteem. She didn't like anyone making a fuss of her and couldn't cope with confrontation.'

In the aftermath of Trevor's death, Hazel did her best to help her two children come to terms with what had happened. Photographs of their father remained on display in prominent places in the house, and sometimes they browsed through the family albums together. Every Sunday, the two children helped to tidy and put flowers on Trevor's grave. Even though he died when they were young, the children had fond memories of their father. He had always helped them with their school homework. Andrew was just seven when his dad took him to have a look around Coleraine police station. He got his fingerprints taken, and remembers being fascinated by it all. Lisa recalls how proud she felt the morning Trevor arrived at her primary school in his police uniform, carrying a savings book she'd forgotten to take with her that morning. Their parents might have been on the verge of splitting up at one stage, but there had never been any arguments in front of the children. After his death, Hazel told them: 'Daddy and I had our problems, but I loved him very much.'

Whatever she had done, it seems that Hazel was a very good mother to her children, and they were devoted to her. She made sure they kept their Christian faith. They were not spoiled, but they wanted for nothing. She read them Bible stories at bedtime and prayed with them before they went to sleep. She admitted to Lisa and Andrew that she had been involved in an affair with another man, and related to them the Biblical story of the seduction of Bathsheba by David. She probably, however, left out the part where David arranged to have Uriah—Bathsheba's husband and his love rival—killed on the battlefield. She regularly told them that their father was in Heaven and was watching over them. It gave them a sense of reassurance.

Meanwhile, Trevor's family did their best to keep in touch with Hazel and to help her move on from the tragedy and build a new life for herself and the children. Victor and Lorna Buchanan were the first of the in-laws to make contact once the aftermath of the funeral had subsided. Hazel had apologised for her behaviour, and they were prepared to be magnanimous, especially for the sake of Andrew and Lisa, whom they adored. They also wanted to make sure the children didn't lose touch with their grandparents.

Trevor's sister Valerie became a committed Christian three years after his death, after a lot of agonising about her religious beliefs while trying to come to terms with the loss of her brother: 'I couldn't get my head around this [Trevor's suicide]. I thought God had the power to stop him. Why did He not stop him? At the end, I came to the conclusion God knew Trevor was going to be even more hurt if he lived. So He let him die. I suppose this was my way of making peace with myself. Now I know he is in Heaven.' Valerie went on to become a founding member of the interdenominational Omagh Community Church. She was keen to renew contact with her brother's widow: 'When I became a Christian, something inside me really changed. I was happier. I had a real relationship between me and God. I believe God was telling me I needed to forgive. I told [Hazel] I realised she never set out with the intention that Trevor would die. She was very grateful, appreciative and pleased that I became a Christian. But as a Christian now, I have to question her Christianity. Why did she do such a thing, when she knew what was right and what was wrong?'

Hazel considered moving away to live in another town. She looked at a house in Ballymena, but eventually decided to remain in Coleraine, even though she felt shunned by some people on the streets of the town. She began to attend services at the Baptist Church in nearby Limavady, where she would sometimes weep as she got to her feet to sing hymns with the rest of the congregation. She never sought sympathy, but others were prepared to forgive, as she attempted to rebuild her life. However, Howell was still very much part of it.

They met at her house on Friday nights. While the children played in one room, they would be all over each other in the next. They played a game called 'Wolf', where the lights were switched off and Howell was blindfolded. The children hid. Howell growled and listened for the giggles and then grabbed hold of them in the darkness. But the lovers were never affectionate in front of the children. Howell's and Hazel's children got on well together. At one stage, Lisa believed her mother might marry the dentist. Young Dan Howell was keen for this to happen too, but one member in particular of the extended Howell family was very much opposed to the relationship being formalised, and asked Howell: 'How can you marry an adulteress?'

But Howell was afraid she would end the affair, and so he asked her to marry him, although an engagement ring was never produced. He wanted them to move away to begin a new life—if not somewhere else in Northern Ireland, then maybe to Scotland, where in 1995 he investigated the possibility of buying two separate practices—in Inverness and Lossiemouth. They discussed selling their homes.

Four years after the deaths, however, Hazel had had enough. She didn't want to marry him, saying that she wouldn't be able to cope with his children as well as her own and that she was reluctant to lose her police pension. She wanted out altogether, in fact, although Howell didn't realise it at the time. Many years later, after his arrest, he told police: 'I wanted to believe that we were an item and to keep on going. Maybe the only way that I could keep that dream alive was to control the situation . . . I didn't read the signs. I didn't listen. She was saying: "This is a disaster. This will never work." I was . . . trying to find a solution, to make these arrangements and present her with a package that would make things better for her and that she would accept.' By the time he was in custody facing a life sentence, he admitted: 'I committed adultery with a sad adulteress. She became my way out of a black hole.'

As time went on, the relationship became more and more strained. Hazel knew the writing was on the wall, but it was a long, protracted goodbye. Many years later, in the course of police interviews, she would say that the affair had been 'very serious' when it first started, and that she had initially she thought she was 'in love' with Howell. But that changed: 'As time went on, and things happened, my feeling changed. I could see a different person. Maybe he knew I wasn't as keen. It wasn't a natural or normal relationship. From the church point of view, we were not allowed to be together.' However the toxic couple might have explained it to themselves, the truth was probably that the heinous crime they had committed together, but never discussed, slowly but surely poisoned everything between them until they could ignore it no longer.

———

Hazel claimed in later years that she had tried to break off the relationship a number of times, but that Howell would always manage to win her over again: 'He is someone who is very controlling, very. He gets his own way in one shape or form. Whether he fools you, or cons you, whatever, he will get you. If he wants something, he will get it . . . I was going out with someone that I thought that I loved at a time and had turned out quite obsessive.' Howell's retrospective account, however, suggests that Hazel was not quite as helpless or as sincere in her attempts to end things as she might have wanted others to believe.

Although Howell was desperate to keep the relationship going, in his heart he knew it was only a matter of time before it finished. He gave Hazel money to pay for petrol, telephone bills, and even clothes, but he knew he had to let go. Anyway, she was already two-timing him with a man she had first met 20 years previously: Trevor McAuley, a print worker with the local *Coleraine Chronicle* newspaper. Howell quickly realised that she was seeing someone else: he of all people recognised the signs. Years later, he would say: 'Whenever you're a deceiver, you know when you're being deceived. You know the tricks.'

He used to stand in the forest behind Hazel's house to watch the comings and goings, and he had noticed a strange car—a green Mazda—in the driveway at a time when she was supposed to be entertaining one of her sisters. She had told Howell to stay away because, she claimed, her sister did not like him. And then one night, he walked into a Chinese restaurant in Glengormley on the outskirts of Belfast, to stumble upon Hazel and the new man in her life having a meal. It was a place which Howell and she had frequented of old when they wanted to be on their own. Trevor McAuley recalls that night: 'I never saw shock on anybody's face like the shock on hers. She could hardly speak. They just said hello to each other. He had a couple of his children with him and you can imagine the atmosphere. It was very tense.'

Deeply jealous, Howell kept returning to spy on the Buchanan house. He pulled up in his black BMW to see who was there and would then drive off at speed. One night, as he stood on the other side of the fence at Mountsandel Wood, Hazel saw him from her bathroom window and quickly summoned McAuley to see for himself. He remembers: 'It was pitch black. He must have had a torch and found his way up through the forest. He was just standing as if he was a statue. It was very spooky. It alarmed her. I remember telling her: "He'll not bother me. I'll sort him out if he approaches me." She replied: "You be very careful, because you don't know what he is capable of."'

McAuley's relationship with Hazel Buchanan lasted eight years. It was good in parts, strained at other times and finally ended in acrimony after a weekend in Dublin in the summer of 2004. Trevor McAuley spoke at length with the author about the relationship. As with Howell and her husband Trevor, Hazel would eventually cheat on him too—with an ex-police officer she met at the Fitness First gymnasium in Coleraine, and would go on to marry.

Hazel and Trevor McAuley first set eyes on each other when they were teenagers in Portrush in 1976. She had been working at a guest house in the seaside town where Trevor and his friends used to tour in their car on the look-out for new and friendly faces. Once Hazel finished preparing the rooms and clearing up the dishes at her place of work, they would spend time in Barry's amusements arcade, walk the West Strand, and from time to time buy chips. It did not last long—maybe two to three weeks—before the girl from Omagh returned home. She was a Baptist, but smoked at the time. Trevor recalls: 'She was quite the tomboy. I remember her in a little black jacket with two white stripes. She had dark hair. It was all very innocent. We kissed, but sex was an absolute no-no.'

Twenty years later they were reunited after he spotted her in the car park of the Irish Society Primary School in Coleraine, as he waited with his sister to collect her children. By this time he was divorced with three children of his own. He noticed the woman with a vaguely familiar face in the car park near the school. He remembered all the talk about the two suicides at Castlerock and then realised it might be the girl he had fancied when he was a teenager: 'But this girl hadn't prominent teeth, not the same teeth as I remembered she had. It was only later I realised Howell had done this fancy cosmetic work. I thought: "Hmmm, might be, might not be".'

They were properly introduced a few months later. A friend who attended Coleraine Baptist Church suggested that they should meet: Hazel was on her own, feeling lonely and might be glad of the company. The two agreed to go for a walk on the beach at White Rocks, outside Portrush—along a stretch which passes below the famous golf links of Royal Portrush. Trevor remembers of this first meeting: 'She knew that I knew what had happened. I didn't want to ask questions. I didn't want to know anything about the affair. I didn't want to know anything about the suicide. I told her that and she appreciated that . . . I didn't want to be put off by it. I needed to focus on the future and not look back. I felt the girl deserved a chance. She talked very little about him, her husband. I knew about Howell because he was pestering the life out of her. When I met her at the White Rocks, as far as I was concerned, she was out of that relationship. It was a dirty and sordid thing. As far as I was concerned, Trevor Buchanan committed suicide because he couldn't stand it any longer.'

As well as working as a compositor on the local newspaper, McAuley was also extremely useful with his hands and skilled at DIY, just the sort of man the houseproud Hazel needed to have about the place. He came from a working-class Protestant housing estate called Windy Hall on the outskirts of Coleraine, just off the main road to Ballymoney.

Even though Hazel insisted that the relationship with Howell was well and truly over, and even though she was in a new relationship, the dentist, it seemed, held out lingering hopes of a reconciliation with his old flame. Trevor remembers how Howell did his best to discredit him in Hazel's eyes: 'Howell was bad. He said to her at one time: "What would it take to get rid of that boy from Windy Hall? That boy is only from Windy Hall." It's a wee estate, but I'm proud to be from Windy Hall and proud to be associated with anybody who comes from it . . . I could see what Howell was doing . . . He was trying to manipulate her brain and make her wonder if she would stay with this boy McAuley. To make her feel that, if he wasn't on the scene, she was finished financially. And finance was her big thing.' Howell was applying heavy emotional pressure to Hazel too: 'I remember her telling me how much it was upsetting him—her going out with me. He wasn't able to eat and he was stopping the car and being sick. All he had eaten the whole day was a banana . . . She hadn't the brains to see that he was working her head.'

Perhaps Howell was not the only one not quite ready to let go.

Unknown to Trevor, Hazel twice met the dentist behind his back—once when she invited him to have sex at her house, after jumping up and down on his knee, stripping to her underwear and throwing herself onto a bed. In his account of the incident during Hazel's trial in 2011, Howell claimed he made his excuses and left. He said: 'I stood at the end of the bed and just said: "I don't want any more." She got dressed and I left.' He added: 'I knew Hazel was still very needy of the relationship. She knew it. She wanted it to end, but she couldn't let it end.'

There was also the time Hazel contacted her ex to see if she could borrow some equipment which her son Andrew needed to go on a camping expedition. Trevor McAuley was not best pleased, especially after she also told him she wanted Howell to continue treating her two children at the Ballymoney clinic, even though Howell had told her: 'Well, if we're split up, we're split up. Everything you had from me is now gone.'

The first signs of a rift and uncertainty between the new couple began to emerge. Hazel wasn't quite the woman Trevor McAuley had hoped. Not only was she emotionally demanding, but financially too: 'I couldn't earn enough money to keep her. I said that to her many times: "I nearly feel I can't afford you. I shouldn't have you because I can't afford you." She would have used Howell and his wealth, his money, to make me feel I should be taking over that [side of things]. [As if] she was [saying]: "He's not there anymore, I've got rid of him. You need to take over here now. I can't cope without it."'

Money quickly became a major issue, as Trevor recounts with some anger: 'It was clothes and the house. The house bugged me so much. I put thousands into that house and that doesn't include the time. How do you put a price on the time? I did all the work. Redecorating, putting in a new kitchen, tiling, bathrooms. There isn't a room in the house which I didn't re-do. I put Amtico floors in it. Then those two [Hazel and David Stewart] sold that house when they got married.

'Most times, [I] would have bought her clothes. But . . . sometimes, she would have bought them on her credit card. But whenever the credit card bill came in, half the time she didn't have the money to pay for it. I ended up paying the credit card. She never paid anything towards the holidays. She didn't even take spending money on a holiday. We went with her children. We went to the south of France, Majorca, Benalmadena in Spain. Good hotels were expected . . .

Whenever you were in that coach being transferred—from the airport—I was always worried the hotel would not meet her standards ... It would have been bad if it failed to match her expectations ... The first holiday we had was in Benalmadena and I remember sitting shocked on a little wall, because all she wanted was to buy presents for friends. But she hadn't brought any money. And I had to buy them. That was the first time I looked at Buchanan and began to think to myself: "I'm in a different league here. Financially I'm not sure I'm going to be able to cope with this relationship."'

McAuley, with three children of his own from his first marriage, soon found his own modest financial resources stretched to the limit in his efforts to meet Hazel's demands: 'There were times I had nothing. There were times when I hadn't a penny, when it all had to go to her. The first time I had to give her money, I came round to the house and I just knew there was something not right. I remember her patronising me. I said: "There is definitely something wrong. You're not yourself at all." She replied: "You are a very sensitive man. You can pick up on that ... Financially, I am not making it at the minute." Being the big man, I said: "What do you need?" If anybody had ever needed a few pounds, I thought they'd be talking about £30 or £40. She was talking £300 to £400. I wasn't with her that long and for me to hand that over was a big thing. It left me with nothing. I was looking after three of my own children. I was paying the Child Support Agency as well. I was keeping her, and her children. I pretended I didn't ever need anything. I never got very much, but she would have pressurised me into buying myself a shirt. I couldn't afford it. It sounds pathetic, but that's the way it was.'

Hazel expected the best of everything, no matter the cost. Trevor recalls: 'If we went to look at a new kitchen and it cost £10,000 in one place, but £20,000 for the exact same somewhere else, she would have bought the one at £20,000. I couldn't pay for it, but I know her mother gave her money towards it ... There was nothing which needed to be done that could lie undone. It had to be done. She had very expensive tastes in life. She could have gone to a clothes rail and picked out the most expensive item straight away. It seemed to be something she could do. She was like a professional shopper. She used to get really, really cross and frustrated when she couldn't find things ... She'd be running here and there, and I was a bundle of nerves.'

He found Hazel's style of communicating her feelings and needs very difficult to handle too: 'She wouldn't be angry, but you'd know, even though she might not say anything . . . There used to be serious mood swings. It got so bad at the end, I would pretend I was playing football matches, so I didn't have to go to her house. She was a very depressive person. When I left at night, until I came back the next day, I never knew what . . . to expect. If the mouth dropped, the reason was always money. It was lack of money . . . The only way I could lift her out of depression was by spending money . . . Trevor's death played on her mind. She used to talk about how she felt. She used to say: "I'm useless. I'm for nothing. I am no better than a worm, crawling below the ground." Because of what had happened and because of the abortion, she likened herself to a worm many times. It wasn't just once, when she was down. I would have tried to lift her up out of it.'

There were some lighter moments in the relationship, according to Trevor. Hazel did display a sense of humour from time to time: 'She could be funny in her own way, though it wasn't very often. She could be witty and she enjoyed a joke. But . . . you always had to gauge her mood.' The only way to cheer Hazel up, it seemed, was to go shopping: 'I knew that if the mood was really bad, the only therapy [for her] . . . was to spend money. To shop and buy things. That was the only thing that pulled her out of bad form.'

Fingering the clothes rails in search of a new outfit worked wonders to lift Hazel's spirits, apparently. She was a regular in the more upmarket fashion stores in and around the North Coast, although some staff, especially in Coleraine, found her aloof, even snobbish at times. Trevor concedes: 'She was so good at finding what she wanted. She could find a needle in a haystack. She would have made a good fashion buyer, rather than doing something involving figures. It was another case of going in the wrong direction.'

At the time, Trevor attended the Church of Christ in Coleraine. Hazel was going regularly to Limavady Baptist Church, sometimes three times on a Sunday. But, as McAuley confirms, she yearned for the day when the ban would end, and she could return to Coleraine Baptist: 'That was a goal she had.'

She eventually got her way in 2002, when Pastor Jim Smyth from Limavady made an informal approach to Pastor Edwin Ewart, who had taken over from Hansford in 1996. Pastor Ewart called with Hazel to discuss her reintegration and he advised her to do it quietly and then gradually build up her attendance over a period of time. The fact that she had moved on, and was now with Trevor McAuley, was an important consideration in the 'amnesty' being granted, as Trevor recalls: 'Whenever it was established that we were in a relationship, she got it [the ban] lifted.' In relation to Hazel's approach to life in general, he remembers: 'There had to be a goal at the end of everything she did, an advantage.'

Trevor got on famously with the Buchanan children, and many a Sunday night was spent driving them back to Belfast where they were students at Queen's University and the College of Art. He thought the world of them: 'Lisa and Andrew were fantastic. They never cast up anything to that girl about their father, which always amazed me. Their loyalty was incredible. They thought their father had committed suicide because of an affair she had with Colin Howell. It didn't matter to them. She was their mother and they loved her to bits. They were totally committed. I used to take them to Belfast on a Sunday night at my expense, but Buchanan would have stayed on in the house and many times on my way home, I used to think: "Why didn't she come with me for the company?" There didn't seem to be a heart there. Maybe because of the deaths all her feelings died. They died along with Trevor Buchanan.'

When it came to her new boyfriend's three children though, Hazel just did not want to know, or have anything to do with them: 'She made that clear from the start, when she said: "I'll never be anything to your children." It put me under terrible pressure. I recall having them for a week [they lived with their mother] and she didn't even know they were there. I remember one night being caught out. We were in a Chinese restaurant. I popped in for a carry-out and she rang the mobile. My boy answered. I was supposed to be working and she was asking: "What's he doing there?"'

The couple kissed and cuddled, but that was as far as their intimacy went. Trevor felt that Hazel deliberately kept him at a distance during the years that they were together: 'The sexual side of it was driving me mad. There were times when things would have happened, but it wasn't a sleeping together thing. Even on holidays, there was nothing. In eight years, I could count on one hand [the number of times] when we got close. She didn't want me to. It was a powerful strain.'

He would try to bring up the subject of marriage and buying a home together. Trevor harboured exciting thoughts of a future together. Hazel clearly had serious reservations, although she rarely confided her doubts. They once talked about buying a plot of land. Another time, Hazel asked him to check with estate agents in the area and find out what houses were available for sale. They went to see some for themselves. But Hazel was not happy with any of them. In retrospect, Trevor sees that this was just her way of stalling: 'If you had Buckingham Palace, it wouldn't have been good enough. When I look back on it now, it's only because she didn't want to marry me. It wasn't because the house wasn't good enough. It wasn't because Buchanan wasn't ready. It was because I wasn't good enough. I couldn't fuel her life. And her life needed to be fuelled.'

In fact, Hazel had never wanted to marry Trevor McAuley. Years later, in police interviews, she would sum up the eight-year relationship with some considerable detachment: 'I didn't feel anything for him. I liked him as a person, but I felt with my life, and what had happened and everything, that I could never marry again.'

The relationship may have lasted a number of years, but tensions and tantrums over money put it on hold several times. Sometimes the separation lasted a week, sometimes just a couple of days. Trevor was desperate to secure a new and loving wife, but Hazel's desire to keep the relationship going was only motivated by self-interest, it seemed. It was the start of another long, slow goodbye on her part.

As time went on, Trevor's family made their feelings on the relationship felt. Initially, his mother and sisters had been willing to give Hazel a chance, knowing what a difficult time she had been through. But as it became obvious that there was nothing reciprocal about the relationship—that Trevor was doing all the giving and his girlfriend all the taking—they tried to reason with him that it would be better all round for him to disengage.

On his death bed, Trevor's father left him in no doubt about what he thought about Hazel. He was having chemotherapy for terminal cancer in Antrim Area Hospital, when he took his son by the hand, looked at his sad eyes and asked him to make a solemn pledge. Trevor recalls: 'My father was a plasterer with big hands, and I remember him taking my hand and he said: "You promise me you'll not go back to that bad woman." That was a big thing for him to say, because they knew how unhappy I was. This was after we finally split. I would say we were finished maybe two weeks, or a month. When it all finished, I was devastated. There were times I wanted to go back, but I knew I couldn't go back, because it . . . was never going to be any different.'

It all ended in July 2004, after they returned from an open-air Simon and Garfunkel concert in Dublin. They took the train from Belfast. As they pulled up at Connolly Station, Trevor could sense an impending separation which this time, he feared, would be permanent: 'I'll never forget the morning we left. There were times there was a distance between us, but this time it was greater. In the train, I remember going and sitting beside people we had gone with. I could get no conversation out of her. I thought it might have been because we had gone on the train and she didn't really like that. She might have considered it a bit common . . . The weekend was really, really strange. She was in total withdrawal. Even at night, she would not come down out of her room. I was quite embarrassed because of the people I was with. I went up to see what was wrong, and there was absolutely nothing. Then that night she finally told me she was concerned about the way she was treating me . . . I don't know whether it was genuinely eating her. She just couldn't convey to me the way she was feeling.'

They did not enjoy the concert. Apart from Hazel's sullen demeanour, Simon and Garfunkel had not lived up to either of their expectations. Hazel's mood darkened even more afterwards, when it started to rain and Trevor couldn't flag down a taxi. By the time they arrived home in Coleraine the following night, the town was at a standstill, as thousands of people gathered on the streets for a parade of teams to mark the start of the annual Milk Cup, an internationally renowned youth soccer tournament. Trevor's failure to make a speedy getaway because of the crowds just added to the gloom: 'Everything was irritating the life out of her. We finally got home and it was eating me what was wrong . . . I went into the house, took her bag in, but before I knew it, she had gone to bed. She never even said "cheerio". I went to her room and sat on the edge of the bed, asking her what was wrong. I said: "Do you not think after all this time we really need to take a decision to get married?" This is what she said, and this was the final straw: "Trevor, I don't know if I ever loved you. I don't know if I love you now, and I don't know if I'll ever love you in the future."' He reeled back in stunned silence for a few seconds, as the impact of the harsh words hit him. He then walked out of the Buchanan home, never to return.

The end of the relationship impacted on Trevor's health and state of mind. He walked the roads at all hours, agonising about what might have been, if only Hazel had been prepared to give him a chance: 'After that night, I lost it. I must have lost the guts of two stones. People thought I had cancer. I walked the roads. If it wasn't in the morning, then it was the middle of the night.'

The previous Christmas, Trevor had signed Hazel up for a year's subscription to a local gymnasium, so that she could work out and relax as she pleased: the monthly fee was debited from his bank account by the gym. If she saw him walking the roads when she was in her car, she would sometimes stop for a few brief words. The very last time Hazel stopped to say hello to him, she was wearing all her gym gear, including the bottoms and top he had bought her that sad and miserable weekend in Dublin. He remembers their exchange clearly: 'She says: "It's terrible. I'm still at Fitness First and you're paying for it." I said to her: "No, I'm not. I've stopped it." I was so pleased with myself. It was really brave and she looked shocked. She was stunned.'

Stunned she might have been, but Hazel had moved on. She already had a new man on her arm. David Stewart was a former Chief Superintendent who once served as a staff officer to Sir Hugh Annesley, the Chief Constable of the RUC. Stewart, a divorcee with a family, had retired from the police in 2001, just before the RUC became the Police Service of Northern Ireland. Tall with greying hair, lean, tanned, well-spoken and keen to keep himself fit, he was introduced to Hazel in the gym by a policeman friend. The two had shared spiritual interests too: David was taking a fresh look at his Christianity around the time they met. It was love at first sight on the treadmill and at the spinning classes.

After they finished working out, they would meet for coffee. It was early 2004 and Hazel was still in a relationship with Trevor McAuley, but when Stewart left for Latvia for a year on a policing project—he now worked in a consultancy business—he kept in contact with the woman he was already besotted with. When he returned home that summer—just after the time Hazel had been in Dublin with Trevor — the ex-policeman was keen to progress the relationship. Just months after she ditched Trevor, he proposed, in January 2005. They did not tell their families at the time, but announced their engagement in April. They got married on 18 July 2005. The couple attended Coleraine Baptist Church for a brief period before switching to

Portstewart. They moved into a new home at Ballystrone Road in Coleraine in late 2006.

David Stewart had once attended Colin Howell's surgery as a patient, but Hazel warned him never to mention her name if he ever went back to the Ballymoney practice for treatment. On their first proper date, she told Stewart that she had been having an affair with the dentist at the time of her husband's death and that she had had an abortion. She also said that she felt trapped by Howell and was unable to break away from him.

The last time Trevor McAuley and Hazel spoke was at his father's graveside in September 2004. He needed a white shirt for the funeral and she had told him to get one. Trevor recalls: 'She put her arm around my waist and said: "Did you get the shirt in Next?" How bizarre is that?' Friends had told Trevor how she had met Stewart in the gym while he was still paying her subscription. Everything became clear to him then: 'So that's where she got the confidence to put me out of her life and not take me back. But it was the best Christmas box I ever bought anybody, never mind her. Because the day I saw her on television coming out after the first court appearance with that man [David Stewart], I said to myself: "That could have been me."' Trevor has since remarried and lives with his second wife in Coleraine.

Stewart spoke glowingly about his wife to police who interviewed him in December 2009: 'Hazel is my wife and I know her extremely well. She is a kind, trusting person with a soft nature. At times she can be too trusting, something she has in common with other members of her family. She is quick to defer to those she thinks know better than her. She has always enjoyed working with children and tends to lack a critical judgement on people. Hazel will always tend to see the good in others. These are admirable qualities, but need to be balanced with the realisation that not everyone is as helpful and as sincere as they appear to be.' He insisted that she was a dedicated mother, tireless in all her dealings with her two children, and added: 'The love and affection they share is very apparent. I find it difficult to express in a statement that may go before a court, how I feel about Hazel. She always puts me first and we have a great and trusting relationship. She is my best friend and the better part of me.'

Trevor McAuley's verdict on the woman with whom he spent eight years of his life is less positive: 'I think Buchanan is a total grabber of opportunities. Nothing was ever good enough . . . She was materialistic to the hilt. Cold-hearted. She should have told me at the start she didn't want me. She should have been straight with me from the start . . . She [only] wanted me around because I could do everything she needed . . . To me, she was as clever as Howell. She had me round her little finger. She could make me do anything, including spending money I didn't have . . . She could work me like no other woman worked me and I hated that.'

Chapter 15
Money, Money, Money . . .

Once Colin Howell had finally decided to move on from his 'sad adulteress', Hazel Buchanan, he lost no time in finding someone else. In December 1996, a policeman friend, Steven Cargin, brought a young American divorcee, Kyle Jorgensen, along to a Christian 'singles night' at Howell's house. Steven introduced them to one another and very quickly they began dating. It was a whirlwind romance. Colin and Kyle married the following year, on 2 May 1997. A fortnight later, she announced she was pregnant with the first of the five children they would go on to have within less than a decade.

Kyle Jorgensen, originally from New York, arrived in Northern Ireland with her two young children, Dylan and Katie, in 1996. She had only recently managed to extricate herself from a deeply unhappy four-year marriage. Wanting to make a fresh start for herself and her children, she had decided to cross the Atlantic to study Irish history. She had applied for a place at Trinity College, Dublin, as well as Queen's University in Belfast and the University of Limerick, and was finally accepted at the University of Ulster at Coleraine.

With her course due to start in October 1996, Kyle rented a house that July in Portstewart—at Millbank Avenue, an area of the town where many students lived. Following her brother Arnie's religious conversion a year previously, Kyle had only just rediscovered religion herself. And so, soon after she settled in the town, she became a regular attendee at Portstewart Baptist Church, where she met the friend of Howell who subsequently introduced her to her future husband. At 30 years old, Kyle was eight years Howell's junior and in many ways a vulnerable young woman, having just arrived in a strange country with two small children and still in the throes of an acrimonious divorce.

The newly-weds lived for a short period at Howell's house at Knocklayde Park, but with six children—Kyle's two and his four— and another baby on the way, space was at a premium. Howell decided to build what would be a very lavish family home at Glebe Road, but as they waited for the building work to be finished, they moved into a rented, semi-detached house on Freehall Road, also in Castlerock.

Like Lesley before her, Kyle quickly found that her independent pursuits—in her case, her university studies—had to be sacrificed in the interests of family life. Howell helped with the children whenever he could, but much of his time was spent at work. He was extremely driven and single-minded and felt that his role was to provide financially for his family. He felt his wife's place was in the home.

Underneath Howell's very traditionalist view of the sexes, however, was also an intractable core of misogyny, it seems. One former female employee recalls his clear attitude that women were basically inferior to men: 'This was Colin's attitude [quoting Genesis 3:16]: "And to the woman he said, I will greatly multiply thy pains and thy groanings; in pain thou shalt bring forth children, and thy submission shall be to thy husband, and he shall rule over thee."' In the surgery, he would make life difficult for some female members of staff and take any opportunity to upbraid them over tiny, insignificant shortcomings. At home too, he was a strict and sometimes brutal authoritarian who was never slow to let his wife know if she stepped out of line.

With six other children in her care as well as baby Erik, who had been born with a problem of the digestive system and had to stay in hospital for some time, the summer of 1998 cannot have been easy for Howell's new wife. She had also had to undergo major treatment after Erik's birth because of an infection. And her ex-husband in the States was still making waves in her life with his bid to win custody of Dylan and Katie. Apart from a couple of church acquaintances, she hardly knew anybody in the area, and even though Northern Ireland was moving towards a peaceful new era, with the signing of the Good Friday Agreement in April 1998, Kyle was still bewildered by the politics of the place.

Just 18 months after they married, Howell made a confession to Kyle which hit her for six. They had just finished dinner and, for the first time in ages, were more or less on their own, sitting in the lounge as Kyle fed baby Erik. Howell, who hadn't eaten much, seemed on edge and distracted. He said there was something he had to tell her. In the moments which ensued, Kyle Howell would get a terrifying glimpse into the hitherto hidden depths of her new husband's soul— and a first intimation of the nightmare into which he was to drag her in years to come.

When they first met, Howell had been quick to tell Kyle all about what had happened with his first wife—or rather the official version of what had happened. Lesley, he explained, had taken her own life because of his affair with another woman, and he took full responsibility for having driven her to such a tragic end. She had suffered from depression, and had been taking prescription drugs as well as self-medicating with alcohol. Howell described how he routinely came home to find her drunk and the children running around the house unattended. He said his lover's husband, Trevor Buchanan, had taken his own life as well. But beyond this, he had not entered into any more detail in his explanations to Kyle. There had been an unspoken understanding between the two of them that it was probably best left at this.

But now, as Kyle sat on the sofa with Erik on her knee, Howell began shaking and suddenly blurted out: 'It's my fault. It's all my responsibility. I did it. I killed Lesley.' Stunned and utterly incredulous, the young American found herself involuntarily shifting to the other end of the sofa. But he continued with his shocking admission. While he didn't describe fully what happened, he told her how he had used a garden hose when he had killed Trevor Buchanan too.

Once she was able to compose herself enough to speak, Kyle's first response was to tell him that she wanted to call the police, there and then. But Howell urged her not to do so—not straight away, anyway. Pleading with her to stay calm and think of the future, he told her: 'Take a deep breath. Take a deep breath. It's been seven years and surely you can wait one more day. We need to sort the children. We have to make sure they are financially okay. Let me try and put the practice up for sale. We can take our time and make sure everything is in place.'

This was a man Kyle no longer recognised. She felt confused and disorientated. Next, she was struck with fear for the children's safety, and her own well-being. She felt she had been duped. Her head was crowded with all sorts of thoughts and emotions. She felt alone and trapped, far from home and anyone she felt she could really trust or depend upon. Not knowing what she should do, for the remainder of that evening she allowed Howell to talk her down and listened while he reasoned that they should carefully plan how to protect the children's future, before he would surrender himself to the authorities.

The following day, after Howell left for the surgery as usual, she telephoned her mother in the United States. She didn't say anything about her husband's startling admission, but simply asked: 'Mom, what do you do when you know somebody has done something illegal, but they're now a Christian?' Her mother just replied that she didn't know. Next Kyle rang her brother Arnie with the same question—but again, without a word about what Howell had just told her. Arnie assumed that Kyle believed Howell had cheated again, and the conversation was left at that. A day later, while out for a walk with some acquaintances from the church, she called an elder aside, and quietly asked him, again without disclosing any specifics, the same question. The man paused for a while, before replying: 'Well, if it goes before the cross . . .'

Kyle was in turmoil. She thought about Nicky Cruz, well-known founder of Nicky Cruz Outreach, an evangelical Christian ministry based in the States. Cruz was the ultimate example of how bad men could turn good, with God's help. Originally from San Juan, Puerto Rico, he had once headed up one of the most feared criminal gangs in New York City—the Mau Maus, named after the anti-colonialist uprising in Kenya in the 1950s. But once he had discovered God, Cruz had turned from a violent life of crime to that of an influential and peace-loving Christian evangelist whose mission was to preach the Gospel. Maybe Howell was like Nicky Cruz, Kyle found herself thinking. Or maybe he was some kind of Irish terrorist, like the ones she had heard about, who had killed people and spread death and mayhem during the years of the Troubles. Had she been manipulated by a charming psychopath?

She rummaged through Howell's personal belongings and discovered Lesley's death certificate, which confirmed she had died from carbon monoxide poisoning. Perhaps her husband had simply exaggerated the extent of the role he had played in Lesley and Trevor's death, because of the guilt he felt over his affair with Hazel Buchanan?

People in the church were always telling Kyle what a wonderful man Colin was: a good father who loved his children. Some had even hinted that Lesley and Trevor Buchanan had taken their lives, because it was they—and not Colin and Hazel—who had been having an affair. Perhaps that was where the truth lay after all?

Maybe it was because she herself had been the victim of an abusive marriage for four years that Kyle was ultimately prepared to keep quiet and stand by the new man in her life. Maybe it was because by this time, she felt a huge responsibility to Howell's four children too. Maybe it was because she was alone and isolated and without any support from close family. She had no money of her own, and no qualifications to help her get a well-paid job: she had worked as a waitress before coming to Ireland.

After his confession to his wife, it seemed at first that Howell had every intention of coming clean and handing himself in to the authorities. He began to make plans to sell his practice, so as to set Kyle and the children up financially. It was September 1998 and her parents were due to come to Northern Ireland. Howell booked rooms at the Burrendale Hotel, Newcastle, County Down, and invited his own parents to join them for the weekend. He had decided that he would make an announcement to everyone and then hand himself over the police. But the night before, his father called to say that he was unable to come because he had been asked at the last moment to stand in for a preacher at a church event. And so the family summit was called off.

While Howell was at church that weekend, a girl whom he later referred to as Sandra approached him and said: 'Colin, I don't know why I'm telling you this, but you just need to know all your sins are forgiven and forgotten by God.' She also quoted a verse from First Corinthians 4:5: 'Therefore judge nothing before the appointed time: wait till the Lord comes. He will bring to light what is hidden in darkness and will expose the motives of men's hearts. At that time, each will receive his praise from God.' It was the sign Howell needed—he decided to abandon his plans to surrender himself and confess to his crimes. He was more than happy to believe that Sandra's words were a communication from God. The Lord was clearly telling him all had been forgiven.

As time passed, and the memory of the evening he had confessed the shocking truth began to recede, Kyle herself gradually let go of the idea of telling the police. While she could never completely erase the revelation from her mind, she was prepared to move on. And Howell certainly was too. He was very convincing when he told her that he knew God had now forgiven him. Kyle Howell agreed to stick by her husband. But she also warned him that if he stepped out of line at any time in the future, she would call the police and tell them everything.

———

By the end of the 1990s, Howell's life was beginning to look up on other fronts too. Financially, things were on a far more healthy footing than during the last fraught years with Lesley, when the bank manager had been constantly on the phone and Howell had been forced to secretly put the new family home on the market and to sound out his former employers about taking the Ballymoney surgery off his hands. Friends and acquaintances quickly noticed Kyle's influence in the way in which he adopted a far more structured approach to financial matters. The substantial injections of cash from which he benefited in the aftermath of Lesley's death helped enormously too, of course.

Once the inquest of May 1992 was out of the way, Howell received £120,000 from Lesley's life insurance. He had been in two minds about what to do before putting in the claim. He read the small print of the insurance policy carefully to ensure that there were no exemption clauses covering the case of death by suicide, and discovered that no such clauses applied. He knew that he was committing fraud—since Lesley's death was the result of murder and not suicide—but he felt others would be suspicious if he failed to lodge the application. He later insisted that financial gain had never been a motive for the killing of Lesley. However, there was no doubt that this money—and the sum of £212,000, of which he was also the immediate beneficiary after Lesley's death (as a result of her late father's will)—must have helped to alleviate his financial difficulties considerably. Howell had invested a third of the life insurance money in the purchase of a bungalow in Portstewart, which he rented out to students, and which he sold for a very satisfactory profit (£13,500) shortly after he met Kyle.

Meanwhile—thanks in some part also to the improvement in his financial circumstances—Howell's career in dentistry was going from strength to strength. The Ballymoney practice was flourishing, and in February 1999, he was able to take on another new associate—a Robin Alexander from Irving in Scotland. Alexander, whose wife Patricia, a dental hygienist, was originally from Ballymena, had qualified in Glasgow and had ten years of professional experience before he came to work for Howell. The two men got on very well, and four years later in 2003, Alexander bought a share in the practice for £220,000.

With Robin Alexander full-time in Ballymoney, Howell started to shift his focus to an area of practice in which he had become increasingly interested—implantology. It represented more of a challenge than his standard NHS and private patient work and the driven and the ever-ambitious Howell was only too aware that it was a financially far more lucrative field to be in. The prospect of the greater earning potential was a huge draw for him, especially with an ever-expanding second family to support. In 1999, he opened his Causeway Dental Implant Studio, having converted part of the first floor of the Ballymoney premises. The two businesses—the general dental surgery and the implant studio—shared the same reception, but the practices operated more or less independently of each other, with Howell concentrating exclusively on implants and cosmetic work. Alexander managed the general and more routine side, and there were days and sometimes weeks when the two dentists would hardly see each other. Howell also owned the top-floor apartment, from which he was able to make some additional income as a rental property.

As ever, Howell applied himself with great energy and dedication to developing his new specialism and to keeping things ticking over in the general practice. Life was very busy at the time. He was forever on the go and, with a big family to look after, he never found himself with much free time. He always seemed to be in a hurry and often worked through lunch. When occasionally there was a gap in his appointment schedule, he might pick up a newspaper down in the reception, quickly flick through the pages and have a word or two with whoever was on duty, before rushing upstairs to his office again. He was an exacting boss and colleague, and expected those who worked with him to display the same dedication to the job as he did. One ex-member of staff remembers when he first opened in Ballymoney: '[Howell] was a workaholic and very, very driven in terms of what he wanted to do and achieve, especially when it came to making money.

He would have come in at 3 a.m. to see a patient. He expected the other dentists to do the same . . . He was plausible about the whole thing. He would say to patients: "I know you are working nine to five with a family and can't come in to see me. But listen, I'll go home and have my tea and I'll see you at 8 p.m." He made it sound as if he was bending over backwards to help people. In actual fact, he was helping himself. It was all part of the image he was trying to create: this really caring, conscientious person.'

Howell rarely discussed religion inside the practice, with his staff at any rate. But he did not miss an opportunity to make his dedication to his religious principles and his status as a deeply moral member of the local community felt among those who worked with him, often in a rather sanctimonious way. At staff nights out, he would drink very little and generally either arrive late or leave early, citing church or babysitting commitments. One summer, he refused to attend a staff outing to the Grand Opera House in Belfast to see the musical *Mamma Mia!* Asked by one of the girls who were booking tickets in advance for the party whether he would be joining them, he pronounced loudly that his conscience would not allow him to go: 'I'm sorry. *Mamma Mia!* is about a woman who does not know who the father of her daughter is. I cannot make myself go to a show about that. I don't approve of it.' It was 2008, shortly before he confessed all to the church elders and then the police.

After work and family, church affairs dominated the devout dentist's life. There would be Baptist breakfast meetings at the Lodge Hotel in Coleraine. Every now and again, he would ask friends and acquaintances to join him. Not all accepted. One businessman became so exasperated with the repeated invitations that he eventually said to him: 'Colin, no harm to you, but don't ask me again. I'm just not interested.' Howell drank very moderately—maybe two glasses of wine with dinner—and exercised assiduously, playing golf, squash, five-a-side soccer, and regularly going cycling and running. He also had an array of gym equipment at his home.

The implantology practice was soon thriving and bringing in substantial sums of money. In 2003, he paid £75,000 for a share in a practice in Bangor because, being close to Belfast, it had a much larger catchment area and was an ideal location from which he could promote his work and develop his reputation. He was based there two days a week. His partner in the Bangor practice was another dentist who specialised in implantology and cosmetic work. In 2004, Howell took on another Scot—David Wilson from Glasgow—as an associate in the Ballymoney practice. Wilson's brief was to take on a number of Howell's NHS and private patients in the general practice with Robin Alexander, so that Howell could devote himself full-time to growing the cosmetic side of the business.

In the late 1990s and early 2000s, implantology was very much at the cutting edge of dentistry in the UK and Ireland. A dental implant is typically a small, screw-shaped attachment, usually made from titanium, which is inserted into the jawbone to take the place of a missing tooth root. Once the bone has attached firmly to the implant, a replacement tooth is secured to the top of the implant. The new tooth can look, feel and perform just like a natural tooth. It is also possible to use multiple implants to support a denture or bridge. Implants are more comfortable than conventional dentures, because there is no slippage or movement, and even though it is an expensive process—generally in the region of £2,000 per implant—which can take between three and nine months, the benefits are immediate. Implants help maintain the shape and structure of the jaw bone, and can do wonders for the self-confidence of the patient.

Like other dentists at the time, Howell was quick to recognise that implantology was a growth area in commercial dentistry. But unlike others perhaps, it seems that he did not have any great qualms about presenting himself as an expert, even though he had very little training or experience. Several of his contemporaries have claimed that he declared himself a specialist in implantology after undergoing a course in Manchester in 1999 which lasted for a mere couple of days. Howell even lectured occasionally to students at the School of Dentistry at Queen's and, through his connections with a big UK pharmacy company, organised courses and talks on various aspects of implantology. At one time, he was hosting regular monthly sessions at the Lodge Hotel, Coleraine. Here, he might talk for 45 minutes or so to an audience of up to a dozen dentists, after which they would all have an opportunity to participate in group discussions on specific cases. After completing a certain number of sessions, those who had regularly attended were given a certificate. Howell also became a Fellow of the International Team for Implantology.

The dentist's thirst for professional recognition knew no bounds, and was not tempered by any consideration that he might not have the substance to back up his claims of expertise. One dentist commented: 'This was all part of his growing stature. There was a thin veneer of truth, but very, very thin. When you scratched the surface, it wasn't all as it would seem.' But Howell was not about to let such concerns stop him. Ever the risk-taker and always the opportunist, he was determined to make the most of whatever breaks came his way to further his thriving career.

In July 2005, after graduating in dentistry in Belfast, a young man called Mohammad Husban from Jordan arrived at Howell, Alexander and Associates in Ballymoney to take up his first job. In many ways, the arrival of the young Jordanian on the scene at this particular juncture would be a godsend in terms of Howell's commercial interests. And perhaps that is exactly how Howell would have seen it himself at the time—as an opportunity sent directly from God.

Mohammad's father, Yasin Husban, was a top Jordanian dentist. He had held the rank of Major General in the Jordanian Royal Medical Services—during which time he treated King Hussein himself on one occasion. He opened his own private dental practice in Amman in 2000. Yasin had done his Master's degree in Dentistry at the University College of London's Eastman Dental Institute in the mid-70s, and had been keen for Mohammad, the eldest of his three sons, to be educated in Britain as well. It had been a couple of professors from the School of Dentistry at Queen's, who met Yasin during a trip to Jordan, who suggested that his son go to Belfast to study. After all, it had one of the best universities in the UK, particularly for the medical sciences. Mohammad duly arrived in Northern Ireland to begin his studies in September 1998.

When he started working for Howell at the Ballymoney practice in the late summer of 2005, Mohammad found his new employer to be very welcoming and hospitable. In fact, the young man lived for the first eight months of his three years in the County Antrim town in Howell's top-floor flat above the surgery, some of the time rent-free. He was very quickly made to feel like a valued member of the staff, and enjoyed taking part in regular team-building days involving all sorts of outdoor activities, which including camping in County Fermanagh, as well as staff nights out to the theatre in Belfast. According to friends, Mohammad considered Howell to be an excellent dentist who treated him well during his three years' training. He would always be financially reimbursed when he bought any fittings for the apartment, and Howell would refer some of his private patients to the young dentist to do fillings and whitening.

The Howells were also very hospitable when Mohammad's parents, Yasin and Hana, came to Northern Ireland to visit their son. They put the couple up in the lavish family home, showing them around their son's workplace and taking them out for dinner at the fashionable Ardtara Country House outside the village of Upperlands. One night, however, Howell forgot to inform staff that his guests were of the Muslim faith, and there was an awkward moment when the main course arrived with bacon trimmings. The plates were sent back to the kitchen, as the host apologised for any offence caused. Luckily the guests just laughed it off. Howell got on famously with Yasin, and, as well as their common interest in dentistry, they were both avid soccer supporters of Manchester United. The dentist did not miss the opportunity to let the local media know about his high-profile guests: the local newspaper, the *Ballymoney Times*, ran an article about them that week, which featured a photograph of the smiling Howell and his staff with the two visitors from Jordan, and was headlined: 'A Crown with a Difference for Local Dentist'.

Friends of Mohammad's were in no doubt that Howell used his father's fairly limited connection with the King of Jordan to promote his implant business. And given how well the Husbans' visit to Northern Ireland had gone, it was hardly surprising that in May 2006, when Yasin, as Chairman of the Congress Committee for the Jordanian Dental Association, was charged with organising their 20th annual conference at the luxurious Le Royal Hotel in Amman, Colin Howell was one of the delegates from Northern Ireland invited to give a presentation. It was a hugely prestigious and high-profile international event. Other speakers invited included two representatives from the School of Dentistry in Belfast, Professor Tom Clifford, head of Prosthodontics and Professor Philip-John Lamey, Professor of Oral Medicine. Naturally, Howell jumped at the chance.

The Amman conference was a huge and impressive gathering. There were 1,500 delegates from all over the world, including Italy, Germany, Australia, Lebanon, Greece, Iraq, UAE, Syria, and the United States. The conference covered all aspects of dentistry, including prosthetic dentistry, conservative dentistry, endodontics, orthodontics, implantology, oral and maxillofacial surgery, the use of lasers in dentistry, periodontology and paediatric dentistry. As well as the lectures and courses, there were many social events to attend outside the conference hall. Organised tours were laid on, with trips to see the Roman ruins in the city of Jerash, the ancient settlement of Petra and the Dead Sea: delegates were taxied everywhere and accompanied by attentive guides. Howell was in his element as he smeared himself with the mineral-rich black mud of the Dead Sea shoreline, before lying back to float in the water. Sociable and outgoing when it suited him, he quickly made an impression on those around him. One delegate remembers: 'He was a very outspoken guy and you could become friends with him really easily. People liked him because of his friendliness. He was interested in people and their culture, and he was not afraid to ask questions. He could also share a joke.' The night before the conference started, Howell and his party were invited to the Husbans' family home.

On Day One of the conference, the ambitious Northern Irish dentist delivered a lecture entitled 'Implant in the Aesthetic Zone'. He focused mainly on the cosmetic side, but covered other aspects of dentistry as well, such as cross-infection control in general practice, bone-grafting products and techniques, and implant design. On the second day, Howell performed a relatively complex procedure for his audience, by completing the final stages of some implant work on a patient. Forty dentists in a lecture theatre at the King Hussein medical centre were also able to watch Howell at work via video link. He rose to the occasion admirably and his performance was well-received. Some of the delegates, however, had their doubts about his bona fides, one of these remembering: 'The lecture he gave was all about how *he* did things, and what *he* thought. There was no evidence-based scientific analysis to prove to people what [he was] saying was correct. It was all wishy-washy stuff. There was no scientific paper. It was all about Colin. It was all about Colin's ego. It was typical Colin.'

Once he was back at home, Howell wasted no time in capitalising on the success of his Jordanian venture, and maximising the kudos of the high-profile contacts he had made. He placed an advertorial in the *Sunday Tribune* newspaper, which was headlined 'Operation Smile', and included text which claimed: 'In fact, he counts the Jordanian Royal family, its government ministers and dignitaries as some of his more high-profile patients.' Howell himself was quoted as saying: 'The King of Jordan wanted his team of dentists brought up-to-date on procedures, and I actually performed live surgery at a lecture I was giving on quality dental implants . . . with over 400 dentists watching.' In the same piece, Howell recommended a particular make of implant, which he described as the 'Mercedes of Implants', adding: 'If it's good enough for the King of Jordan, it's not too shabby for us mere mortals.' He claimed that there were only six practices in Northern Ireland with the experience to provide the range of treatments he offered, and insisted that price was very important and a measure of a dentist's expertise. He generally quoted between £1,600 to £2,100 for one implant, complete with a crown, and he warned patients against those quoting any less: 'If you are being quoted [a] lower price, then you probably shouldn't go there, as either the dentist is a very inexperienced dentist, or is using budget implants.'

Some of Howell's fellow professionals were less than impressed by his credentials and his inflated claims, as one confirms: 'There was something in a dental magazine which claimed that he treated Queen Rania. It just wasn't true. Somebody raised it with him. Colin said it must have been an error by the guy who wrote the article, and he would let them know. But to the best of our knowledge, he never did.' Another dentist remembers: 'He inflated the truth of exactly what he did. He was taking full-page adverts in glossy magazines and it was a strategy which seemed to work. Patients came from far and wide, including the Irish Republic. I never heard of any complaints, but obviously there were some. He certainly performed treatments that would have been stretching the normal rules of clinical practice and maybe sometimes breaking them.' Another dentist felt equally critical of Howell's work: 'I think that patients were disappointed when some of the procedures didn't work out. These . . . may have been outside the realms of traditional dentistry. They seemed to be risky, unpredictable and therefore more likely to fail, which meant it made it harder to go back and do corrective work . . . I have had to do that corrective work.'

Howell was keen to create and feed the impression that he was a major global authority on implantology who treated the rich and famous. But specialists in the field were more than a little sceptical about his abilities and ethics: 'We viewed him as a common or garden general dental practitioner with a particular interest in one area of dentistry, in the same way as somebody with a special interest in orthodontics. It was an extra string to his bow, but nothing special. He was never considered by any of us to be somebody we would look up to.'

But there were plenty of patients who were more than impressed by his PR and, taken in by the hype, were happy to travel to Ballymoney. His customer base expanded ever more rapidly, with many patients travelling up from the Irish Republic, where dental charges were twice and sometimes three times as expensive. Dentists in Dublin, Cork and Galway, who might have spent three years being trained in implantology at some of the top units in the United States, were coming back home looking for a fairly quick return on their investment, but not all of their patients could afford the prices for root canal treatment, crowns, fillings and implants. For such clients, even Howell's fees were considerably lower.

By the mid to late 2000s, the dentist's earning capacity was huge and he was making substantial sums of money, year on year. There was never any shortage of people in search of a brilliant new smile. One couple paid him £35,000 for cosmetic treatments over a three-year period and were delighted with his work.

Things were on the up and up for the Howell family. They had moved into the fabulous new property just off the Glebe Road. Painted a primrose colour, down a narrow, stony, twisting lane with a trout lake nearby, the house had wonderful views across open countryside and ample, well-landscaped gardens, as well as a terrace at the front which caught the sun.

By 2008, the Howells had also purchased a site for a house in Florida, near where Kyle's parents lived, on Sanibel Island. They liked to spend as much time as possible in Florida with the children, and the proposed house for construction would enable them to stay there for longer periods. They also enjoyed family holidays to exotic locations such as Costa Rica.

The couple had a good circle of church-going friends with whom they socialised regularly, and even with such a young family, they would eat out from time to time on their own, sometimes at the well-known local restaurant, Ardtara House, which had an excellent reputation for fine dining. Life had never been better for Colin Howell. What had happened in the past was now firmly in the past, and surely there would never be any need for him to revisit the dark days of May 1991 ever again. Or would there?

———

In August 2008, the entire staff of Howell, Alexander and Associates gathered at Galgorm Manor hotel, near Ballymena, for a farewell dinner to mark the departure of Mohammad Husban. The young man had spent three happy years in Ballymoney, and was sorry to be leaving. He was a popular member of the surgery's team. During all that time, Howell had never once raised the issue of religion with the young Jordanian. But as Mohammad sat quietly at the restaurant table, having just been presented with a wallet, cufflinks and House of Fraser vouchers from the staff, Howell started to talk to him about God.

One of Mohammad's friends recalls the young man's account of the conversation: 'He [Colin] asked Mohammad about forgiveness and said how in his religion, Jesus had died for their sins. Whatever you've done, you would be forgiven, and would go straight to heaven. Howell told him that if he believed in Jesus, then that's where he was going, no matter what he did in life. He then asked him how people of the Muslim faith viewed that opinion. Mohammad told him it was God who decided who went to heaven and who went to hell. God's forgiveness depended on how bad the things you had done were. It didn't matter if you stole something, or murdered somebody—you could be a really good Muslim, and then commit a crime. But would God forgive you? It would be up to God to make that judgement.'

Howell suddenly began to shift in his seat. He was looking uncomfortable and his face was flushed. He said he needed to go to the bathroom and excused himself. It seemed that Howell had been more than a little unnerved by the conversation, as Mohammad's friend relates: 'He eventually came back. Mohammad was preparing to engage again and pick up where they left off. Howell changed the subject completely. Religion wasn't [ever] mentioned again.'

Chapter 16
The Wages of Sin

AUGUST 2006

In the summer of 2006, Colin Howell was devastated by the death of a close friend, Fritz Hoffman. Hoffman, an American pastor whom Howell first met in the early 1990s while doing free dental treatment for orphans in Romania, had contracted a fatal infection after developing an abscess on an erupting wisdom tooth. As the infection spread into his lower jaw and then into muscles of his neck, Fritz was left gasping for breath. His wife Ady had phoned Howell in a panic from their home in Romania, but there was nothing he could do, other than to urge her to call an ambulance immediately. But it was too late. Even as Howell and Ady spoke, his great friend took himself off into the bathroom—well away from his children—where he collapsed and died.

Fritz had visited Castlerock a number of times, and in the year before his death, Howell had treated him for some bridge work at his Ballymoney practice. This treatment had absolutely no bearing on the infection in Hoffman's wisdom tooth, which developed many months later and from which he would ultimately die. But Howell could not help blaming himself for what happened to his friend. Others reminded him that Hoffman's general health had been poor in recent years, and that he had refused to look after himself properly, despite being urged to do so by all those who knew him. None of this made any difference to Howell's frame of mind: he still felt Hoffman's death had somehow been his fault. No matter that his friend ate too many Big Macs, drank too many sugary drinks and was massively overweight, or that in later years, Hoffman had suffered from breathlessness and chest pains. The persistent feeling of guilt never left Colin Howell.

The two men had been particularly close, ever since meeting in 1993 in a town called Baia Mare in the Maramureş district, near the Ukraine border in Romania. Howell, who was there as a church volunteer dispensing free dental treatment to destitute orphans in the area, had set up a makeshift treatment centre in a caravan, just beside the huge Pentecostal church in the town centre. Hoffman had previously been a pastor in the US Army in Germany before he left to live in Austria and then Romania. During the Ceausescu era, he had smuggled Bibles into Romania and done his best to offer practical help and spiritual succour to those who were suffering and most in need. He was an honourable man, and widely respected in church circles, and he admired Howell's philanthropic streak. The two men hit it off immediately. In later years, Hoffman would even name his only adopted son after the kind man from Northern Ireland who was always so generous with his time and money.

Howell had told his new-found friend about the death of his first wife. But it was all lies, of course. Hoffman felt for him and later told friends he believed Lesley had been the guilty party, because she killed herself and left Colin with four children to bring up alone—to his mind, this was a far greater sin than the dentist's adultery. When the pastor set up his own church—Couriers for Christ—in Baia Mare, he was quickly able to move it from its humble beginnings in the two-roomed flat in which he lived, to an old Baptist Church building which he secured with the help of some of Howell's money. As far as Hoffman was concerned, his friend from Northern Ireland was a deeply committed Christian determined to do the Lord's work and make a better life for children who were otherwise without hope. He died of course before the full truth about Howell was exposed.

———

APRIL 2007

Less than a year after Fritz Hoffman's death, tragedy struck once more for Howell. If he had been deeply affected by the loss of his friend in

Romania, it is hard to imagine the extent of the emotional body blow he suffered on 30 April 2007, with the death of his eldest son, 22-year-old Matthew, in a freak accident in the apartment block where he had been living in St Petersburg, Russia.

Matt had been there on an overseas semester as part of his university course: he had died after falling 40 feet down a stairwell from the fourth floor of the building. The death had a cataclysmic effect on Howell and was undoubtedly a crucial catalyst in the process of emotional and spiritual disintegration which he experienced in the months which followed. Just like his friend Hoffman's death, the loss of Matthew left Howell destabilised and tormented. Suddenly, it must have seemed to him that death was everywhere he looked. He became increasingly possessed by the notion that God was finally punishing him for his past sins. He could not cast off the feeling that his previous conviction—that he had been forgiven—was nothing but empty self-delusion.

––––

Matt Howell had been a very bright, popular young man who had many friends both at Dalriada Grammar school in Ballymoney, where he was a pupil until the age of 18, and later at St Andrews University also. He was unassuming and quietly spoken, but he had a sufficiently strong sense of himself to resist pressure from his father to follow him into dentistry. After achieving top marks in A-level Spanish, Religious Education and Classical Civilisation in 2003, Matt took a year out to work in South America for the Christian charity, Operation Mobilisation. On his return, he took up a place at St Andrews to study Russian, Spanish and International Relations. He was a great traveller, and, as well as his time in South America, he had been to Nicaragua and then the United States, where he spent three months working for Microsoft in Washington DC. At the time of his death, he was also making plans for a trip to China.

According to close friends, Matthew's relationship with his father had not been good for some time, largely due to Howell's controlling ways. One friend of the young man remembers: 'Matthew hated his father. He was always pushing him. Matthew was always a quiet guy, a lovely young man. His father kept telling people: "He's going to follow in his dad's footsteps." It was a simple as that. There was to be no argument ... They didn't get on, and Howell had no right to say they did.'

After being informed of Matt's death, Howell had caught the first available flight to St Petersburg, accompanied by his church friend, Willie Patterson. Kyle's sister, Elke, and her husband Joe Woo, an opinionated Chinese-American, also travelled to Russia, from Costa Rica, to help Howell with the repatriation process. When the grieving father arrived in St Petersburg, a team from St Andrews was already there and, as they assisted with the paperwork to secure the early release of Matt's body, Howell returned to the apartment block to see for himself where his son had met his death.

The details of what exactly had happened on that fateful night were now emerging. Matt had been in the apartment with a friend, Geoff. The two young men had some kind of argument, and Geoff left around 4 a.m. Just as he reached the exit door of the building downstairs, he heard his friend cry out twice.

Matt had followed his friend out of the flat, apparently to throw him a key to let himself out of the building. He was in his sock soles, and slipped on the well-polished floor on the outside landing. He lost his balance, but managed to grab a low handrail as he tumbled over. At this point, he cried out and Geoff looked up and saw him dangling. At first he thought his Irish friend was playing some kind of joke, but suddenly realised that he was hanging on for his life. Geoff turned and sprinted up the stairs, pulling a calf muscle two-and-a-half flights up. Just then, he looked on in disbelief as Matt's body passed him in the shaft of the stairwell, striking the handrail at the bottom. He heard a thump and then a heavy thud. Matthew Howell moaned, but was dead within a minute of hitting the floor.

Howell's brother-in-law Joe Woo had his doubts about the death. Could it have been anything other than an accident, he wondered. Maybe it was suicide? Or could Matt even have been murdered? Who knows what could happen in this particular part of the world if a young man had strayed into the politics of the place and mixed with the wrong company? Howell quickly dismissed such theories, but decided to find out for himself what had happened in the moments before his son died. When he went to the apartment block to see the scene, he brought with him a stopwatch and three coins. He was going to carry out an experiment.

The blood stains from Matthews's head wounds were still in evidence on the concrete floor near the exit door when Howell got there. He took out the stopwatch and proceeded to climb the stairs. He estimated it would have taken five seconds for Geoff to realise his friend's life was in peril in the early hours of that morning—and then some 10.5 seconds to run up the two-and-a-half flights of stairs. Next, Howell went to the spot from which his son had fallen and dropped a coin to see how long it took to hit the ground. He did this three times and each time it took precisely 2.1 seconds. Howell calculated that between the time of his son's first shout for help and the moment his body landed, it would have been something like 17.6 seconds. It must have been a terrifying ordeal for Matthew, but at least Howell left the building with some peace of mind—in the knowledge that his son was only briefly traumatised before he fell to his death.

The action was typical of Colin Howell in many ways: his detached, almost clinical approach when in extreme circumstances; his determination perhaps to create some sense of control after the event, over a situation which he never could have anticipated or imagined. The precision and methodical nature of his 'experiment' speaks volumes about an obsessive personality in the grip of a grief which threatened to overwhelm him completely. Although Matthew's death was not the final tipping point in Howell's decision to admit to murder, it certainly was a defining moment. He believed it was God's way of punishing him for what he had done 16 years earlier.

———

Over 600 people attended Matthew's funeral at Portstewart Baptist Church, where his father and stepmother Kyle, his brother Dan, and close university and school friends, paid fulsome tributes to the young man. At one point in his address to the congregation, Howell asked: 'How did we produce such a wonderful son? I believe that it was his love of Jesus in him that came out to make you feel welcome.' Lesley's name was never mentioned.

Ryan Wilson, Matthew's closest school friend, also shared some of his impressions of the young man: 'He was incredibly popular. When times were good, Matthew would be there, sharing your joy and laughing with you and when his friends faced challenges and difficulties, he would be there, willing to cry with you, or offering a judiciously chosen word of encouragement that would make you see this situation in a different way . . . I'm privileged to count myself in a number that were moulded and shaped by Matthew's wisdom and guidance at that formative time. It was his compassion, his conviction, his enormous friendliness, his principled yet grounded and down-to-earth outlook on life that people so admired.' Andrew Brown, Howell's dentist friend, simply said: 'Matthew was really good at drawing people out. That's what came out time and again. He was brilliant at making everyone feel as though they were his best friends.'

In the immediate aftermath of his son's death, Howell issued a statement, to be printed in the local press, which read: '[Matthew] was the oldest of ten children and a son who honoured his parents and brought us great pride. His home church, The Barn Fellowship in Ballymoney, will miss his energy and loving smile, as well as his frequent reports of his international travels. Matthew will be missed and we thank God for the gift of his life and the time we were allowed to enjoy him. His race is finished and we thank God for His greater knowledge and wisdom in allowing him to go to be with Jesus so soon.' The words reflected a serene acceptance of the promising young man's death. And to many of those around Howell at the time, it seemed that his response to the loss of Matthew was just that—almost unbelievably calm and accepting. He took a month off work in the wake of the bereavement, but by the time he returned to the surgery, it seemed that his life had moved on. He told his patients and staff not to worry, because Matt was now in a better place.

One of the first patients into Howell's chair when he returned from leave was a businessman from north Antrim who had been having extensive cosmetic work done—the final bill came to some £15,000. This man's appointment had to be rescheduled because of the funeral arrangements, and he was slightly apprehensive at the idea of meeting Howell again so soon after the tragedy. How do you commiserate with somebody you don't know particularly well, who has just lost his eldest son? The patient remembers the day well: 'Matthew's death didn't seem to affect him the way I thought it should have. He just accepted it. It was as if it was God's will. God had called Matthew home. He quoted a few Biblical sayings, as if to justify what happened. He went on with the work and didn't seem to be in the least concerned. That's what shocked me. I know how I would feel if I lost a son. I would be inconsolable for a long, long period of time, but he was dealing with it in a way I just didn't expect . . .' Other patients and acquaintances would have the same impression at the time: that Howell's apparently measured acceptance of his oldest son's death was somehow disconcerting. It was as if some part of him was simply able to detach himself from the reality of what had happened.

———

But the tragedy had affected Howell far more than people imagined, of course. He found himself wondering what Trevor Buchanan's father, Jim, must have felt, as he struggled to come to terms with his son's death and deal with all the unanswered questions which surround an unexplained suicide. At least, Howell realised, he had had some degree of closure about Matt: he knew what had happened, and that it had been an accident. Sixteen years after the deaths of Lesley and Trevor, the killer had gained some insight into the true extent of the misery and suffering he had inflicted on so many others back in 1991.

Chapter 17

All that Glitters

D espite his deeply conservative outlook on life, Colin Howell had always had a reckless streak, a part of him that enjoyed the thrill of living on the edge and close to danger. And while his skills in financial management had improved over the years—particularly since he had married Kyle—he had never been very good with money. But even this does not explain his decision in mid-2008 to get involved in an outlandish scheme to recover lost gold in the Philippines. In so many ways, as those around him could see only too well, it was a crazy course of action, which could only ever end in disaster and financial ruin. But maybe, at this stage in his life, deep in his heart, that is what Colin Howell really wanted. Perhaps he was already set on a course of self-destruction over which he no longer had any control.

The only type of precious metal which Colin Howell had bothered with up until this point in his life had been the gold that he used for the fillings he gave to some of his wealthier patients when he first started to practise. Yet in April 2008, he joined a treasure trail which would begin at a branch of the Northern Bank in Coleraine and extend all the way to the exotic islands of the southwest Pacific. As a friend later remarked about the whole affair: 'Sometimes truth is stranger than fiction.'

Howell had plenty of spare cash on hand. He had sold off his half-share of the practice in Bangor, and David Wilson was going to pay him £300,000 to become a full partner in the Ballymoney surgery. Howell retained his share in the building and owned the two-bedroom flat on the top floor. Although he faced two hefty tax bills, the implant business was still thriving and bringing in a very healthy income.

Before this, the dentist had dabbled a little in property. He had bought a site for building a house for the family in Florida, and at Christmas in 2006 while on holiday in Costa Rica with Kyle's sister and her husband, he decided to make another investment. His brother-in-law Joe Woo already owned properties in Costa Rica, Hong Kong and Nicaragua. From Costa Rica, the two men boarded an eight-seater plane which touched down on a grassy runway in Granada, Nicaragua, where they spent the day checking out derelict sites for building. They identified one, and Howell paid £45,000 for his half share. It was supposed to be a fun investment which they believed might—just might—make them some serious money. It all depended on the volatile politics in that region of Central America. Provided the electoral fortunes of the Sandinista movement were kept in check, the two men reckoned their site could in the future be worth up to ten times what they paid for it.

The Nicaraguan deal was of limited risk, relatively speaking, but the Philippines project was in a different league altogether. When he was first approached at the beginning of 2008, Howell had been advised by friends—especially one in The Barn Fellowship—not to get involved. Kyle had her doubts as well. He heard about the venture through a friend who had connections with an American missionary who was, it seemed, heavily involved in coordinating a scheme to recover gold which had been buried in underground bunkers during the Second World War on the orders of Japanese generals. Or at least that was what Howell was told.

The gold had allegedly been stolen in Southeast Asia by Japanese forces and then hidden away in caves and tunnels in the Philippines. It was named after the Japanese general, Admiral Yamamoto, but was never found, despite claims that some of it had turned up. Various experts have challenged and disputed that it existed at all, but the quest by treasure hunters from across the globe still continues.

Howell was told that some of the soldiers who had hidden the gold were later murdered after it emerged that its whereabouts had become known—secrecy was therefore absolutely vital. A man known as 'Alan' was the contact in Manila and, Howell's friend told him, it was to Alan that a former general, now in his 80s, had handed maps identifying six different sites where the gold was stashed, some of it up to 100 feet underground. The operation to recover it had started, but additional funding was needed. It was a tricky and delicate operation, apparently, as the bunkers were booby-trapped with explosives and filled with poisonous gas.

An Englishman and five Americans were already involved in the project, Howell was told. And so the God-fearing dentist from Castlerock agreed to invest. He had, after, all plenty of money at his disposal. It was a hare-brained idea, but he stumped up £50,000 as an initial investment. He confided in friends that he believed he could make between £10 million and £20 million from the scheme. He was convinced, in any case, that his return would be more than sufficient to finance a long retirement, pay for the upkeep of his extended family and their third-level educational requirements, and generally keep him in the style to which he was accustomed. He also wanted to be able to teach his young children at home. His outstanding tax bills could also be settled and money would be set aside as well to help various charitable projects and organisations to which he was committed. These included Family Spectrum, which deals with adults who had been victims of child abuse, and the Christian Family Centre in the village of Armoy, Country Antrim, which has close links with The Barn Fellowship. There would be money as well to build schools and orphanages in India, where Howell had been the previous October with his son Jonny and stepdaughter Katie, to check out potential sites in the state of Karnataka, where a Baptist friend from Ballymoney, Shankar Sankannawar, had once done some missionary work.

Howell made arrangements to begin transferring the money to his contact, and if anyone at the bank asked him where it was destined, he just replied: 'It's for charity. It's church work.' He mostly filled in the forms himself, but from time to time he called on others to help with the paperwork, especially in the days before he left for the Philippines, when he was very busy at the surgery.

As the months passed and Howell pumped more and more money into the project, he must have begun to wonder if his wife's reservations and the caution of his friends had been justified after all. But when, in the autumn of 2008, he was assured by the man in Manila that the excavation process was very nearly finished and that there was just another 40 feet to go, any lingering doubts he had simply disappeared. Although he had never met 'Alan', they were in regular e-mail contact and he trusted him implicitly, along with the others he knew were involved in the project. And the gold diggers were so, so close.

But Howell's resources were rapidly draining away. He and Kyle had joint bank accounts, although she didn't have any of the PIN numbers and was happy to leave her husband in full control. He realised he would have to cash in their ISAS—tax-free savings—worth about £50,000. Even this would not be enough, however, and so in desperation, the dentist then began to approach business contacts on the North Coast, to see if they would consider getting involved. He also sounded out a fellow dentist as to whether he would be interested in making an offer for the implant clinic. Howell told him that he was thinking of going to live and work in America.

Not surprisingly, none of Howell's business contacts was willing to take up the offer. One man who was approached said he simply couldn't believe what he heard when Howell came to his house to discuss their proposition. He recalls: 'I thought to myself: "Are these people wise?" But they were dead serious. There was all this hidden gold, but they [the Japanese] had put explosive devices around it. There was gas which had to be neutralised. It was all heavily guarded. All they could see was a hole in the ground and they needed more money. Howell told me he had put in £100,000 and he was going to take out millions . . . He told me the Lord's hand was in this, and he was going to get money for doing the Lord's work, funding some sort of missionary exercise. I just . . . laughed to myself. I asked him: "Who owns this gold? Is it the Japanese? Which government? Is it the landowner? Who owns the titles to the gold?" He seemed to be taken aback, because it was obvious he hadn't really thought about it. My impression is that the £100,000 [he was asking me for] would have gone to Colin Howell. It would never have seen the Philippines. It was all supposed to be very secretive, but rather than give an immediate answer, I waited and called to tell him I wasn't interested . . . It was pie-in-the-sky stuff. How could you dig up gold, bring it home without a legal contract? Colin said he could get one, but I told him it wouldn't be worth the paper it was written on . . . He then asked if I would give £80,000, £50,000: £20,000, even . . . They were nearly there: they had to pay medical bills; somebody had been injured; somebody had died. They just needed more money. He needed an answer by [the] Monday.

'Colin, I'm told, never managed money very well . . . He was never a businessman. These were supposed to be fine Christian people from a strong evangelical Christian background and, even though they took the view that the Lord provided for them, this was stretching it a bit too far. Who would want to get involved in this sort of carry-on?'

In the run-up to December 2008, staff at Howell's surgery noticed that he seemed increasingly distracted and on edge. There were whispered telephone conversations behind closed doors, and plans to spend the festive season out in Florida with Kyle, the children and his ageing father Sam began to drift. All the money the Howell family had in savings—including much of the cash he had made on the sale of the Bangor practice and what David Wilson had handed him over the previous month in return for Howell's share in the general practice in Ballymoney—had gone. A total of £353,000 had been poured into the seemingly bottomless pit of the Philippines gold venture. There was nothing left.

On 7 December 2008, Kyle left for America with her younger children to spend Christmas and the New Year with her family. Howell left Northern Ireland around the same time, but travelled in a different direction, taking a flight from London to Singapore and then a connection on to Manila. It would be the dentist's first time in the Philippines. As far as the reason for his current trip went, he didn't feel unduly worried. He confidently expected to see some of the long-awaited gold for himself, even though he had been told that some additional money was needed to buy a special neutralising chemical agent to solve the problem of the toxic gas in the tunnel.

'Alan' had arranged to meet the dentist at his hotel. Howell was expecting to see two bars of the gold which had already been recovered. At the agreed time, his man in Manila arrived, carrying two old tin ammunition boxes. Fearing that they might be booby-trapped, Howell insisted they should not be opened in his room, and so they moved elsewhere to view the contents. But as Alan opened the boxes with a flourish, Howell's face dropped. All he could see were some silver dollars and old bank notes which amounted to about $30.

Flabbergasted, the dentist immediately realised he had the victim of an elaborate scam. Looking directly at Alan, he said: 'You're a fraud, aren't you?' 'Why do you ask?' responded Alan. Howell just replied, wearily: 'Because I'm a fraud. My whole life has been a fraud.' The house of cards of Howell's expectations, of his greed and his grandiose plans for the future, had collapsed in that very moment. He had been duped by a tall story and some Filipino charm. He had handed over all the family's savings to a brazen conman.

That night, Howell paced up and down in his hotel room. He was in a daze, telling himself what an idiot he had been, reproaching himself over and over again for having been so foolish. All at once, he was distracted by the view from the fourth-floor window. Down below, he could see crowds of young girls walking up and down on the streets, offering themselves for sex. Provocatively dressed, with their pert figures on full display, Howell thought they looked so young and so pretty. He would later tell staff at the surgery about how he had watched Manila's street girls. Such a disclosure—that he had been distracted and fascinated by the spectacle of prostitutes at work at a time when his life was in crisis—from a man of such deep religious convictions, was as strange as it was unexpected.

Howell didn't eat or sleep for the next 48 hours. He thought about flying to Florida to see Kyle and break the news of their catastrophic losses, but then decided to simply go home. He returned to Ballymoney a broken man. When he managed to gather himself to go into the clinic, he told staff: 'I'm trembling inside. I don't want to talk about it.' Eventually he explained a little more, informing some of them that an investment project had gone spectacularly wrong. 'It's been a disaster,' he confided.

Some of Howell's staff were very concerned about his mental state. This was a completely different person from the one who had left for the Philippines. One of this team later told police: 'It was just like when Matthew died. He was withdrawn, not focused and completely deflated. He just wasn't thinking rationally. He wasn't thinking straight. He'd lost weight. Normally he was the driving force, but you had to take him in hand and show him what to do. We were worried about him. He seemed almost disorientated. I thought he was going to kill himself.'

Andrew Brown, his dentist friend and confidant, and also a member of The Barn Fellowship, was so concerned that he contacted Dental Protection—the professional indemnity association for dentists—to seek advice, although he did not give the identity of the person on whose behalf he was making the enquiries. He believed that Howell was no longer capable of treating patients.

Kyle had returned from Florida at the beginning of January, ordering her husband to be out of the family home before she got back. She too had fears about Howell's state of mind, and would not allow him to take one of the boys to a rugby tournament in Dublin because she was worried for the child's safety. It was different when he called in to the family home each evening, to say goodnight to the children—then at least, she was close at hand and could keep an eye on what was going on. But she was not prepared to take the risk of entrusting her son into the care of a man who was clearly losing touch with reality.

Howell's financial situation was now critical. Not only had he squandered all their savings in the madcap investment venture, but he had serious debts. Patients had paid him a total of £230,000 up front for various treatments he might not be able to complete. The dentist also still faced two huge tax demands: one for capital gains on the sale of his share of the practice in Bangor, and the other a projected income bill from the Inland Revenue. His tax bills were estimated at £250,000.

He was in emotional, spiritual and physical meltdown. After all these years living a lie and deceiving so many people, it had suddenly hit him just how much of a cheat and hypocrite he had been for so long. Now he had no choice but to face the music and accept the harsh reality of what his life had been all about. Like all deeply troubled evangelicals, it was time to bring everything—all those desperately dark secrets—'to the Cross'.

It just was not just the loss of all his money, of course. Howell had known when he packed his suitcase in Manila and ordered a taxi to the airport, that much, much more had taken him to the dead end he now found himself in. Like Matthew's death, the fiasco in the Philippines was another defining moment for the killer—and almost certainly the tipping point. Perhaps, as his friend Andrew Brown later surmised when he spoke to police, it really was the workings of Divine Providence which had led him here. The bright light of the truth was about to shatter his dark world. There would be no escape for Colin Howell this time.

Chapter 18

'Hiding, but not Hiding . . .'

FEBRUARY 2009

A t North Antrim Magistrates' Court in Coleraine on Monday, 2 February 2009, Colin Howell was formally charged with the double murder before District Judge Richard Wilson. He spoke twice: once to confirm his date of birth, 8 March 1959, and once to say that he understood the charges against him. Even though he had only lived there for a month, his address was given as Sea Road, Castlerock: the caravan park where he had been staying since Kyle had ordered him out of Glebe Road. It was the opening phase of a quite remarkable legal process. The courtroom was packed. Members of Trevor Buchanan's family sat to his left, towards the front. Howell, who had been led handcuffed into the dock, was flanked on either side by two prison officers. Expressionless, he just stared at the floor in front of him.

Detective Inspector Ian Magee gave evidence of the arrest and said he believed that he could connect the accused with the two murders. When he had first been charged, Howell answered: 'I'm sorry.' His defence lawyer Francis Rafferty said there would be no application for bail, and the prisoner was quickly led away.

On the day of his arrest, Howell had been questioned in an interview room at Coleraine police station by Detective Constables Alan Devine and Anne Henry. Devine, the lead inquisitor, invited him to speak: 'Is there anything you want to tell us, Mr Howell, in your own words?' Howell replied: 'Can you advise me on what the starting point is?' Over the next three days—off and on—the two officers sat and listened, sometimes in disbelief, as Howell proceeded to recount, calmly and matter-of-factly, what had happened at his home that night in 1991, and how he had ended up with two bodies in the boot of his car in Castlerock in the early hours of the next day.

There was never any doubt in the minds of the police investigation team as to his culpability, not even when he pleaded 'Not Guilty' when he was sent for trial the following year. The plea did not, however, represent a change of mind on Howell's part. The lengthy delay in publicly admitting what he had done was due to a legal process which required that his mental state be investigated. Could the accused have been suffering from some form of diminished responsibility when he gassed his wife and Trevor Buchanan? If so, then the court would have to take that into account. And so the prisoner had to undergo a series of searching psychiatric assessments in order to try to establish what his state of mind might have been at the time, and if he was suffering from any form of mental disorder.

After he was charged, Colin Howell was remanded in custody to Maghaberry prison, where he would stay for almost two years before the completion of the legal process. Although Howell would become a model prisoner, settling relatively well into his new surroundings, there was a time, shortly after he was first incarcerated, when life in jail became unbearable for him. At this point, he would require psychiatric intervention which had nothing to do with the proposed examinations by consultant psychiatrists to establish, on behalf of his defence team, his state of mind at the time of the murders and in the intervening years.

The crisis happened in the months after he was charged, when Kyle left him without any farewells and returned to the United States with their five children, with the intention of beginning divorce proceedings. Howell had more or less anticipated that she would leave the country at some point, but the manner of her departure without warning left him devastated.

He was found one day sitting in a chair in his cell, rocking back and forward and sighing from time to time, with his head in his hands. Later, in the prison hospital, he tried to push his head under the handle of an oxygen trolley. He had lost weight and looked unkempt. Medical staff were worried about his deteriorating mental state and general well-being. He was considered a suicide risk and was admitted for an extended period to the prison's healthcare unit for close observation and psychiatric assessment. Howell was claiming he had been bullied and threatened, and that he was being watched and followed. He had difficulty sleeping and became acutely agitated, expressing thoughts of a dramatic and nihilistic nature, and claiming that he heard intrusive voices 'telling him to kill, cook and eat his family members, and then himself'.

Howell was due to undergo a series of psychiatric examinations anyway, as we have seen, as part of his defence. These were to be conducted by Professor Nigel Eastman and Dr Philip Joseph, both from London, as well as Dr Helen Harbinson from Bangor, County Down—each consultant would carry out their own independent assessments. Eminent and highly respected psychiatrist Dr Harbinson met with the prisoner six times in total. She first assessed him in May 2009, when he was still in the throes of his apparent mental breakdown. At this point, Howell was not considered to be in a fit state to face further questioning by the police, who wanted to enquire in greater detail into allegations of inappropriate behaviour with some of his female patients.

Dr Harbinson, who noted that the prisoner had had no previous psychiatric history, found him on this occasion to be tense and perplexed throughout their exchange. His speech was slow and very hesitant, and it was difficult to follow his train of thought. He had lost his appetite and, accordingly, a lot of weight. Before he was admitted to jail, medical records showed that he had weighed 85 kilos, but, the consultant noted, the clothes he wore now looked loose. He had difficulty sleeping, and during the day felt tired and tormented. He had vivid dreams of destruction, hell and demons.

In her report on this first session, Dr Harbinson recorded Howell's repeated claims that everything had a meaning, and that the meaning in each case related to the matter of his destruction. Television programmes referred to him. For example, in soap operas, there was always a character who tried to trivialise how he had treated others, until he was suddenly confronted with the reality of his life. Such men had no friends and no family support, and Howell believed there was a message for him in this. He then went on to insist: 'My whole life has been on television,' describing a film called *The Truman Show* starring Jim Carrey. The chief character in this film, he explained, had been on television since birth, but did not discover this fact until he was in his mid-40s. Dr Harbinson recorded: 'He believes his life is like that and he did not realise it until he came into prison. He believes his whole life has been scrutinised since he was born.' Howell claimed that he was the only one who did not know he was on TV.

He told the consultant that he struggled with denial and reality: 'At times, I see clearly and can say certain things to certain people. Most of the time, I hide from what's happening.' He described his dreams as hellish and himself as 'forced into resistance'. He now believed he should have taken time and learned how to live with the people in his life. When asked who he thought was scrutinising him, he replied: 'God sees everything and we all have to give an account to him some day.' God's attitude towards him, he claimed, was one of destruction and that would not change. His future was not good. God was in control and had chosen to destroy him. This annihilation would take the form of some sort of ritualistic event, when he would be burned or attacked by warriors from a sect or group, using knives or swords. The ritual, Howell explained, would be the sort which would have been engaged in by the Romans, Spartans or Aztecs.

Howell was asked if he thought of killing himself. He said he was not in control of that, but that it was not in God's plan for him, and even if he tried, it would not work. Torment was God's plan for him and there was a 'whole system' geared against him. He said that it was hard to describe this system: it was unreal, he explained, and yet most of the time it was happening. He concluded: 'It's as if I'm the focal point of everyone's future. My destruction is part of that future.' Everyone in the world thought his destruction would save the world, he said, but he knew it would not. He was intimidated and controlled by others, and that too was part of God's plan. The fact that he had been given medication against his will was part of the plan, he told the doctor. He was on anti-depressant medication, but, he told Dr Harbinson: 'No medication will fix this.'

Howell said he wondered if Satan controlled his mind, or if he could control it himself. He described his mood as more 'oppressed' than 'depressed'. It did not matter, he claimed, what choice he made—the outcome would always be negative. When asked by the psychiatrist to give her an example of what he meant, he told her that he got up early one day and felt he ought to clean the ward bathroom. He had stopped cleaning, however, because he had a bad feeling about it. A prisoner, he said, told him that he had disturbed a dragon's den, and so he decided not to clean any more. He believed the prisoner was right and that it was all connected with his dreams of demons and torments.

When Dr Harbinson asked Howell if he believed that he deserved to be tormented, he replied: 'There should be a limiting factor. This punishment may not have a limiting factor.' What did he deserve to be punished for, she queried. Howell responded darkly: 'I had a purpose and calling. That would have prevented billions of people from being destroyed.' He said he was not sure whether he was like Noah, who rescued a small number of people, or Moses, who rescued a whole nation. He was then asked if he deserved to be punished for killing his wife and Trevor Buchanan. Howell replied: 'I didn't go back that far.' He said he believed the system would set him up, but he was not sure if he had been set up already. God was behind the system.

Howell said he could often hear a voice inside his head, and that at times it was his wife's voice (he did not say whether it was the voice of Lesley or of Kyle). His concentration was poor. He jumped from one thought to the next. He could not read a newspaper. His memory was poor and he was frequently forgetful. He did not talk to staff or other prisoners. Howell then told Dr Harbinson that he had been spending a lot of time in bed, 'hiding, but not hiding', and concluded: 'You can't hide from your thoughts.'

It had been a very strange interview. Dr Harbinson's report concluded that Howell had 'depressive, religious, grandiose and persecutory delusions'. But was he really, as the highly experienced psychiatrist suspected at the time, going through some kind of psychotic episode? Or was it merely a case of the scheming and manipulative Howell at work again, trying to bluff the authorities by preparing the groundwork for a psychiatric defence? The various claims and convictions he had voiced were bizarre in the extreme, almost the stuff of casebook psychosis as sometimes featured in horror films and TV dramas. Was Howell play-acting, trying to create the impression that he was suffering from some form of madness? On one occasion, displaying the classic symptoms of paranoia, he asked staff if he could see Dr Harbinson in a storeroom in the prison hospital, because he feared the area where the visits normally took place was bugged. The psychiatrist refused his request.

During Hazel Stewart's trial some 18 months later, the killer admitted that during his early psychiatric assessments, he had indeed adopted a strategy in a bid to get a reduced sentence—although he also conceded that he had been in a very fragile mental state at the time. Before he had surrendered himself to the police, he recounted, he had powered up his computer and Googled prison tariffs, to check the length of the sentence he could expect to receive for a double murder. He discovered that if he pleaded guilty to manslaughter because of diminished responsibility, he might get eight to ten years, instead of the 30 he anticipated the court would otherwise impose. It was an option he seriously considered. Kyle was no longer in the country, and he had thought to himself: 'Who is going to catch me?' As he told the court: 'I became seduced into the whole idea [of securing a lighter sentence] because I was mentally sick, so I went through a phase of manipulating and deceiving, knowing that I had something going wrong and I was distressed mentally—but also manipulating and deceiving something in the legal system that I knew would be a huge benefit to me.'

He had cheated the legal process before, but ultimately, he decided that he would deceive no more. There would be no more lies. He was now on a journey of truth: 'I wanted to be free from all of the delusion that you can fall into, that psychiatrists bring you into. It's a personal conviction. It's a system that is used and can be abused.' And then he would add, as only Howell could: 'I have been told not to preach by my [legal] team, but I have to say it. Based on my faith and based on what the Testament said, if you confess your sins to God, Jesus is faithful and just, and will forgive your sins and cleanse you from all of the unrighteousness.'

When Dr Harbinson examined him again the following month, she found his condition considerably improved—although, she recorded, he continued to be distressed by the loss of his freedom, the consequences of the murders, and the impact on the families involved. Although he was intelligent, Howell told her, he had little insight or wisdom. He did, however, try to rationalise his confession as the doctor's notes detailed: 'He thinks that perhaps he confessed because at some level, he realised the need to come into prison to appreciate fully the consequences of what he has done. At the time of his arrest, many things in his life were out of control, including his finances and his marriage.'

Unlike other prisoners, Howell told the consultant, he was giving evidence against himself and was finding his decision difficult: 'I'm struggling with the consequences.' He was still on suicide watch, but, he insisted, that was not necessary because he had no intention of committing suicide, as Dr Harbinson's notes confirmed: 'He wants to experience the consequences of his behaviour. Therefore he will not take his life. He said to do so would be like shooting himself in the foot. Had he been going to commit suicide, he would have done so, instead of confessing.' Howell said he now felt less tormented, and believed he had been mentally ill and that there was a spiritual dimension to it. Demons he believed, could manifest as illness, in the way they did in the Bible—such as epilepsy, deafness and lameness. The mind could also be altered by demons, but helped by medicine, although medicine was not a cure.

Howell told Dr Harbinson that when he killed his wife and Trevor, he had had a choice, but did not feel at the time as if he had. Similarly, while he now had to face charges of sexual assault, he had not, he insisted, wanted to sexually assault any of his victims and he had regretted it afterwards: it had been like an addiction. He had known it was wrong, and so he had to hide it. Since going into prison, he was now saying, he had gained logic. Everyone had areas of weakness, and sex was his Achilles heel. With hindsight, he realised that what he had done was avoidable. He had now lost the compulsion and fully understood the consequences of his actions.

Howell also told the doctor that he was no longer experiencing any auditory hallucinations. As for his paranoia, he now believed there had been an understandable reason for it. Before he was transferred to the prison hospital, he explained, he had been frightened by a number of Polish prisoners who were playing pool. One of them had been staring at him incessantly and then a number of them slowly manoeuvred their way across the room and blocked one of the CCTV cameras. He felt that it had been rehearsed and that he was at risk. He had heard rumours that he would be harmed, and believed that had he stayed in the same position, he would have been attacked. So he moved. He mentioned it to another prisoner, who told him he was paranoid. At the time he believed he heard a voice telling him to move, but he was no longer troubled by voices.

Dr Harbinson then asked Howell again about the incident in the ward bathroom—when he had thought that by cleaning the place, he was disturbing a dragon's den. Dragons, he told her, were like demons. He believed that the prisoner who told him about the dragon's den had implied there was witchcraft at work. There had been a number of items set out in an orderly way in the bathroom, which he took as an indication of witchcraft. At that stage, his instinct told him it was witchcraft. He now believed that the other prisoner was mentally ill. Howell also confided that he was no longer preoccupied with sacrifice and rituals and the belief that he would be killed in a ritualistic way.

When the doctor mentioned his ideas about his life appearing on television, he now explained that these had been triggered by his belief that God could see everything. He described how in the Old Testament, King David had committed adultery with Bathsheba and then arranged for her husband, Uriah, to be killed on the battlefield. That had all been done in God's sight. He no longer believed, however, that his whole life had been played out on television.

Howell repeated that his criminal behaviour was compulsive and that his sexual behaviour had been like an addiction. Death and murder had not bothered him 18 years ago, he told the doctor. Lesley had had three pregnancies terminated before they married; Hazel had had one abortion, although he was not sure if he had been responsible for her pregnancy. They were wrong, but he did not see that at the time. He now viewed abortion and suicide differently. He explained that his actions had been carried out in a situation of intense emotional strain: 'I couldn't see outside the pressure cooker situation which I had created. I couldn't see any other way out.'

As for his confession, some days he thought it had been the right thing to do. On other days, however, he regretted it. And at times he felt selfish because he had distressed so many people. He had thought that it would be important for Lesley's memory and honour, and for the Buchanan family as well, that he should be truthful. Now, he believed he had not thought through his confession or the consequences properly.

During this interview, Dr Harbinson recorded, the prisoner appeared relaxed and composed. His speech was spontaneous; he was not depressed, deluded or experiencing hallucinations; his concentration and memory were good. He was preoccupied with religious and spiritual matters, but only in a way that would be in keeping with his faith. Commenting further on this aspect of Howell's mindset, the consultant noted: 'It can be difficult to distinguish between deeply-held religious beliefs and delusions. A delusion is defined as a fixed, false belief out of keeping with the person's culture and background. There is no doubt, however, that Mr Howell's belief that killing his first wife and Trevor Buchanan was merciful was peculiar to him. Religious themes featured prominently in his delusions in 2009, following his imprisonment. A religious faith can give hope, meaning and purpose and can contribute to a sense of mental well-being. I think that in Mr Howell's case, the church provided an environment where his needs for attention, admiration and control were met.'

The report for the second session concluded: 'His presentation is consistent with a personality disorder, principally narcissistic in type. This would predispose him to psychotic episodes. His personality disorder is evidenced by his grandiosity, his need for admiration and his lack of empathy. Disregard for the feelings of others and a sense of entitlement permeate his thinking and behaviour. This grandiosity and need for admiration were particularly evident during his second interview with me, where he described himself as 'a small god' who needed to be worshipped by women. The aetiology of his personality disorder is not obvious. There is no evidence that he experienced the abuse or neglect found in the case histories of many children who go on to develop personality disorders.'(During Hazel Stewart's trial, Howell challenged the 'small god' observation, claiming that Dr Harbinson misunderstood what he had said.)

By the time of Howell's final interview with Dr Harbinson in April 2010, his anti-psychotic and anti-depressant medication had been stopped and he appeared to have fully recovered from the psychosis he had suffered from in the early months of his stay in prison. Although she now considered him fit to plead, Dr Harbinson said there was evidence of a deterioration in his mental state which would require further monitoring.

All three psychiatrists questioned Howell at length over a number of months about his personality, his psychosexual history and his relationships with Lesley, Hazel and Kyle. All three doctors more or less came to the same conclusion—that Colin Howell was bad, but not mad. He exhibited a narcissistic personality disorder, and there might have been evidence of mental disturbance at various points in his life. He was a fantasist who could manipulate, deceive and control;

he took chances and was often delusional; he was 'a charming, controlled psychopath'.

———

18 NOVEMBER 2010

It took almost 20 years for Colin Howell to stand up and publicly admit his guilt—and just under 10 minutes for a judge to sentence him to life imprisonment.

The prison van which had brought him to Belfast Crown Court arrived late, after making a detour to avoid flooded roads in the Antrim countryside—but everybody was ready and in place in the courtroom on the fourth floor when the cell door opened. The prisoner wore handcuffs as he made his way to the dock and, after what seemed like an eternity, a woman warder turned a key to free his wrists. He sat grey and gaunt, wearing a pressed light grey suit with a white shirt and brown and navy tie, and braced himself for what was to come.

Howell spoke just three times: to confirm his name, and then, when the two murder charges were read out by a court clerk, to reply 'Guilty' in each instance—just loud enough for those in the crowded public gallery behind him to hear. Trevor Buchanan's two sisters, Melva and Valerie, and his five brothers, Gordon, Victor, Jackie, Raymond and Robert, were all there, as were Lesley's brother, Chris Clarke and her son Dan and daughter Lauren.

Six days later, plans to swear in a jury for the start of Hazel Stewart's trial had to be delayed, after it was confirmed that Howell had made a new and lengthy statement to police, which ran to 43 pages. He had agreed to be the so-called 'star witness' to testify against his former lover—raising speculation that he was going into the witness box in return for a reduced sentence. But, as was later confirmed, there had been no such 'deal' in place.

29 NOVEMBER 2010

At Howell's pre-sentence hearing, the formidable Richard Weir QC said he had been instructed by Howell to express his profound regret and deep remorse. These were not merely hollow words, since his client had made a voluntary confession long after the murders had been committed and when the wisp of suspicion had completely faded. Weir continued: 'The perfect crime is an unwholesome concept, and if its definition is the evasion of prosecution and a subsequent pronouncement of guilt, then Colin Howell's crime fulfilled that. But that definition leaves out the existence and action of conscience which is what we say ultimately led to these crimes being admitted.'

Anyone knowing the bare facts of the case could legitimately describe the crimes as monstrous, Mr Weir acknowledged. But, he continued, anyone knowing Colin Howell before and after the murders would find it unimaginable that he could do such monstrous things, because he was an upstanding, effective and worthy member of society—not a monster: 'It was quite plain that it was grossly distorted thinking which led to this appalling and monstrous crime. The distortion of reason might be viewed as bad enough, but the plan which sprang from it—and the activation of that plan—was caused by Colin Howell's departure from all that was his true self: a decent, upstanding, hard-working, religious and valuable member of society . . . Whatever chemistry there was between him and Hazel Buchanan, one of its by-products was undoubtedly the toxin that enabled the plan, not just for him to kill his wife, but to kill them both and for them to be together. He always accepted his role in the planning and conduct of the crimes and he had never attempted to minimise that.'

After the murders, Mr Weir told the court, Colin Howell had been visited by unhappiness, discord and tragedy, brought on by himself. Having escaped detection, he did not live happily ever after. He made a revelation to his second wife Kyle in the late 1990s, and later to the police. It was an instance of someone whose conscience had eventually ruled him and brought him to this point. Howell regarded the death of his son Matthew in an accident as another awful outcome from the sins he had committed and concealed. He also went on to invest in a scheme in the Philippines which was almost transparently a fraud: 'The court might take the view, or at least ask the question— was that a symptom of Colin Howell seeking out his own destruction, his downfall?'

Mr Weir's concluding remarks asked for due consideration to be given to Howell's sense of remorse and the fact that he had been moved to confess to his crimes, albeit so many years later: 'He accepts entirely how bad and monstrous these matters are, but there is a man there, not a monster—a man who allowed distorted thinking, a loss of reason, and illicit passion to completely destroy the lives of his victims. On any reading he will be a very old man before he is even considered for release . . . There must be some significant credit for the fact that he has confessed, and confessed without any external force upon him. Only by reason of conscience and knowledge that he is a fraud of the worst kind, who destroyed people's lives, family life. That is an indicator of the genuine remorse he has.'

3 DECEMBER 2010

Just before he handed down the duration of the sentence, Judge Hart revealed that, had Howell been convicted by a jury, he would have sent him to jail for a minimum of 28 years. Then, for the best part of the next half hour, the prisoner closed his eyes and sat head bowed, as the judge detailed how he had murdered innocent people and deprived six children of the love of their mother and father.

Judge Hart summed up: 'These were truly heinous crimes, constituting as they did the cold-blooded, carefully planned and ruthlessly executed double murder of two people who Howell saw as standing in the way of his adulterous desire to be with Hazel Buchanan. Each murder was carried out when the victim was asleep and thus entirely defenceless. Even when they stirred in their sleep, Howell did not draw back and spare their lives, but physically subdued their faint signs of approaching consciousness, thereby ensuring their deaths.' The judge recounted how he had studied a number of confidential statements from relatives in both families, all of which showed that many lives had been gravely affected for many years by the murders. By staging the deaths as suicides, Howell had caused further irreparable damage in the lives of the children of Lesley and Trevor: 'The reputations of their innocent parents, who had already been wronged by Mr Howell, were further stigmatised by the false implication that they had taken their own lives in a suicide pact.'

The only mitigating factor in the case, the Judge said, was Howell's confession and his willingness to give evidence for the Prosecution. The confessions were a factor that had to be taken into account in his favour, not least because, had he not confessed, he would never have been brought to justice for the crimes. He had accepted his guilt and given practical expression to his remorse. The judge concluded: 'Unpalatable though it may seem to many, the courts recognise that criminals who plead guilty should receive a lesser sentence than would have been the case had they been convicted after a trial, because by doing so they publicly accept their guilt. Tragically, murders of those who are seen as standing in the way of the fulfilment of lustful desires are not uncommon in this jurisdiction.'

Judge Hart then sentenced Colin Howell to life, with a minimum jail term of 21 years.

Chapter 19
A 'Joint Venture'?
The Hazel Stewart Trial: Part One

Hazel Stewart had always been a smart dresser—designer labels only, if she could possibly help it. And in the months before her arrest, she had never looked better. On the night of the Police Chief Constable's Ball, 5 December 2008—when the great and the good on the North Coast sat down to a sumptuous meal and then danced into the wee small hours at Portrush's Royal Court Hotel—she had looked dazzling. That evening, Hazel was in her element as she moved into the pre-dinner reception, nursing a glass of white wine, her usual tipple. At her side was her husband, an ex-Chief Superintendent, who, long divorced from his first wife but now hopelessly in love again, had persisted in his efforts to persuade Hazel to marry him. For a woman with such deep religious convictions and heady social aspirations, surely life could not get any better?

Just a few short months later, Stewart was a changed woman, however, in circumstances which could not have been more different. The tanned good looks and shapely figure, which she maintained with regular sessions in the gym at Fitness First, where she once attracted so many admiring glances as she worked out in her lycra all-in-one, had gone. The woman who appeared at Coleraine Magistrates' Court on Monday, 2 February 2009 was pale, gaunt and drably dressed—and so distressed that she could hardly get to her feet when called to rise, so she could be formally charged.

By this time, Stewart was living at a beautifully fitted-out, recently built detached house in the countryside on the Ballystrone Road, Macosquin, a few miles outside Coleraine. This was where she had been arrested the previous Thursday by the same three police officers who had arrived on Howell's doorstep. Sergeant Soren Stewart and Detective Constables Kidd and Parish were met at the front door by David Stewart, who invited them in. His wife, he told them, was at the dentist's, but would be back soon. The officers would not tell him the reason for their visit, and asked Stewart not to contact his wife because they feared she then might not return to the house. They sat waiting for 45 minutes in a small room, no doubt admiring the quality of the décor which had all the hallmarks of Hazel's expensive tastes.

Eventually the woman of the house pulled up in her black VW Golf. She was wearing a cream coloured three-quarter length coat, dark jeans and ankle boots—but the colour drained from her face when she realised who was waiting for her. The police officers did not even have to introduce themselves: she knew why they were there. It was what she had always feared—the knock on the door, the tap on the shoulder which would signal the end of life as she knew it. Hazel began trembling and fell into a chair with a look of resignation. She was allowed a few private minutes with her husband and then taken to the waiting police car. As she was driven to Coleraine police station, she did not say a word. At the reception desk when they arrived, she asked: 'Am I going to be here long? Will I be getting out later today?'

Although Howell had been remanded in custody when he had been charged, Richard Wilson, the district judge who presided over the hearing, took a different view in Stewart's case—despite police objections to bail. Inspector Magee said that the application to refuse bail was based on the grounds of the accused's welfare and safety: 'There is a clear intimation to me, and my team, that, should she be released, she may well take her own life. It would be my main concern.' While he acknowledged that she had the support of her husband, he added: 'It is very difficult to keep an eye on someone 24 hours a day.'

Stewart's husband David, who addressed the court that day, insisted, however, that their home would provide Hazel with a much safer environment than the women's prison at Hydebank in Belfast— a view shared by Stewart's solicitor, Stephen Hastings. Mr Stewart declared that he was convinced that his wife would not cause him or her children any difficulties if she were allowed to remain at home with them: he would do everything to keep her safe. His wife, he said, had an extremely close relationship with the children: they considered her to be their best friend.

District Judge Wilson said he was prepared to grant bail, provided that certain conditions were met. Stewart would have to surrender her passport, report daily to the police in Coleraine, and sign off on bail terms totalling £15,000: a sum which would be forfeited if she failed to turn up for her next court appearance.

Stewart returned home in a deep depression. In the weeks that followed she lost weight, found it difficult to concentrate and sleep, and her family were deeply worried about her general health and mental state. Obviously bewildered by the turn of events, David Stewart asked his wife over and over again to explain her actions: what exactly had happened that night in May 1991? These questions on his part would continue over a number of weeks—sometimes for as a little as ten minutes at a time, but generally for longer. He repeatedly asked one question in particular: 'Why did you not shout and scream and warn Trevor when Howell came to the house?' Stewart's son and daughter, Lisa and Andrew, also struggled to comprehend and come to terms with the truth of the circumstances of their father's death. But they never for a moment, it seemed, entertained the idea that their mother was culpable. They remained, unwaveringly, 100 per cent loyal to Hazel: as far as they were concerned, Howell was solely and completely to blame.

Meanwhile, Stewart's sisters took her for walks on mostly deserted nearby beaches in an effort to try and raise her spirits. Of necessity, but by choice too, she became a virtual recluse. She no longer frequented the gym in Coleraine, which she had so zealously attended previously. She also stopped going to services at Portstewart Baptist Church with her husband.

Eventually, Hazel's mood picked up. She began travelling to Omagh sometimes to visit her mother Peggy, and even though this was not the Hazel of old, she gradually got out and about again, taking herself off to places where she would not be instantly recognised. She was once spotted in some of Belfast's fashion shops wearing a large pair of sunglasses. Later, she even felt confident enough to return to her part-time job as a clerk for a local pharmaceutical company. Hazel had been working there for several years before her arrest. All talk of her predicament was banned in the office, as one of her then colleagues confirms: '[Hazel] was likeable, efficient and very good at her job. Nobody was allowed to speak with her about the case.'

As the date of her trial for murders drew ever closer, Stewart's sense of apprehension began to loom large once more. Although the hearing had originally been scheduled for November 2010, she was given a few months' further reprieve, due to the fact that her psychiatric assessments had not yet been completed. There was also a last-minute change on her legal team, and so the Judge agreed to postpone her trial until the following February.

The trial turned out to be the most dramatic and sensational in Northern Ireland for many decades. While Hazel might have been beginning to regain a little of her old sparkle in the latter months of 2010, by February 2011 she once more cut a very sombre figure as she took her place in the dock at Coleraine Crown Court. Thin and drawn, she was only a shadow of her former self. She was dressed in dark slacks and a plain tweed coat, which she kept tightly buttoned for most of the lengthy time she spent in the dock. The only adornment she wore at all times was a rather prominent silver cross around her neck.

––––

From the beginning of the court case, and even during the four long days that Howell would be in the witness box, Hazel Stewart seemed to be somehow removed from what was happening around her. She just sat there, day after day: expressionless, her head tilted to the one side, never making eye contact with the former in-laws sitting to her right, or with Howell, as he swept past her more than once to take the stand. The only time she seemed to show any signs of animation was when she peered over at the strained faces of her husband and two children on the left of the courtroom, seeking to make eye contact with them and when she did, mouthing as if to say, 'Don't worry. I'm alright.'

She was frisked every time she presented herself at the entrance to the dock, and would hold her arms wide as one of the wardens ran her hands down her sides, before she sat down—just left of centre—on the wooden bench. Two officers, sometimes both female, sometimes one of them a man, sat on either side of her.

The jury was chosen in less than an hour. No objections were raised by Mr Ciaran Murphy, QC, counsel for the Public Prosecution Service, or by Mr Paul Ramsey, Stewart's QC. Each of the 12 jurors was offered the choice between taking the oath and making an affirmation. All took the oath. As chance would have it, the jury selected for Stewart's case comprised nine men and three women: whether this would work in her favour or not would of course remain to be seen.

One of Northern Ireland's top judges, Mr Justice Hart, who was presiding over the trial, then requested that all the Crown witnesses be brought into the courtroom. As Stewart caught sight of some of the familiar faces of those who crowded into the court, it must have seemed like a Coleraine Baptist Church reunion, from the days when so many young couples and their children, some of them new to the borough, took their places each Sunday in the Abbey Street church. There was Linda Brockbank, who had been so good to her at the time of Trevor's death; Derek McAuley, husband of Hilary, her then best friend, and the man who had steamed open the letter Howell had given him to deliver to Hazel on the day of Lesley's funeral; Dr Alan Topping, who had been a great friend of Trevor's. There was Topping's wife, Margaret, who had visited Lesley just days before she was murdered, and Jim Flanagan and former detective David Green, the two church elders who had found the bodies that fateful morning.

Some of Lesley's closest friends were to be called as witnesses too. These included Shirley McPhillimy and Carolyn Young, Gillian Alcorn and Ruth Middleton; also Tania Donaghy and Betty Bradley. Leslie Clyde, the former police colleague of Trevor's, and Trevor McAuley, Hazel's loyal companion of eight years, were also among the witnesses who crowded into the courtroom.

Mr Murphy began by outlining the Prosecution case. He ran through the shocking and gruesome details of how Lesley and Trevor had met their deaths almost 20 years previously, as a result of a 'joint plan' conceived by the two accused; he spoke of how the murders had been covered up by Howell and Stewart; he touched upon the way in which Stewart, when confronted by arresting officers in 2009, had exclaimed: 'What? What? What evidence? What has been said?' In conclusion, Murphy summed up the key premise of the line the Prosecution would be taking: that—'Hazel Stewart knowingly entered into this agreement and assisted Colin Howell in ensuring he could safely kill her husband, and afterwards they both covered up the whole thing.'

The first of the Prosecution witnesses were called: Jim Flanagan, a former languages teacher at Coleraine Academical Institution, and

David Green, the ex-detective who had gone on to open an art gallery in Coleraine. Green spoke of the suspicions he had had from the outset, and Flanagan described Howell's demeanour after he had been told that his wife was dead: 'There was no overwhelming sadness as one might have expected.' Next up to the stand, Margaret Topping disclosed how Lesley believed Howell had tried to electrocute her as she was having a bath; she also spoke of her friend's dismay at the affair, telling the court: 'She was very sad, embarrassed, very hurt and kept asking: "Why was I not number one?"'

Alan Topping told the court of his astonishment that the relationship between Howell and Stewart had continued after the deaths, saying that there had been questions in people's minds about the deaths at the time: 'Everyone did not believe it was a suicide.' When his turn came, however, Jack Hutchinson, the detective who headed up the inquiry, insisted to the jury that no one raised any such suspicions with him. He chose his words with caution: 'People felt bad about what had happened, but nobody made any categorical insinuations of criminal complicity.' It was clearly a well-rehearsed answer.

Leslie Clyde, Trevor's former police colleague, revealed that his devastated friend had told him that the church wanted the affair kept quiet. He recalled Trevor's words: 'In other words [the church was saying], "Let's not tell the whole world, but try to get it sorted out in the church."'

John Hansford, the church pastor who had counselled the two couples in a bid to save their marriages, had travelled with his wife Liz from their current home in Javea, Spain in order to give his testimony that day. No doubt his new role—ministering to a Baptist congregation of ex-pats on the Costa Blanca—is a far cry from the trials and tribulations of his days in Coleraine at the beginning of the 1990s. As he now took the stand to address the court, Hansford must have been struck by the dramatic change in the appearance and circumstances of Hazel, one of his former Sunday School teachers. He related how, just weeks before the murders, he had brought the two husbands together in his office: how an apparently penitential Howell had held out his hand in an act of reconciliation: 'He offered his sincere apologies for what he had done and sought his [Trevor's] forgiveness.' Howell was, of course, being his usual deceitful self, but neither the pastor nor Trevor was to know this at the time.

The next Crown witness, Trevor McAuley, was clearly nervous about having to testify. The man Hazel had turned to after walking away from Howell, and had subsequently kept at arms' length during a long and sometimes difficult relationship, was able to corroborate the bizarre details of Stewart's claims to him that Howell sometimes sedated her before sex. When Neil Connor, Mr Murphy's junior counsel, asked why Howell might have done such a thing, McAuley replied: 'So he could enjoy sexual gratification with her without her feeling guilty about it, while he was able to have pleasure.' The witness was not the only one in the courtroom to shift uncomfortably in his seat as he offered the explanation.

Next, Lesley's brother, Chris Clarke, now a hospital anaesthetist in the north of England, talked of his surprise at the time when he learned his sister had had £212,000 in her will—money which, he claimed, was subsequently pocketed by Howell. Then it was the turn of the dentist's old school friend, Marshall Reilly, who said that he too had been taken aback when, in the months after Lesley's death, Howell had repaid him the £10,000 he had borrowed from him: 'He told me one of the consequences was the life insurance had come in and he was now able to pay me back.'

Graham Stirling and Willie Patterson, two of the three elders from The Barn Christian Fellowship who were privy to Howell's astonishing confession, described the dramatic events of the day Howell handed himself over to the police. Patterson told Mr Justice Hart: 'He was stressed to the point of being distressed. He was agitated, his eyes were staring. He was jumpy and nervous.' Stirling commented: 'I think there was an element of bravado about [Colin's] endeavour to hoodwink the police . . .'

With more and more details of the terrible events of the night of 18 May 1991 emerging, as well as the bizarre and shocking revelations about the double life which both Howell and Stewart had been leading in the 20 years since, the opening three days of the trial were taxing and intense for all those in the courtroom, especially of course for the accused, her family and the families of the victims. But the drama was about to be ratcheted up to a whole new level. It was now the turn of the Crown's star witness to take the stand.

Chapter 20
'Waltzing Together in Time'

The Hazel Stewart Trial: Part Two

14 FEBRUARY 2011

Colin Howell had waited almost two years for this moment, and the timing of his arrival in the witness box seemed to be just right. He slipped into the seat, set down his reading glasses, pushed aside a small plastic water tumbler and then adjusted the microphone, to make sure the jury and all those inside Court No. 2 could hear his every word.

It was St Valentine's Day, and with his former lover and one-time confidante sitting just yards away, his entry on this day of all days could not have been more fittingly choreographed in the latest episode of the dark tragedy in which he and she had the leading roles. Hazel Stewart might have caught a fleeting, sideways glimpse as he emerged from the cells behind and made his way to the witness box. The woman with whom he was once besotted and had wanted to marry all those years ago, dropped her head and looked away as he stepped out and brushed past the glass panel separating her from the rest of a courtroom already filled to capacity in anticipation of his appearance.

Was this really the same fit and healthy Howell who used to run and cycle the roads, who played indoor soccer and had a fiercely competitive streak? The one who always had to be first across the line or on the winning team? Even though he had busied himself as an orderly in the prison hospital and tried to keep himself in shape, his period of incarceration had obviously taken its toll. Dressed in the same grey suit, pale tie and striped shirt as on a number of previous courtroom appearances, he had not aged well.

Howell's pulse rate must have quickened as he made his way to the front of the courtroom to take his place just below the Judge's bench. He had a determined look about him: clearly keen to tell his side of the story, and, as far as he was concerned, set the record straight. Minutes earlier, Mr Justice Hart, bewigged and resplendent in his scarlet robes, had entered the courtroom, bowed, pulled up his chair and checked with the various legal representatives that everything was in order. Just before he nodded to the official standing at the door of a side room, to indicate he was ready to proceed, he took time to issue a word of warning to those assembled before him: 'Let me make it clear to everyone in court that if there is any disturbance whatever, however minor, any exclamations, any comments, the public galleries will be cleared.' Pausing for a moment to let the full impact of these words sink in, he finally gestured to the man standing over to his right: 'Very well, have him brought in. Bring the jury in.'

———

Day Four of Hazel Stewart's trial was under way, and the star witness was in a place he could hardly have imagined. Here was a self-confessed double killer presenting himself before a jury, asking them to endorse a testimony which would come close to defying belief. Hazel Stewart, as they would hear later, had already damned herself with her own words—but could the panel of strangers sitting opposite accept anything which Howell would now say as true?

Those in charge at the Public Prosecution Service must have thought long and hard before embracing his offer to give evidence against his co-accused. Thoughts that he might secure a lesser sentence in return for his testimony had never been entertained by the authorities—there had been no deal on offer to Howell prior to sentencing—but, with him now prepared to reveal all, the case for the Crown against Hazel Stewart would be strengthened immeasurably. Yet there were many important questions as to his integrity as a witness. Was he motivated by a sense of vengeance, out to get even with a woman who was not prepared to admit that she was just as culpable as he was? Could he withstand an inevitable and hostile inquisition as to his credibility, with justifiable claims that he was a devious and controlling manipulator? Or would the court accept that he could, in any sense, be a reliable and objective witness?

Yet Howell was the only person who knew what had really happened. Even though there was a risk Stewart's defence team might be able to take the dentist's testimony apart and therefore raise doubts as to her guilt, surely he of all people could provide the corroboration which was absolutely vital to secure a conviction? After all, he had masterminded everything, and Hazel, as he would confirm, was a willing accomplice.

The witnesses who had been called before Howell took the stand had given evidence about what went on before and after the bodies were discovered. But it was only Howell himself who could detail exactly what had taken place that night—in his house, at the Buchanans' home, and in a garage above the village of Castlerock.

And so the jury—the nine men casually dressed in open-neck shirts, some of them wearing pullovers, the three women slightly more formally attired—filed in to take up their places. Each one of them carried a manila folder containing documents, including maps and diagrams detailing the layout of the scenes of the crime.

Howell was invited to stand up, take the Bible in his right hand, and swear by Almighty God to tell the truth, the whole truth and nothing but the truth. It was not the first time he had been asked to take such an oath on the first floor of that red brick building, which looked so out of place in the middle of the neighbouring residential properties of the Mountsandel Road. Back in May 1992, in the very same venue, he had attended a Coroner's Court inquest—the one held to investigate the circumstances surrounding the deaths of his wife and Trevor Buchanan.

Fast forward almost 19 years, and, as Howell surveyed the courtroom in front of him, he would have recognised some familiar faces. His daughter was there that morning: now Mrs Lauren Bradford, sitting with her new husband, Michael, the man she married in Belfast the previous year. Trevor Buchanan's brothers and two sisters and some close family friends sat tightly together in the public gallery, just to the left of the main door. On the opposite side, Hazel Stewart's second husband David, and her son Andrew and daughter Lisa McConnell (she had also married the previous year) sat in the front row, with their aunts, Hazel's sisters, directly behind them.

Family rooms had been set aside for the duration of the trial: one for the Buchanans, on the ground floor at the end of a corridor running from the foyer, and one for Hazel's relatives, upstairs in a room just off one of the main public waiting areas. There were flasks of tea and coffee, some food, and piles of glossy magazines, mostly for women. Not surprisingly, given the unprecedented level of media coverage of the case, and her photograph on every front page, no newspapers were provided for Hazel's relatives.

Once Howell was sworn in, the courtroom fell silent for just a few seconds, as the Prosecution's Ciaran Murphy QC got to his feet. He asked Howell to face the jury, before posing his opening question: 'Why did you go to the police in January 2009?'

Howell's voice was cracked and low, as if he had not quite cleared his throat: 'I just knew that the time had come when the truth had to be told. I was overwhelmed by my conscience with hiding this crime for such a long time. I believed that there still were scars that needed to be put right and I wanted to tell the truth. That's the only motive.'

He went on to detail the early days of his relationship with Lesley. How they had met when she was a nurse at the Royal Victoria Hospital in Belfast and he was at Queen's University, studying anatomy at the Medical Biology Centre as part of his dentistry degree. How they had married and then moved to Coleraine, where he secured his first job. How, through Coleraine Baptist Church, they got to know Hazel and Trevor Buchanan.

Howell could not have been in the witness box for more than five minutes before he revealed that the relationship with Lesley was in trouble even before they exchanged their wedding vows. She was the first one to express doubts, once they were already married, but as a dutiful husband he wanted to make it work: 'I think we came into the marriage with unhappiness, but hoped, and I believed we both sincerely wanted, to make it work. But it didn't.'

It was Howell as never before, speaking publicly—and at length— for the first time. Those in the courtroom were no doubt surprised by the degree of his composure, his soft yet assertive tone, his cultured accent and the precise, highly articulate way in which he expressed himself. He was steady. He took his time. He was almost clinical in his delivery. Was this the man who had planned and carried out the cold and merciless actions which were now under intense scrutiny?

Apart from his daughter at the back of the room, he was without friends and completely on his own. But he rarely showed any signs of vulnerability or stress. Only once or twice did he seem to choke on his words—especially when recalling the birth of his first son Matthew in 1984. But then he composed himself again, and needed little encouragement from Mr Murphy, as he went on to disclose, in at times exhaustive detail, an astonishing double life which involved love, greed, drugs, sex, deceit, religion, and then the planning and execution of the greatest sin of all.

Howell's initial statement for the Crown would take up one full day of his four long days in the witness box. By any standards, it was an extraordinary and compelling testimony, electrifying at times, and occasionally theatrical. It was as if he wanted to divest himself of the dark, horrible secrets he had kept for all those years. Maybe he was following in the time-honoured tradition of all troubled evangelicals, looking to rid themselves of their guilt—he was 'bringing it to the Cross' in full, graphic and sometimes lurid detail. It quickly became clear, however, that Howell was not only determined to make the most of this opportunity to exorcise his guilt in such a public way, but that he was also positively relishing his own performance. Now, finally, he was centre stage.

The question-and-answer exchanges between Howell and Mr Murphy of the Prosecution were relaxed and almost leisurely: it was as if the two men were having an informal conversation. But with the cross-examination the next day, led by Mr Ramsey QC, the pace quickened considerably.

Ramsey is widely acknowledged as an extremely able and competent advocate—but in Colin Howell, he faced a formidable and challenging individual with a level of intelligence equal in some ways to his own. The star witness for the Prosecution was no ordinary adversary, no run-of-the-mill witness. Ramsey's brief—to prove his client's innocence, and establish that Howell's real motive for the killings had nothing to do with love for his mistress, and everything to do with money—would be a tough and demanding one, which would seriously stretch him in spite of his considerable abilities. He conceded that Hazel Stewart had perjured herself by lying at the inquest a year after the deaths, that she had withheld information and thus perverted the course of justice. But, he repeatedly insisted, she was absolutely *not* guilty of murder.

Hazel's lawyer quickly set out his stall. 'Some ground rules before we start,' he said to Howell. 'I should tell you that some of the matters I am going to ask you about will relate to 20 years ago, or beyond that, and obviously if you are not sure about something, or can't remember something, don't try to guess at it. Alright? Try and direct your answers towards the ladies and gentlemen of the jury, so that they can hear your evidence and [finally] – if at any time you want a break, or want to stop, let us know. And subject to his Lordship, we can make arrangements.' Howell listened attentively, without flinching.

Ramsey's opening question was remarkably similar to that of the Prosecution: 'Mr Howell, why are you here?'

Howell replied: 'I am here as a witness to the events in 1991, because this is the trial, the case. I can expand, if you wish?'

Mr Ramsey: 'Yes, of course.'

Howell: 'It was only when I acknowledged . . . to myself, that the truth of what happened 20 years ago was bigger than myself . . . Whenever I . . . saw that the truth was bigger and more important . . . I made the decision to get rid of all the deception in my life, and that included the events of 20 years ago. I believed that the impact of that was still alive and affecting people . . . It began after the death of my son and other events [which] made me begin to realise, because I had been so selfish and lived within my own world, that was still having an impact . . . When that wound is opened, a lot of people bleed and I realised that there are victims, and the closest victims to me are my children . . . Other children were affected . . . And I am here because of them . . . I know I set myself up to be a punch bag for all of the wrong that I have done. I am here under great personal shame. I have brought disgrace on myself and on many other people. But that is no longer the most important thing. I am prepared for what is coming today . . . I have been in preparation for that for a long time . . . It gives people a chance for the wound to be closed. I wouldn't dare beg or ask forgiveness from any of my victims, because then I would be really selfish. If anyone chooses to forgive me, then that will be a good thing because I believe that a person never truly recovers from an injury until they forgive. So if anyone chooses to forgive in the future, I would like that, but it would be for their sake, and not for any personal selfish reasons . . .'

Mr Ramsey responded: 'That is a rather lengthy answer to a straightforward question, but effectively you seem to be saying that it is a noble gesture on your part to in some way give some closure to the victims of this. Is that right?'

Howell replied: 'That's right. Well, if it *was* noble. I have done nothing that is noble. Everything I have done is ignoble. You misunderstand or misinterpret my lengthy answer. If you thought I was trying to be noble, I have no merit to be noble and that is not what I am trying to achieve by my lengthy statement.'

Ramsey: 'You have no other agenda? You have no other reason for being here, other than to give closure to the victims today and heal the wounds that you have opened?'

Howell: 'There is no personal benefit to me, but I am willing to bare my own disgrace.'

Even at this stage of the proceedings, it was obvious Howell was determined to make his point at all costs, and that he would spare no detail in his explanations and explications. He was almost eager to engage in polemic with Mr Ramsey on matters of morality, religion and philosophy—even semantics. In a typical exchange, he took issue with the Defence's definition of the word 'clever':

Ramsey: 'You told Dr Harbinson . . . that . . . you understood forensic medicine and you regarded the manner in which you killed Lesley and Trevor as clever, would that be right?'

Howell: 'I don't remember saying that . . . I don't remember using the word "clever". Dr Harbinson made some errors which I notified my brief, my solicitor, about and she made several errors in the statement which I objected to and she wasn't willing to change anything, so I don't know if that is one of the—if I used that word or not.'

Ramsey: 'Dr Harbinson's report was put before his Lordship at your tariff hearing, isn't that right, relied upon and put before the court, isn't that correct?'

Howell: 'Yes.'

Ramsey: 'Yes?'

Howell: 'Then I will have to accept I used that word, I don't remember using it.'

Ramsey: 'So—in this confession that you made in 2009—were you not a victim of circumstances, the way things were going for you financially, your marriage, everything else and you found yourself in that situation?'

Howell: 'No, that's not right.'

Ramsey: 'Was it a true confession, a real confession?'

Howell: 'What do you call a true confession?'

Ramsey: 'Well, what do you call a true confession?'

Howell: 'I call a true confession when you have made a confession about what you did.'

Ramsey: 'Were you properly contrite when you made that confession? . . . No residual feelings of "how clever I was, how sharp I was to fool the police all those years ago"?'

Howell: 'Absolutely not, I never even had a notion of that. I was so ashamed and regretted what I did . . . That has been inferred obviously by you by picking up a single word like "clever". Perhaps I used that word, but it wasn't clever in the mischievous sense of the word "clever".

Ramsey: 'Alright.'

Paul Ramsey found that even the most determined attempts to pin Howell down on almost anything proved difficult, sometimes simply impossible. The smallest, even the tiniest, inaccuracies of speech, and what Howell believed to be unfounded assumptions, were challenged. Ramsey's exasperation with the witness understandably came to the fore every so often: 'So therefore, you are going to agree with me [on] things you said to Doctor Harbinson that suit you, and if it doesn't suit you, you will disagree with it, is that the position?'

Having attempted to make some sense of Howell's motives for testifying, Ramsey moved on to try to establish something of his essential character. His intention was no doubt to demonstrate to the jury the extent to which, at the time of the murders, the accused had been in thrall to an extremely domineering and even dangerous Howell.

Mr Ramsey: 'So, are you controlling?'

Howell replied: 'I don't believe I am. I believe I *have been* in some situations.' He was asked to expand. And off he went on another lengthy exposition: 'There is legitimate control. Judge Hart is in control of this court . . . If a defendant goes into the box, he can become manipulative, deceptive and therefore he has to be controlled, which means he is sentenced and put into prison, found guilty, and that is legitimate control. If I am a father, then I have legitimate control of my children and I have the right to tell them what time to come in at night. If they are under 16, I have the right. If they want a tattoo up their back, I have the right to say, you can't do that, and so on. So there is control that is legitimate.

'In church situations, there are pastors and elders. In the same way, if someone breaks the rules . . . then there has to be a certain amount of control. That is a good thing, otherwise society would break down and situations would break down. And no matter whether it is a church organisation or a club, there has to be a certain amount of control, because there are rules. But there can also be deviousness and manipulation.

'Then there is illegitimate control. When you take control of a person or a situation where you don't have the right to do that, or if you do have the right, and you then abuse how you use that control, then that is dominance and abusive control. So I just wanted to clarify that, so that when we do talk about control, I recognise and acknowledge and accept that there is legitimate control.'

Howell's attention to detail, his insistence on following every tangent and indulging in lengthy explanations, was often taxing and extremely trying for all those who listened. This was compounded by the fact that the courtroom was free of any natural light. Although there was always a plentiful supply of tap water available, the atmosphere was dry and dehydrating, and the presence of so many people in such a confined space meant the air was stale and stifling. Even the judge found it difficult. Mid-afternoon on day two of Howell's testimony, when he was being cross-examined about his planning of the murders, Mr Justice Hart suggested a brief adjournment: 'I don't want to interrupt, Mr Ramsey, but it's getting extraordinarily warm in here. So I think we'll break for 10 minutes.'

When proceedings resumed, Ramsey questioned Howell on his attitude to women. Was he something of a ladies' man? Did he— as psychiatrist Dr Helen Harbinson claimed—think of himself as, in his own words, 'a small god who needed to be worshipped by women'?

Howell's response was characteristically long-winded: 'As with most beautiful females or handsome men—however you want to label people—there is often a great insecurity and low self-esteem. So whenever someone, an attractive female, shows [you] attention, it serves that neediness. So yes . . . my success . . . perhaps . . . my status as a dentist and therefore my wealth in proportion to the community . . . made me attractive to some females and I got a positive response. Am I a ladies' man? Well, let other people hold that opinion. I never had that opinion about myself.'

As for his comments to Dr Harbinson, Howell claimed—not for the first time—that he had been misunderstood: 'I said I believe that in the fantasy world of sex . . . when men fantasise about a woman, it doesn't matter if you are short, fat, ugly and bald. But you will believe that you are, and I used the words, "like a god". You have a self-belief . . . part of the fantasy world. So that was the context of the conversation. But I never said I am like a small god.'

The cross-examination moved on to Howell's relationship with Hazel. What was she like? The star witness quickly dismissed Mr Ramsey's suggestion that his client was a shy, somewhat naïve, and softly-spoken woman. Howell had clearly anticipated the question: his answer seemed well-rehearsed: 'I would describe Hazel as an advertisement for an orphanage in India. You see these pictures of a little child with a big teardrop and dark brown eyes, and you just want to get your wallet out and give money to it, and help it. But I have been to India twice, and I have discovered that those adverts often have two businessmen behind them, collecting money off wealthy people and putting it into their back pockets.'

Trying to shrug off the rather chilling effect of this deeply cynical description of Stewart, with its subtext which hinted that materialism was her driving force, Ramsey swiftly moved on to quote some of Howell's words during a police interview at the time of his arrest: 'This is what you said at the time, Mr Howell: "Well, I know that she was finding it hard to take in information, IQ-wise. She was very simplistic, she wouldn't be academic and that is what I was getting at when I said . . . if you explain everything, she'll not understand . . . . So, yeah . . . she probably was easy to control if I wanted to control her, and vulnerable to somebody, someone like me. Okay." . . . Is that your view of her, that she was someone who was fairly simplistic and was easy to control if you wanted to control her, and vulnerable?'

Howell quickly hit back: 'You see, some of us say: "Oh, wee Johnny is easily led by his friends . . . And that is why he got the tattoo on his arm." But in fact, wee Johnny is a very determined, manipulative child who disobeys his parents. So we have this wrong perception of people who are easily led. People who have the disguise and guile to appear innocent . . . A word [sic] that Hazel used about herself is "I'm just soft" . . . and I believe that is part of the huge deception [sic] that I was under about Hazel.'

In spite of all that Ramsey tried to put forward in terms of Hazel's personality being passive, easily intimidated and submissive, Howell was insistent that she had made her own choices and had to take responsibility for them. Speaking about how things were between them in the months after the murders, he recalled: 'I would phone her because I couldn't take the pressure of missing her so much. We were so dependent on each other because of our dark secret and it was hard to break that tie. Then sometimes a week would pass and I wouldn't contact Hazel, and she would phone me in soft silk tones that she would be missing me.'

According to Howell, Stewart had been the one to seduce him at the beginning of the affair. He described the power she had over him in dramatic terms: 'I walked into the spider's web. Now, flies go into a spider's web because they might think there is some food for them there. So I willingly went after the bait and we [got] caught together in a trap and it proved to be so because of the end result.'

Everything Howell said about his former lover reinforced his claim that her true personality was very far from the naïve innocent she presented herself as. Their relationship was far more one of equals than the Defence were trying to imply. 'Control is a very complex thing,' he declared at one point during the cross-examination. 'So if I was controlling in one area, Hazel was controlling in another area. It was a dance between control and manipulation when two people are in a relationship like that.' Howell picked up this particular metaphor again later in his testimony, in words which resonated beyond the courtroom: 'And so Hazel and I were waltzing together in time ... All of the side-stepping was done together. I may have been the lead partner in the waltz, but Hazel was dancing in cooperation with that dance. I wasn't dragging her around that floor, making her put her foot to the left or right. She was doing it in perfect harmony, on her own and willingly. She has lots of issues of control, manipulation and deception, but to try and highlight me as the controlling one and Hazel as the soft, manipulative one—that is not true.'

Howell's testimony in court was remarkable in many ways—not the least of these was his clever and very persuasive use of language. He took every opportunity to hammer home to the jury his conviction that Hazel had been a willing accomplice in the planning—and the execution of the plan—to murder their spouses. He frequently used the same key expressions, 'joint venture' or 'joint enterprise', which encapsulated one of the main arguments of the Prosecution's case: that the murders had been a mutually agreed undertaking between him and Hazel: 'If you look at the joint venture of the abortion. Hazel wanted it and I facilitated it. If you look at the murders—I wanted it and Hazel facilitated it . . . Nobody was dragging anybody in the wrong direction . . . When it came to killing two people, the decision to have an abortion with Hazel was extremely significant. That joint cooperation was so significant to how the two of us could do the same together.'

He also talked of the abortion and then the murders in terms of a contract between himself and his former lover: 'It [the abortion] was like a blood contract that Hazel and I had secretly signed between each other, which is [was] to murder an unborn baby . . . It meant then when it came to me coming to Hazel with my idea to have a joint venture to kill Trevor and Lesley, that we had already—six months earlier, whatever it was—signed a contract in blood that it is okay to kill a human . . . It is [was] a very powerful bond that we had, one that we were not in control of . . .'

Media attention to the trial in Ireland was massive, and the story was picked up with interest in mainland Britain too—although in a more restrained way. The public's fascination grew exponentially as Howell's detailed and increasingly lurid revelations about his sex life with his former lover were brought under the spotlight.

Each morning men and women queued in the waiting area of the courthouse for two hours and sometimes longer, all in the hope of getting a seat in the courtroom. There were just 19 places available in the two public galleries on either side of the dock. Three extra chairs were brought in at one point, but this was not nearly enough to accommodate those who waited outside. The courtroom was big enough for the trial, but woefully inadequate for those whose only motive for attending the proceedings was to satisfy their own curiosity. On the rare days when places were available, only a handful of those waiting were admitted. But the others stayed anyway, in the hope of catching sight of Stewart arriving with her family each morning, and they would then while the time away until the afternoon, when they could see her leaving the building again, after the day's session in court was over.

One woman, who apparently made the journey most days from her home in the countryside outside Derry, was philosophical about not getting a seat: 'It doesn't really bother me. It's the atmosphere. I just want to take in the atmosphere.' The Northern Ireland Court Service took calls daily from hopefuls inquiring about the availability of seats. One caller asked if staff could find room for 30 to 40 of her friends, all women: she explained that she was hoping to organise a special bus trip from Belfast for the day.

Howell spared the court no detail as he elaborated on the nature of his sex life with Hazel. He revealed how sometimes, particularly in the run-up to the Coroner's Court inquest in 1992, they would pretend that they never had sex, even when they did: 'This myth began to develop and that became a pattern from then on. The other form of denial that both of us had is that sex is only full penetration and sex isn't if you fiddle around to only about an inch of your penis into the vagina. Let's be crude. So there is a whole thing about what is sex. In the last few days I have had it clarified that legally sex doesn't matter if it is an inch, or eight inches, or what it is. It is sex. So, if you asked me did I have sex with Hazel for four years, I would have said no. But now that I know what it means legally, I will now be saying that I had sex with Hazel on a regular basis during these four years. But . . . the climax was always followed up by extreme guilt . . .'

Stewart, her husband and two children and her wider family members must have squirmed as he went on to describe in excruciating detail how he would drug her before intercourse, at his clinic and once at her house, where he used to climb in through a back window. He attempted to explain the rationale behind their increasingly bizarre behaviour: 'We got to the point where it was all foreplay and no sex because penetrative sex was a no-no by this stage for both us, although the sexual relationship was still going, fully sexual without full penetration. However, it got to the stage where whenever Hazel got really turned on, she'd say to me: "Well, if you're going to turn me on, you have to have sex, you know. Why are you getting me turned on if you won't have full sex?" So she got angry and insisted that I would have full sex, but I wasn't having full sex . . . So the experiment was: right, I have brought home the liquid sedation, sedated her to give her the same relaxed and uninhibited effect that she would have with the laughing gas, so that then I would be able to give her the full sex and she might not feel guilty. So, that was the experiment.'

Howell was calm and measured throughout his mammoth four-day stint in the witness box. He did not have to be reminded to keep his voice up. Every now and again he took a sip of water. At times he looked and sounded like someone delivering a lecture: clinical, detached, factual. In all the horrors that he revealed, one of the most chilling features of his performance was the way in which he repeatedly referred to the murders as 'the procedures'. When he detailed how he had conceived his deadly plan, it was as if he was back at his desk at the clinic, drafting letters to his client patients, proposing various options, costs, and timescales—only this time, it was he and Hazel, sitting in Trevor's white Toyota Corolla, in a nature reserve beside the River Bann, as he outlined his grotesque plot. And when he described to the court how he had pushed the hosepipe channelling the deadly carbon monoxide under Lesley's blanket while she slept, it was for all the world as if he was administering some therapeutic dental treatment to one of his trusting patients.

Only once did Howell get agitated and betray any real degree of emotion. This was when, without any advance warning to the judge or the jury, Mr Ramsey produced some family photographs of Lesley which had been taken in the weeks before she was murdered. In one photograph, she was holding Lauren, just four years old and wearing glasses because she was having trouble with her eyesight. It was December 1990. Another picture was of her and Howell, dressed up for a night out in February 1991, when Lesley was desperately trying to lose weight and having beauty treatments in a final bid to win back his affections and save the marriage. Then there were two more— taken that April of 1991—in a garden bathed in spring sunshine with bunches of daffodils in full bloom. The young mother was wearing denim jeans and a floral blouse, crouching down, with little Daniel in his babygro on her knee and Matthew standing at her side. Friends had handed these photos over to the police—four images of a young woman radiating happiness and contentment. But behind the smiles, this was someone struggling with her emotions and a man who had all but abandoned any lingering hopes of reconciliation.

Glancing at the pictures, Howell shifted in his seat, removed his spectacles and glared at his inquisitor. He declared that one of the reasons he pleaded guilty was to keep such details confidential, and not add to his daughter Lauren's plight: 'For her to see this exposed now because there's now a trial by the co-accused, is a prolonging and an extenuation [sic] of her pain . . . I believe you have brought this out in terms of discrediting my character. I know my character, but I did not want this to happen. I wanted that to remain private and not to go to trial . . . not become public to the Press, to the book writers and the storytellers in the future. Unfortunately [it] has been brought into the light and I don't like it for the sake of my children, who now have to share in that humiliation.'

As the cross-examination drew to a close, Mr Ramsey came back one last time to the question of Howell's motives for testifying. He challenged him that these were questionable, to say the least: 'You want a platform, [Mr Howell]. Your ego demands a platform. In an effort to rehabilitate yourself and reinvent yourself . . . that's what you are doing. That's what the exercise has been over the past few days, hasn't it?'

Unwilling to give an inch here, as at any moment throughout his epic stint on the stand, Howell was having none of it. He fired back: 'What I have demonstrated is that, no matter what the cost of what I lose, there's something much more important . . . to me. If I was calculating for the best, I wouldn't have stepped forward. If it was [just for] self-interest and self-preservation, I would still be free, placing dental implants and having a glorious website and being popular with people . . . So the opposite is true. My actions speak that . . . That's why I'm here.'

No matter what his motives, it was evident to everyone in the courtroom that Colin Howell's testimony had been far too detailed and compelling to be dismissed as mere vindictiveness. It had been a startling performance which clearly made a huge impression on the people who really mattered—the jurors who sat opposite him. The task that the Defence faced—to persuade them of Hazel Stewart's innocence—was now a truly unenviable one.

Chapter 21
'What will Happen to Me?'
The Hazel Stewart Trial: Part Three

H azel Stewart's dramatic and sensational trial was almost over. All the witnesses for the Prosecution, including Howell of course, had had their say. The accused sat silently throughout, maintaining a stoic composure at all times, her face expressionless, even as her former lover described the intimate details of their ever more dysfunctional sex life. Now, surely, it was finally time for her to speak.

But those who had anticipated this moment eagerly, hoping at last to hear the accused explain in her own words what had happened and why she had acted as she did, would be disappointed. For in the final event, Hazel Stewart would not speak a single word throughout the 15 days she was on trial for double murder.

She could of course have gone into the witness box. But her lawyer announced to the court that he did not intend to call her to give evidence or face cross-examination by his colleague, Mr Murphy, sitting to his right. Mr Ramsey said he realised that the jury could draw an adverse conclusion from the decision—but this was, after all, her inalienable right. He turned to the nine men and three women and asked: 'How would your task be helped by observing a contest between a housewife and an eminent and able senior counsel like Mr Murphy? It would be like sending a pub team to play a Premier League side like Manchester United or Chelsea at their home ground. No contest.'

By then in fact, the jury had already heard Stewart speaking for herself—or at least as she had done almost two years previously, in police interviews after she was arrested and taken in for questioning. All these interviews had been recorded on tape and formed a crucial—and indeed critical—part of the case for the Prosecution, as the jury was able to listen to the full detail of Hazel's exchanges with her inquisitor, Detective Sergeant Geoff Ferris. The process of playing back the police recordings to the court lasted for almost two days.

Howell was being questioned in an adjoining room when Ferris had pushed the record button to begin his interrogation of Hazel Stewart. Years ago the policeman had been a useful soccer player when off duty, scoring around 200 goals for a variety of teams in the Irish League. He wore the No. 10 shirt, was quick on his feet and good with the head. But as the court would hear, it took him the best part of three days to negotiate his way past the lady sitting in the dock.

Neil Connor, junior counsel for the Prosecution, got to his feet and invited the jury to listen. They could also follow a written record of the questions and answers which would scroll down—line by line— on monitors in front of them. Ferris positioned himself in the witness box in readiness to leaf through the transcripts, just to confirm that they tallied with what was being broadcast. Mr Connor then asked for the first tape to be played.

The initial interview began with the detective introducing himself and a colleague, Constable Nicola Moore, and noting the time and date for the purposes of the tape: it was approaching 19.40 hours on the evening of Thursday, 29 January 2009. They were in Coleraine police station. Hazel sat at the opposite side of the table with her solicitor Stephen Ewing. She was still in a state of shock.

Ferris began: 'Okay, so you understand, Hazel—you've been arrested now for a very serious offence. It doesn't get any more serious than murder, okay. And we have lots of questions to put to you and to ask you. During the course of the interviews, we will be asking the questions. We will try and ask them in a fair manner, and hopefully you'll understand every question.'

Stewart: 'Hmm.'

Ferris: 'So, can you tell us about your involvement?'

Stewart: 'Well, I'm not going to lie. I had an involvement with Colin Howell. It was intense at times, and he's quite a controlling person. Where do I start? He said he would never leave his wife or whatever at the time. That it was fine, and one day he said to me . . .'

Ferris interrupted and quickly advised her: 'Just take your time. You're okay. Take your time.'

Only a few minutes into the first tape, this was already proving to be a mesmerising and compelling exchange which held the courtroom spellbound. At first, Hazel seemed reluctant to say anything, but Ferris managed to coax her along, quietly and without fuss. Yet he also made her circumstances clear: 'You have to face reality here. Nobody else can deal with this situation, apart from you. Other people will have to answer for what they did. But your knowledge around that time is all down to yourself. We have to deal with that and you have to deal with that as best you can. I know you have lived with it now for 18 years, or whatever the case may be. I am sure that has been difficult for you, but now is the day that you probably thought would never come.'

Stewart told him how the relationship started; how her husband had been 'gutted' when he found out; how he did not want her to leave, although she would have divorced him because she was in love, or at least she thought she was. She spoke about the trauma of having a secret abortion, but insisted time and time again that she wanted nothing to do with Howell's plan to murder. She had never wanted it to happen. She had been terrified.

Each of the interview tapes lasted 40 minutes. Hazel's voice, soft and hesitant with traces of a west Tyrone accent, reverberated around the courtroom. Her replies were brief and sometimes monosyllabic. She could be heard taking the occasional sip of water. She did not eat anything during the entire three days of questioning.

It was now the start of the second day, just coming up to 10.20 a.m., as Ferris noted for the tape. He started the proceedings by inquiring: 'How are you feeling this morning, Hazel?' 'Dreadful, terrible,' came Stewart's reply. Yet she stuck firmly, doggedly to her story: 'I was so scared. I thought, if I say something against this, he'll turn round and he'll kill me. That's how I felt.'

Ferris then asked: 'Did you feel any time that the truth would come out?'

Stewart: 'I always knew. I would never have said. I would have taken it to my grave because of my children and my family. I thought it would be better for me to suffer this every day—which I did—than to open a can of worms and affect so many people after so long.'

Ferris: 'Did you ever think, or would you have had any hint that, "Well, the only person that could tell the truth would be Colin"?'

Stewart: 'Yes. And maybe I had my fears because of the type of person he was.'

Just after lunch on the afternoon of the second day of the interrogation, however, Stewart's version of the facts began to change—albeit only slightly at first. She said she should have stopped Howell murdering her husband. She admitted that Trevor had taken a tablet to help him sleep on the Saturday evening, but said that she had not given it to him. Despite what Howell claimed, she could not recall him ever giving her sedatives to put into her husband's food to ensure he was well sedated by the time he arrived to murder Trevor.

Spotting an opening in her line of defence, Ferris accused her of twisting the truth: 'It's nearly written across your forehead. I know you're finding difficulty with some questions. You're not in here for stealing a cheque out of work, or a burglary, or a theft, or a shoplifting case. You're in here for the most serious of offences under the law in this country. I'm asking you to be truthful.'

At the start of her third day of questioning, Hazel said she felt fine, but the strain in her voice and in the way she responded was obvious to those who were listening to the exchanges between her and the detective. Soon she was claiming—for the first time—that she had told Howell to get out of the house before he had made his way to the bedroom to gas her husband.

Ferris persisted. There was a perceptible change in the tone of his voice now: he was more urgent, more forceful: 'We're getting no satisfaction whatsoever . . . What is important is that we get to the bottom of [this]. All the pieces of the puzzle have to fit, and there are a couple of pieces not right. You're in a situation where you feel totally hopeless, but I'm asking you to tell us everything involving Trevor. He's got a family as well. They need to know the truth, Hazel . . . Next week, we'll walk away from this. We'll be dealing with another murder inquiry. So I'm asking you. Don't be adopting the hardened attitude and try[ing] to fool us. You know you've told lies, and you conned the police away back in 1991.'

Stewart: 'I didn't like doing that.'

Ferris: 'It's gone. It's done. What we're saying to you in here is: "Look, sort it out now." We need to know and we do know the picture. But it has to come from you, Hazel.'

She paused briefly, and then said: 'What will happen to me?'

Ferris: 'Sorry?'

Stewart: 'What will happen to me?'

It was approaching lunchtime on Saturday, 31 January, and it was the first time it seemed to dawn on Hazel Stewart that there was now little or no room for manoeuvre. She still sounded well in control of herself and her emotions, but the pressure to divulge everything was becoming more and more apparent. Her resistance started to wane, as Ferris persisted. There was a short pause in the tape, as Stewart asked for a glass of water. When the interview resumed, she accepted that she had encouraged Trevor to take a sleeping tablet, but insisted over and over again that she had *not* given it to him. But she conceded that the plan to murder could not have gone ahead without her husband being sedated. Yes, she had known earlier that Saturday what Howell was planning to do, and when he arrived at the house with his wife's body in the boot—yes, she knew what the next part of his plan would entail. She could, and should, she admitted to Ferris, have shouted and screamed, but she did nothing to stop her lover. He was on a mission, but he could have been stopped, she agreed: 'I let it happen. Yes, I let it happen.'

She left out the clothes for Howell to dress her husband's lifeless body. She cut up and burned the garden hose which had been used to kill him. She changed and washed the bedcovers in the room where he had fought for his life, and opened the windows to release the lingering fumes of carbon monoxide. Ferris pressed the point: 'You got rid of the evidence. Is that fair?'

Stewart, who had always been so fussy and houseproud, replied: 'I suppose you could say that. I never thought of it like that, but I just felt I had to get the room tidied up.'

By the time the judge and jury heard the fifteenth and final tape, the atmosphere inside the courtroom was electric. And for the first time since the trial began, Stewart's vacant, impassive demeanour changed. Pushing her blonde hair to one side, she pulled out a handkerchief and began to cry. As she listened to the final exchanges between herself and the detective, she held her head in her hands, now weeping openly.

Ferris could be heard pressing on relentlessly, until Hazel now accepted that Howell could not have murdered on his own. It had to have been a 'joint enterprise'—again, those all-important words—

between the two of them, for the plan to work. Finally, the detective sergeant asked her: 'Is there anything [more] you want to say, Hazel?'

Between her sobs, the reply came tumbling out: 'I would like to say sorry to Trevor's family. I can't imagine what it would be like to lose a son. I've a son and I love him very much. To David, my husband I love so much, Lisa and Andrew—they're my life and I have lost it. The biggest mistake of my life was ever meeting Colin Howell. I have paid the price for the past 17, 18 years. Since that happened, I lost so much of my life. I lost joy, a peace, and contentment. It was like living in a black hole. Every day I got up, every night I went to bed, it was there. I thought about it 24/7. It never left me.'

Sitting in the front row of the public gallery of the court over to her left, her daughter Lisa and son Andrew were now crying too, as were some of her sisters in the row behind. David Stewart's face was drained: he looked pale and exhausted. Hazel Stewart's family were reliving every moment of her pain with her. They clearly found it unbearable.

The voice on the tape was now weary, resigned: 'I had to do things for my children and be strong for them. My guilt was horrendous. My shame. I hated him. The relationship went on for years, but only because of him . . . He did not want it to end. Maybe I couldn't say to him . . . I was scared of him, not knowing what he would do. I saw what he had done, how capable he was of doing things. I was scared sometimes for my children. I just didn't feel easy about it at times. They thought he was alright, but they weren't that comfortable with him . . . But life has been horrific for me. I never got over it. I'm going through all this now. The thought of losing my children, losing David, is the hardest thing. Yeah, I destroyed their lives, Lisa and Andrew's lives. Colin's children didn't deserve this, or Lesley. Lesley was a lovely girl. Trevor was very good too.'

Gordon Buchanan's head fell back and he looked skywards. Victor leaned forward. Raymond Buchanan sat with his chin resting on his right hand. Trevor's two sisters, Valerie and Melva, were in the same place as they had been throughout: the front row, sitting at an angle from their former sister-in-law. What must they have thought?

And what must have been going through the mind of Lauren Bradford, Lesley's daughter, who sat with the Buchanans, directly opposite from Stewart's daughter Lisa? During one brief interlude earlier in the trial, Lisa had crossed the room to speak to Lauren. No doubt they had some catching up to do since the days they had grown up in Coleraine, when they had spent so much time together. And the two young women had many other things in common, having both suffered the awful ordeal of losing a parent through suicide, only to find out years later that it had been murder all along.

It had been an astonishing trial in so many respects—not the least because of the extraordinary sideshow being played out on the periphery of the courtroom, as so many shattered relatives and friends tried to confront the devastating fallout of two murders which had happened almost two decades previously.

----

2 MARCH 2011

Hazel Stewart struggled so hard with her breathing that a police officer just to her right feared she was going to hyperventilate. Waiting for the jury to deliver their verdict, she sat in the dock for almost 20 minutes, looking gaunt and forlorn in the same coat she had worn throughout the trial, which failed to conceal her heaving chest and shifting shoulders.

Her children, it seemed, had already resigned themselves to the worst. Even before the jury returned, Lisa sobbed loudly. Her mother looked over and nodded as if to say: 'Don't worry. Don't worry.' Hair swept back into a ponytail, her daughter appeared to mouth back: 'Mummy, I love you. Mummy, I love you.' Andrew doubled up and held his head in his hands, as if he was praying for a miracle. At one stage Hazel's solicitor, Stephen Hastings, left his seat and leaned over to try and reassure the two of them. Sitting beside them, the loyal and attentive David Stewart seemed to have aged 10 years. Red-faced, his tie hanging loose, he looked completely exhausted.

The jury had requested the transcripts of Hazel's last six interviews with Geoff Ferris, which had effectively damned her. Even if she remained convinced of her own innocence, surely some of those who had been sitting on her family's side of the courtroom had good reason to be fearful. In his summing up the previous day, Judge Hart had asked the jury to make a calm and fair decision based on the evidence, and not to be influenced by the sensation which surrounded the case. He stressed that the legal definition of 'joint enterprise' did not mean that Stewart had to commit the murders, only that she was part of the plan to carry them out, and that a plan in itself could take different forms too: 'The word "plan" does not mean there had to be formal agreement about what's to be done: a plan could be made on the spur of the moment, with a nod, wink or knowing look. Put simply, the question for you is: Were they in it together?'

Stewart's personality, the Judge had said, was soft, weak and vulnerable, but she had openly flirted, and was willing to have sex, with Howell. Was Howell controlling or was she perfectly capable of deciding for herself? They had both proved themselves to be capable of sustained deception in the past, although here he cautioned: 'The mere fact the defendant tells a lie is not in itself evidence of guilt. She may lie to protect someone else, to conceal her disgraceful conduct, or in panic or confusion.' The defendant, however, he continued, had not given evidence to undermine, contradict or explain the evidence put by the Prosecution, and the jury could draw such inferences as appeared proper from her failure to do so.

Finally, the Judge asked the jury to consider the crucial question of why Stewart had not intervened to stop the killing: 'Did she do everything, or as much as she could have done, to prevent the murders or at least the murder of her husband? Why did she not tell someone beforehand what he was planning on the night Howell came to her house and committed this murder? Why did she not wake her husband, keep the door closed, scream the house down, run to a neighbour to raise the alarm and get help?'

The jury retired at 10.47 a.m. on Wednesday, 2 March. They examined the transcripts, deliberated and had lunch before returning to the court again. Looking at his watch, a court official was able to calculate that it had taken them exactly two hours and 29 minutes to reach their decision. The foreman—a man in his late 30s or early 40s, with a receding hairline—got to his feet.

The court clerk asked him: 'Have you reached a verdict on count one?' [The murder of Lesley Howell.]

The reply came quickly: 'Yes.'

'What is your verdict—guilty or not guilty?'

'Guilty.'

'Have you reached a verdict on count two?' [The murder of Trevor Buchanan.]

'Yes.'

'What is your verdict—guilty or not guilty?'

'Guilty.'

The distress of Hazel Stewart's two children was painful to witness. Lisa cried out: 'Oh no. Oh no. It's not fair. No, it's not fair. It's not fair.' Hazel reached for her handkerchief to rub her eyes, and for a moment seemed not quite sure what to do next. Her son, husband and sisters all looked towards her, weeping as well. Some of the Buchanan family sitting on the opposite side of the room hugged one another. One or two shed tears, but there was no sense or sign of triumphalism—just relief that justice had been done, had been seen to be done, and that this long nightmare was nearing an end at last.

Once the verdicts were announced, Mr Justice Hart wasted little time in passing sentence. The defendant was asked to stand. He told her she had been convicted of two murders and the only sentence open to the court was that of life imprisonment. It was mandatory and the length of time she would have to serve in jail would be determined at a later date. He then beckoned two prison officers on either side: 'Take her away.'

———

16 MARCH 2011

For the sentencing of Hazel Stewart, Court 12 of Belfast Crown Court was packed with relatives and friends, as well as many other people who had no connection with anyone involved and were there out of sheer curiosity. Solicitors and barristers involved in cases in adjoining courtrooms on the fourth floor also congregated at the door. To the left of the dock was the senior police officer who headed the 2009 investigation: Detective Superintendent Raymond Murray had taken time out from his annual leave to be there. Beside him was his number two on the inquiry team, Ian Magee.

Stewart had three prison officers sitting with her this time, not two as before. She looked more drawn than ever, desperately tense and fearful, her face pale and without evidence of makeup, her eyes lowered and fixed on the ground before her. Only occasionally did she lift her head to look at the Judge. She was dressed in grey slacks and her customary buttoned-up, plum-coloured coat. Just before she was asked by a court official to take her seat 'with his Lordship's permission', she turned and looked over her left shoulder to seek out familiar faces in the crowd behind. Unlike the day she was convicted, this time there was no drama or tears.

As the hands on the wall clock directly above the dock approached 10.23 a.m., Chris Clarke, Lesley's brother, rushed into the courtroom just in time to hear the Judge announce the sentence. His flight from Liverpool had been held up because of fog.

It took Mr Justice Hart 22 minutes to deliver his judgement in *The Queen v Hazel Stewart*, which ran to seven pages. He said that by its verdict, the jury had accepted that she and Howell 'were in it together'. Stewart's culpability was 'exceptionally high', because she knew in advance what Howell was going to do and did nothing to prevent the killings: 'She could have told someone else. She could have told the police and, even after Lesley Howell had been murdered, she could have prevented Howell from entering the house and killing her husband by any one of a number of actions, such as not opening the garage door to him, locking the door against him, waking her husband, ringing the police or alerting her neighbour, to mention but a few. Whilst she knew Howell was murdering her husband in another room, she waited and did nothing to save his life. Had she had a spark of compassion for her husband, even at that late stage, she would have tried to prevent his murder.'

Howell, the judge continued, had planned and carried out the murders and persuaded her to take part. She could not claim any reduction in the minimum term, because she had pleaded not guilty. She had repeatedly lied and persisted in attempting to evade responsibility and, while she had expressed sorrow and regret during police interviews, that was more about the effect of the events on herself, her children and her present husband, than the effects of the murders on all the others whose lives had been ended and blighted.

Her former lover, the Judge declared, was undoubtedly a charismatic, manipulative and hypocritical man with a very considerable sexual appetite, to whom Hazel had initially been attracted because he offered the excitement which she felt her marriage lacked: 'She then fell in love with him and was driven by that love and by intense sexual desire, to allow herself to be persuaded by

Howell to play her part in these dreadful crimes, despite her fear that they would be caught, a part which she then concealed for many years. Despite her protestations to the police that she was controlled by Howell, his unchallenged evidence during the trial was that they continued their clandestine and highly active sexual relationship for several years after the murders, and that even after she refused to marry him and they decided to end their relationship, Stewart tried to persuade him to have sex.'

Mr Justice Hart said he had been provided with a number of statements from people, including her two children, asking him to show leniency. One of the letters was from employees of the company she worked for, which read: 'We are as shocked as others by the events of 1991 and this letter should not be construed as any attempt to exonerate Hazel, but we feel that Hazel has had very little positive representation and we are anxious for the Court to be aware of how those who have spent every day for many years with Hazel have thought and still think of her. From our daily dealings and close friendship with Hazel, we can say that Hazel, who has been portrayed as a manipulative, unfeeling, selfish, amoral, devious and wicked woman, bears no resemblance whatsoever to the Hazel we have come to love and respect.'

The judge concluded: 'Tragically, the consequences for Stewart's children and her husband are part of the legacy of the conduct of both herself and Howell. Those factors, and the fact that she has a clear record, cannot carry great weight when placed in the balance when fixing the minimum term for such crimes, but I have given them, and the positive side to her character spoken of in the passage previously quoted, such weight as I can. Taking all of the factors to which I referred into account, I consider that the minimum term that Stewart should serve before she can be considered for release is one of 18 years' imprisonment.'

Chapter 22

A Time of Reckoning

olin Howell has settled well into life at Maghaberry, confident
he will be a free man again by the time he is 70. With a history
of longevity on his father's side of the family, he believes he
can hope to live for another 20 years after his release. He gets on well
with the staff and most of the other prisoners.

He once had his own accommodation inside the prison hospital,
with a television set in his cell. He also has access to a computer—but
not to the online pornography which at one time held so much of his
attention. The former dentist goes to church on a Sunday and studies
the Bible every day, also delighting in ecclesiastical visits now and
again from a few friends from his church-going days on the North
Coast. He occasionally has a go at the crossword in *The Times*
newspaper, which he reads six days a week. After signing up for
creative writing classes organised within the jail by writer-in-
residence Carlo Gébler, Howell is a prolific writer specialising in
Christian-themed children's books. Compulsively driven and needing
to be occupied, he no doubt welcomes the distraction. An outrageous
proposition to the prison authorities—that he could open a dental
practice for the staff and inmates—was rejected out-of-hand, even
before he was struck off by the General Dental Council.

One of Howell's closest friends in jail is another murderer who
also almost got away with it. Ken McConnell, a former police
inspector and notorious womaniser, strangled and robbed a frail,
asthmatic and defenceless elderly widow, Annabella Symington, at her
south Belfast home on Halloween night in 1989. He needed the money
to pay his gambling debts. With unbelievable callousness, he stuffed a

cardigan into his 77-year-old victim's mouth to stop her screaming. Unlike Howell, McConnell never confessed to his crime: he was caught in January 2010, after police were able to match his DNA with that found under the pensioner's fingernails. He was jailed for 18 years.

Hazel Stewart is being held in a women's jail at Hydebank Wood on the southern outskirts of Belfast. She is planning to appeal her conviction, but in the meantime, according to staff, has settled in well after a difficult first few months. She uses the gym four or five times a week. Like Howell, she reads her Bible daily, and prays at her bedside every night. Stewart was heartbroken that she missed her son Andrew's wedding, in May 2011. On the day her son married, she asked prison staff to leave her alone in her cell, no doubt imagining how the ceremony and reception would be going without her at the top table.

After his spectacular fall from grace, Colin Howell is financially ruined, with hardly a penny to his name. He owes former patients an estimated £230,000, which they paid in advance of getting treatment at his clinic. After his arrest, staff at the surgery found a £20 I.O.U. note in Howell's petty cash box.

At present, he retains a substantial property portfolio, with his name still on the deeds of his seven-bedroom house outside Castlerock, a half-share of a derelict building in Granada, Nicaragua and the flat at Queen Street, Ballymoney, as well as a share of the rest of the building. His affairs are currently under investigation by the Inland Revenue. After Howell was jailed, the Public Prosecution Service, which claimed he had assets as well in Singapore and the Philippines, set out to recover all he owned under the Proceeds of Crime Order Northern Ireland 1996. The application was later withdrawn without explanation. It is understood, however, that the decision not to proceed was taken because the murders were carried out in 1991, and as such, assets belonging to Howell and Stewart could not be recovered under this legislation, since it has no provision for retrospective confiscation.

Both Howell and Stewart defrauded insurance companies. Outstanding mortgages on their homes were paid off under the terms of the families' respective endowment policies. Stewart also received a police widow's pension between 1991 and 2005, when she remarried, as well as a special children's allowance for several years. Howell has known for some time that one day the insurance companies will come looking for their money: just before he confessed to the murders, he did some rough calculations about what he might have to pay back. During this time too, he destroyed one of his computers. It was a laptop which contained details of his financial affairs, including details of his bank accounts and the ill-fated venture in the Philippines. He had promised the friend who encouraged him to invest in the project that he would never reveal to anyone the names of those involved in it—he was told that to do so would put their lives in danger, especially that of 'Alan', the man in Manila. Howell used a screwdriver to remove the laptop's hard drive, which he then smashed into pieces and dumped in various litter bins in Castlerock.

The 2009 inquiry which followed Howell's confession was a highly sensitive and exhaustive police investigation which was headed up by Superintendent Raymond Murray. One of the Police Service of Northern Ireland's top detectives, with 20 years' experience and a Master's in Criminology from Cambridge University, Murray, 40, is meticulous and demanding. He was also determined that, unlike in 1991, there would be no mistakes and oversights this time around. His was a textbook investigation.

Early on, investigating officers considered contacting the Federal Bureau of Investigation (FBI) in the United States to discuss staged suicide scenes. They also looked closely at the issue of whether to exhume the bodies of Lesley and Trevor from Coleraine Cemetery, where they are buried just yards apart. The final decision, however, was to leave the graves alone, primarily because the self-incriminating statements made by the accused were so consistent and watertight, and also so damning. When considering the possible exhumation, officers had spoken with Simon Cosbey, the toxicologist who carried out the original blood tests in 1991. They all concluded that carrying out further tests would most likely serve no useful purpose: apart from the carbon monoxide fumes as well as traces of prescription drugs, what other toxins were likely to be found, to strengthen the case of two people being deliberately poisoned? The feelings of the families of the deceased and the further trauma they would face were another major factor in the decision against exhumation.

In relation to the death of Harry Clarke, Murray's team consulted Adrian West, the UK's leading criminal psychologist, when Howell was being questioned. West has worked as a profiler on many police

investigations in Britain, including the murder in April 1999 of the
BBC presenter Jill Dando. Howell has always emphatically denied that
he murdered his former father-in-law. But some, including Harry's
son, Chris Clarke, still remain sceptical about his plea of innocence.

————

Many of those who sat in the congregation with the Howells and
Buchanans to listen to Pastor John Hansford's sermons are no longer
members of Coleraine Baptist Church. They have moved on to other
parts and different churches. But they, and those who stayed on, will
surely have reflected on how this tragic affair was handled. Hansford:
'I often wondered why I didn't pick up on Colin's lies, but then he lied
to a colossal number of people. I don't feel too bad that I missed the
signs. I would scrutinise my conscience in many ways, and as I look
back, I feel everything was done that could have been done, humanly
speaking, at the time.'

He says that he feels desperately sorry for Howell, whom he
describes as a Jekyll-and-Hyde character: 'We saw one side of him in
the life of the church, and yet there was another life going. It is hard
to make head or tail of his Christian commitment, and how it all
played out in his life.' The pastor's attitude to Hazel Stewart has
changed over time, as he explains: 'I think Hazel schemed. I picked up
that her marriage to Trevor lacked sparkle and was not very exciting.
She was looking for far more . . . There are many women who find
themselves in that position, but didn't go out and do what she did.
Hazel would have come across to me as being a victim of
circumstances, particularly of Colin's dominant personality. Looking
back now—and this is a personal assessment and judgement—I
wonder whether that was true . . . Initially, one felt the whole blame
resided with Colin, though not exclusively, because it takes two for
this to happen. I can see now that Hazel was far more a participant in
what happened than she led us to believe at the time. She portrayed
herself to be an innocent in the whole thing, but my reading of the
situation now is that I don't think she was. I would see Colin Howell
now as a very broken man. I hope a very repentant man. I still believe
there is forgiveness and grace available if there is true repentance.'

The pastor's final thoughts are for the children whose lives have been so badly damaged: 'I feel desperately sorry for his kids. After telling them their mother took her own life, they had to come to terms with the fact that their father murdered their mother. I want the kids to know the part I played in all this. I want them to know that I have tried, as far as possible, to be as truthful about the whole thing.'

While some in the Baptist Church have had misgivings and concerns, it is the close relations of Lesley Howell and Trevor Buchanan above all who have suffered anguish of an unimaginable level. A number of them have described their feelings in interviews for this book, as well as in personal letters known as 'impact statements' which Judge Hart studied carefully before he passed sentence. Their testimonies are moving and sometimes heart-breaking.

At her home near Omagh, just a year after Howell and Stewart were arrested, Valerie Bleakley, Trevor's oldest sister, confided, in a quiet, halting voice: 'I can't describe what it has done to me. The only way I can describe what I feel is that something inside me has died. A lot of the time I'm quite emotional. I have a pain in my chest all the time. I can't cry and I can't laugh since last January. There has been such deep, deep pain.

'I just couldn't believe that Hazel was involved. I could believe it, but I couldn't believe it. Surely she couldn't have been that stupid. But she was. It was just as if Trevor had died all over again. The emotions were even stronger. That first week, I drifted between shock, anger and at times hatred. Other times, strangely enough, I felt sorry for her. I couldn't work out my feelings, because on the day of the first court appearance I was almost relieved when she was not put in prison that day . . . but I could not understand why. I do have a certain amount of compassion. I think the worst scenario for me would be going to prison and the isolation of it. I just couldn't bear to think of that for anybody. It didn't make me feel jubilant, but she deserved to go to prison because justice must be done and she has murdered my brother. How could she do such a thing and deprive her children of a father who loved them passionately? I think about what were Trevor's last words: who heard them, what did he say in those last moments. There are only two people who can answer that.'

Trevor's father, Jim Buchanan, had been confined to a wheelchair for some time before he died in July 2007, aged 84. He suffered from angina. Hazel went to visit him years after Trevor's death, and even though he was still hurting, he felt he had forgiven her for all the pain and misery.

But he never fully recovered. Mrs Buchanan still lives in Omagh.

Melva Alexander, Trevor's sister, is also regretful and filled with a grief which remains unabated: 'I would just love to know why? If I knew that Hazel had any remorse or even showed any? But she hasn't. She carried this for 18 years . . . She has robbed me of my brother; wrecked mum and dad's lives; left the children without a dad who would have loved and supported them . . . The biggest problem at the time was being told that Trevor was in the back of a car with another woman. I have spent 18 years of my life correcting that statement. I've said that to so many people. It wasn't true. It was bad enough that he took his own life, but there were these horrible stories that he was with another woman . . . Then you had people telling Daddy that possibly he was changing his mind and wanted to get out of the car. What a thing to tell Dad. That haunted us for another while, especially around the time of the inquest.'

Gordon Buchanan took charge of the family throughout the investigative and legal processes. They never missed a hearing, no matter how brief, in the run-up to the day Hazel was sentenced. He also insisted on a second Coroner's Court inquest to make sure the records of the deaths were officially corrected. At that inquest, in June 2011, Senior Coroner John Leckey issued a new verdict of 'homicidal carbon monoxide poisoning', setting the record straight once and for all. Gordon finds himself tortured by the same questions and feelings as the rest of the Buchanans: 'I ask myself how Hazel carried that lie for 18 years, burdening our family with the heart-wrenching pain of loss and the unanswered questions associated with suicide, while leaving Trevor's unblemished character vulnerable to innuendo and speculation as a result of the bodies being placed together. When I saw her in court, I thought: "How did you get to such a low point? How could you do such a thing: take your husband away from the children he was devoted to? How could you do that to someone who you presumably once loved and who loved you dearly? Where did it all go wrong? Where did your good upbringing and your faith go?"

'I feel sadness for the legacy she has left others. I feel no pity towards her because of what she did. She carried this cruel, dark secret without, for a moment, even thinking about divulging it. I feel so much sadness that the children did not get the chance to get to know their father better. I know how much he loved them and I know they doted on him. I know they had a wonderful father who looked after them well, guided them well and would have done anything for them. They have been deprived of that. My heart goes out to them. I hope, now that this matter has been settled in court, they will take time to remember their Dad and know he was a good man who was proud to be their father.'

Like other members of the family, however, Gordon has been determined not to allow his feelings towards the two murderers to develop into a hatred which could consume him: 'I never knew Howell. There was a family bond with Hazel and she broke that bond. What she did amounts to the ultimate betrayal. Howell is clearly cruel and calculating and I will be forever haunted by the knowledge that Trevor was aware of what was being done to him—in his own bed, the safest place one could imagine . . . It would be easy to call them names, but I think they have caused us enough pain and taken up enough of our lives without becoming twisted and bitter. Saying nasty things about them would only take away whatever humanity is left in us. Their own actions speak volumes about their characters. Trevor's reputation does not need to be retrieved, because it was never damaged in the first place. His integrity is untarnished. He was an honourable and kind man. He wasn't a saint and I'm not trying to paint him as one. He was simply a good and decent man who loved his family and his wife . . . His Christianity was the real McCoy. It wasn't a Sunday morning thing. It was all day, every day, flaws and all. He was the genuine article.'

'What do I think of Hazel? I just need to know why she felt compelled to go down this road. Why did Trevor have to die? Was murder easier than divorce? Was money more precious than the sanctity of life? My deepest thoughts are more to do with the loss of Trevor, but the hurt it caused me and my family, the unanswered questions; why it was done in such a cruel and horrible fashion, more than what I actually think about Hazel as a person.'

Former associates and colleagues of Howell were stunned by his arrest, and many of them moved quickly to distance themselves from a man they did not particularly like anyway. Mohammad Husban, the young Jordanian, who spent three years at his clinic, remains shocked and dismayed, as one of his friends confirmed: 'He is absolutely shattered. He used to look up to Howell. Howell was almost a father-like figure to him back then, but he cannot believe that he could have been an evil individual, that he could be guilty of such an appalling act. He will never forgive him for what he did. He thinks all the time about Howell's family and how they are managing, especially the little ones.'

Hazel Stewart's son, Andrew, a graphic designer, and her daughter, Lisa McConnell, a nurse, remain convinced of their mother's innocence. They told friends that the jury's verdict means they have been punished twice—first with the death of their father whom they loved dearly, and miss so much, and then with their mother's imprisonment.

As for Howell's children, only one—his daughter Lauren Bradford—has stood by him. His second wife Kyle divorced him last year, after returning to the United States with their five children, Erik, Jorgen, Jensen, Finn, and little Susanna. Dylan and Katie, Kyle's two children from her first marriage, have also left Northern Ireland.

Lauren continues to go to see her father in prison. At one stage in her life, she had a difficult relationship with him but she is the only one now who has not abandoned him. Lauren never missed a day of Hazel Stewart's trial and found it a dreadful experience. She could not understand why Stewart, who admitted her role in the murders when she was first questioned by the police, could then put both of the families though such an ordeal, by pleading not guilty.

In a letter to the court before Judge Hart jailed Howell, Lauren wrote: 'I love my father, but I will never understand how he could have done this. He and Hazel have impacted on so many people. All that taken into consideration, I am now grateful that he has done the right thing by pleading guilty to [Lesley and Trevor's] deaths. I feel like he has finally restored their honour, albeit almost 20 years later. He could have gone to his grave with it.

'I visit my father in prison on a regular basis. Some people may misunderstand this as me being soft, but the only reason I can do this is because of the remorse he showed to me. I initially went to see him so I could try and understand what happened, yell at him maybe and tell him how much he had hurt me. He was the only one with the answers I needed. I never expected to go back after the first few visits, but with each visit, I began to see the reason why he confessed and I believe he is in prison to pay for what he has done. Every time I am there, without fail, there is a moment when he becomes overwhelmed that I am sitting there. And so he should. Almost any conversation I have with him, he thanks me for giving him time. It does not take away from the fact that I hate what he has done to my mother, to me and to all my brothers and sisters, not to mention the Buchanans. There is a divide in our family that may never be mended, and although the main reason for that lies beyond him, it is just another ripple in the whole mess.

'I would not be able to look at my father if he didn't have the right attitude, remorse and guilt. I am not easily taken in and the only reason I can see him is because I believe his remorse is genuine.

'I am not writing this to ask for a greater or lesser sentence. It wouldn't work even if I did. I believe the Judge to be a fair man. I just want justice for my mum and due consideration for my dad. I want him to pay the consequences for what he has done. Whatever the Judge decides, I will support him and continue to visit him and will always love him. I will probably miss my mum every single day, like I have for the last 20 years and will never get to know the wonderful person that I know she was. But at least I now know the truth and hopefully, one day I will heal.'

Unlike his sister, however, Dan Howell will not be signing the visitors' book at Maghaberry any time soon, to see the man he now refers to as 'Colin', and who once told him: 'Fear the Lord because he is awesome and his wrath is terrifying.' The last time Dan spoke with his father was in the Yoko noodle restaurant in Coleraine on the evening of 17 December 2008. His brother Jonny had been at the table as well.

Dan and his father were never particularly close, and unlike Lauren, he has not been forgiving in the aftermath of Howell's extraordinary confessions. Dan also sent a letter to the court before his father was sent down. This is what he wrote:

'Colin murdered my mother Lesley sometime during the night of my second birthday. He always said this was because my mother had committed suicide and as I grew up, I struggled with feeling rejected, believing that my mother wanted herself dead on my birthday, not understanding why she didn't care. During my childhood, Colin became more and more reluctant to talk about my mother with any of us. We stopped visiting her grave. All contact with her brother Chris was cut. This culminated with us being told we were not to talk about any of what happened among the family. I was denied any memory of my mother, as was my younger brother Jonny . . .

'For all his life, my late brother Matthew had believed his mother left him when he was six and he shared with me the anguish that caused and ways in which he blamed himself for what happened. Colin appeared to have no problem rubbishing my mother's name and allowing us to believe she was a bad mother.

'His actions have left me without a father, but even more tragically, my youngest brothers and sister, children of Colin's marriage to Kyle Jorgensen, are fatherless at very young ages. His deceit and selfishness came as a terrible surprise to them. They thought, as young children tend to, that their Dad was the best thing ever, and now I notice the profound effect that is having on them. They don't like to talk about it, but when they do, they voice anger as well as missing what they once knew. They have been uprooted from their community and friends.

'When I found out about how Colin had murdered my mother, it put a tremendous strain on me. I struggled to do the work demanded of me in my medical degree. It put a lot of pressure on my closest friendships and it has split the different sides of my family apart, leaving me in the middle to try and mediate between them. To describe this as life-changing is an understatement.

'I have known Colin for all my life and I believe I know him well. He is very intelligent and very good at coming across sincerely. People trust his intentions to be good, despite everything he has done. He is excellent at portraying himself in the way he wants people to see him. Everyone thought he was a model citizen, a success story, just before his arrest—during a time when he was having an affair, and there was the sexual harassment and his involvement in this financial situation in the Philippines, all the while concealing what he had done.

'I believe that no one can ever know if he has truly changed, and therefore he remains a danger to society. It is vital in my opinion that he is in prison protected from society for as long as possible, since he has demonstrated how much harm he is capable of causing and how good he is at concealing it.'

Colin Howell has never seen Dan's carefully considered and yet deeply emotional judgement of him. If he did, he would no doubt be appalled, as would any father on learning that his own son believes him to be too dangerous and too much of a liability to society to ever be released from prison again. It is an extraordinary assessment.

But so many things are extraordinary in this barely believable saga. The affair between the driven, ambitious dentist and the bored, dissatisfied housewife was in itself nothing unusual—extra-marital relationships happen all the time, of course. What was incredible, however, was the plan Howell conceived of to enable him and Hazel to have a future together, and her willingness to be part of a plot which involved not divorce or legal separation, but a double murder—carefully planned and brutally executed.

Howell and Stewart have been haunted all their lives. They found no real happiness and there will be little or no public empathy for either of them, especially the self-centred Howell. There is, however, great sympathy for the families so cruelly affected by a merciless man and a callous woman, who deprived children of their parents and inflicted untold loss and distress on innocent people. In many ways, it is the love, togetherness and the determination of these families to keep the memory of their lost loved ones alive which represent the most extraordinary aspect of all in this tragic human story.